Radical Islam

W9-DAH-220

Radical Islam
Medieval Theology and Modern Politics

EMMANUEL SIVAN

Yale University Press
New Haven and London

Copyright © 1985 by Yale University.
All rights reserved.
This book may not be reproduced, in whole
or in part, in any form (beyond that
copying permitted by Sections 107 and 108
of the U.S. Copyright Law and except by
reviewers for the public press), without
written permission from the publishers.

Designed by James J. Johnson
and set in Electra Roman type by Brevis Press.
Printed in the United States of America by
Vail-Ballou Press, Binghamton, N.Y.

Library of Congress Cataloging in Publication Data

Sivan, Emmanuel.
  Radical Islam

  Bibliography: p.
  Includes index.
  1. Islam—20th century.   2. Islam—Doctrines.
1. Title.
BP163.S63   1985   320.5′5′0917671   84-20999
ISBN 0–300–03263–3 (alk. paper)
    0–300–03888–7 (pbk.)

*The paper in this book meets the guidelines for
permanence and durability of the Committee on
Production Guidelines for Book Longevity of the
Council on Library Resources.*

10 9 8 7 6 5 4 3 2

To the memory of my father

Contents

Preface

Perhaps a personal note is in order. Thirteen years ago, having just published a book on Islamic movements of Holy War (*jihad*) in the late Middle Ages, I embarked upon a new phase of my inquiry into Muslim history. Throwing aside the Dark Ages, I ventured into the brave new world of the twentieth century, fascinated by such novelties as nationalism and communism in Arab lands. From time to time, the long bygone past tugged at my shirt sleeve, forcing me to pay attention at least to modern Muslim perceptions of this past—in history-writing, political propaganda, and the like. Yet in these areas it was a matter of the way Muslims made use of the past—for apologetics, for window dressing—rather than a case in which the past had a creative impact upon the present. Survivals of the past—or what looked like such—existed, of course, but they held no attraction for me. I preferred to concentrate on what was new, and what was new was, on the whole, imported into the Middle East from abroad.

Nine years later, strolling in the streets of Cairo and East Jerusalem, I was drawn to the stacks of books by the master theoreticians of the jihad in the late Middle Ages, above all Ibn Taymiyya and Ibn Kathir. These books, smelling of fresh print, were quickly snatched off the bookstalls by people in all walks of life, but especially by youngsters in modern garb. As I leafed through the books,

I noticed that the introductions and commentaries thereof did not consist of sheer fossilized paraphrasing of thirteenth- and fourteenth-century texts, nor did they belong to the shallow propagandistic variety where Saladin was a parable for Nasser, the Crusades for Britain (or Israel), and so on. The reader of these books would note an evident effort—quite learned at times and certainly creative—to reflect upon the meaning these texts could have for a modern and totally different historical situation. Facile analogies were discarded; innovative application of underlying principles of Islam was what the authors attempted.

When I engaged many a book buyer and a bookseller in conversation I was struck by the degree to which the basic message of these writings had been driven home, even though not all my interlocutors had the benefit of a traditional education. It is a response to contemporary problems they sought in these exegeses of five- to seven-hundred-year-old texts, trying to weave them into the texture of their own, quite modern, life. These readers were neither nostalgia-seekers, basking in the halo of past glories, nor simple-minded reactionaries. And yet their ferocious attention to detail in these medieval texts showed this past to be a living reality for them, capable of guiding the perplexed in the later third of the twentieth century in all realms of life, including politics. My interest whetted by these conversations, I embarked upon a scholarly inquiry into this phenomenon.

The extended essay that follows presents what I discovered about the transformation of medieval theology into modern Muslim politics, and the twist given to certain age-old Islamic ideas as they entered the contemporary world. As such, it deals with but one major aspect of the Islamic revival today. That revival, as has been rightly pointed out, is multifaceted: "an evident regeneration of culture, a profound renewal of religiosity, a political exploitation of the Islamic vocabulary by governments that use it to reinforce their legitimacy and to strengthen their power, and a use of religion by a political opposition that is often left with no other means of expression . . . along a scale going from conservative fundamentalism to extreme radicalism."[1] The radical end of the spectrum (which encompasses more than just "extreme radicals," or terrorists) is the subject of this essay. It is only a part of a whole, but being the cutting edge of the Islamic resurgence—its most creative and consistent expression—it may also tell us something about the revival movement as a whole. Moreover, as the radicals have achieved cultural hegemony in that movement and, in some cases, in the society at large, their intellectual and social impact is undeniable; and as any reader of the press knows, the movement's role in politics from the revolt in Hama, Syria, to the assassination of Sadat is growing in importance.

We have not mentioned either Iran or Khomeini, for the essay concentrates on Sunni Islam, which is to a large extent a world apart from that of the Shi'ites and where nine out of ten Muslims live. For reasons that had to do with access to, and availability of, source material, the focus is on the three major Arab countries where the radical movement is particularly active and creative today—Egypt, Syria, and Lebanon. Nevertheless, Pakistan, whence the original inspiration came, will have to be taken into account.

This is an essay in the history of ideas viewed and interpreted in their social context. As field surveys of the radical phenomenon are unfortunately impossible, the psychosocial makeup of the movement cannot be fathomed satisfactorily.[2] (For much the same reasons it was also very difficult to trace the modes of oral transmission of ideas.) An attempt is made, however, to deal not merely with thinkers and leaders but with militants and rank and file as well; with the receiving end as well as with the idea-producing end.

We have used a simplified system of Arabic transliteration without diacritics, except for ' which stands for both 'ayn and hamzah.

Material for the book was assembled during my year as Fellow of The Institute For Advanced Study, at the Hebrew University of Jerusalem. The book was written during a year spent at the Institute for Advanced Study, Princeton, New Jersey. My thanks to both Institutes, their Fellows and staff.

CHAPTER ONE

The Mood: Doom and Gloom

Jeremiads   Let me introduce this essay by discussing the most accessible facet of radical Islam, namely, the mood prevailing among the radicals and their immediate periphery, a mood grounded in a certain reading of the current state of Islam. This reading helped shape the radicals' worldview and spawn their specific reaction.

A good period to capture this mood is the last few years of the fourteenth century of the Islamic Era (which ended on November 19, 1979), when Muslim thinkers were given to stocktaking, evaluating the meaning of that century in the annals of Islam. If one were to believe the Western media, one could have expected an exultant mood, an Islam triumphant. After all, the very last year of the fourteenth century After the Hijra (A.H.) began with the Islamic Revolution in Iran and ended with the attempted seizure of the Grand Mosque in Mecca. And yet the mood of the hardcore fundamentalists was rather subdued. Their vision of the present was bleak. An eminent Egyptian theologian, Dr. Muhammad al-Bahi, in *The Future of Islam and the Fifteenth Century* A.H. (Arabic), speaks of the "eclipse of Islam and the proliferation of the challenges to its call during the fourteenth century A.H." The caliphate was abolished (1924); Turkey, Soviet Central Asia, Albania, Bosnia, Bangladesh, Zanzibar, Afghanistan, South Yemen, and Somalia

1

officially relegated Islam to marginality, if not oblivion: Muslim minorities are persecuted in Cyprus, the Philippines, Burma, China, Ethiopia, and Tanzania. While the author deplores these "crusader-style" offensives, the real dangers, he says, come from within (though often inspired by insidious alien ideas). The elites are becoming secularized and surreptitiously cut the ground from under Islam even if they shy away from declaring a separation of religion and state. Nationalism (be it Arab or Persian) loosens religious solidarity and virtually replaces it. The Islamic establishment stands powerless because it is completely subservient to government, looking only for ways and means to justify the latter's actions. It is all the more unable to stem the tide as its economic basis, the waqf, came effectively under the control of the powers-that-be. No wonder that materialism and individualism run rampant in *Dar al-Islam*.[1]

An underground publication of the Syrian Muslim Brethren depicts a "war to the death" waged by the regime in place against the Faith, while a major Syrian thinker, Sa'id Hawwa, in exile in Jordan, laments the absence of Islam from all realms of human activity. In consequence, a Lebanese writer, Fathi Yakan, considers that Islam faces today the worst ordeal in its existence, menaced to be reduced to insignificance and relegated to the dustbin of history; the Lebanese Civil War is for him a prime example of that process. A compatriot of his, Muhammad Mahdi Shams al-Din, detects this very danger as coming above all from the unflagging warfare carried out by the proponents of secularism who accuse Islam and its "metaphysical mentality" of responsibility for all the calamities that had befallen the Muslims (especially since 1967).[2]

Similar views were put forward by the Pakistani theologian Abu-l-A'la al-Maudoodi (who died in 1979) and Iran's Ayatollah Khomeini.[3] At a less lofty level one finds these views in the fundamentalist Muslim press. A perusal of these organs in Egypt (*al-Da'wa, al-I'tisam*) and Syria (*al-Ra'id, al-Nadhir*) during the last year of the Islamic fourteenth century comes up with an array of articles on, for example, the Communist danger, difficulties in re-

introducing Islamic law, attacks on Michel Aflaq and George Habbash as proponents of secularism, protest against sterilization
operations and against sycophant ulama singing the praise of unor-
thodox rulers, on the Islamic Associations youth "defending themselves" against malevolent press campaigns, the perverting influence
of television, the dangers of scholarly criticism of the Sunna, the
diminishing role of Islam in school curricula, permissive women's
dress, and so forth.

   Islamic revival—while activist and militant—is thus essentially
defensive; a sort of holding operation against modernity. And though
it has no doubt a sharp political edge, it is primarily a cultural
phenomenon. Its very strength proceeds from this alliance of political and cultural protest.

   The Global Village   The refrain of all fundamentalist litanies is
                           "Islam is isolated from life." This is no-
where more evident, in their eyes, than in the mass media. Television comes in for most of the blame because it brings the modernist
message in the most effective, audiovisual form into the very bastion
of Islam—family and home. But the same holds true for radio and
for tape cassettes, be they specially produced or recordings of radio
programs. The electronic media carry out a "destructive campaign"
that overwhelms the efforts of religious militants by "broadcasting
indecent and vulgar songs, belly-dancing, melodramas on women
kidnapped in order to serve in the palaces of rulers, and similar
trash."[4] Pop music, Arab style, comes in for more criticism than
explicitly sexual plays (or films), perhaps because of its popularity.
According to a field study quoted by *al-Da'wa*, preference for variety
programs was expressed by 60 percent of Egyptian viewers and lis-
teners (as against 54 percent for Koran reading). They are all the
more dangerous for being indigenous and at the same time impreg-
nated with "the Western poison." A content analysis of the lyrics
propagated by popular singers like Umm Kulthum, Muhammad
'Abd al-Wahhab, and 'Abd al-Halim Hafiz comes up with "terms

and ideas diametrically opposed to Arab and Islamic concepts, encouraging loose morality and immediate satisfaction, placing love and life and its pleasures over everything else, totally oblivious of religious belief, and of punishment and reward in the Hereafter."

Sociological surveys revealed indeed that love songs take up to 37.8 percent of Egyptian broadcasting time compared with 9 percent for religious programs.[5] Worship of TV-, film-, and singing stars—generated by the media itself—only tends to make things worse, as it creates idols that subsume the superficial character of this popular culture, lionized for achievements based on image and not on substance. Popular mourning over the death of 'Abd al-Halim Hafiz, given an aura of respectability by the participation of prominent intellectuals and pundits, made one commentator scoff: "All the martyrs of Sinai and Golan . . . did not get the same amount of solicitude from the media. . . . To hear their eulogies, one could think that insipidity is heroism, vulgarity is an uplifting experience, and singing is tantamount to glorious struggle. The populace learned that their problems, grief, and suffering are of no significance, compared with the death of that entertainer." TV "personalities" build up a trivialized hero worship around themselves, enabling them to spread consumerism all the more efficiently by incorporating commercial publicity into their talk shows. Even worse is professional sports, which brings the idolatry of pagan-inspired body worship to a peak.[6]

Not that the sexually explicit products of popular culture are made light of; it is only that as Islamic criticism of modernity became more sophisticated, it learned that the indirect approach is sometimes more dangerous, precisely for being implicit. But articles on the permissive morality of TV dramas and films (let alone underground pornographic films, whether imported or produced locally) are legion. Here Egypt is no doubt the most prolific center of production in the Arab world, although Lebanese writers find much to complain of about Beirut. This is less true of pulp novels and popular magazines—whether of the implicitly or explicitly sexual variety—but their availability to the public, even in the proximity of mosques, is often lamented. Buttressed by other forms of popular culture such as beauty contests, the result is inevitable: "the weakening of family bonds battered by the unleashing of carnal appetites." "Rare are the films and plays in which one cannot watch at least one of the following: seminude dancing, wine cups filled, easy-to-learn tricks to woo young females, criticism of the conservative older generation for blocking marriage between lovers, description of the beloved merely in terms of sex appeal, justification of the adultery of a young woman given in marriage to an old man or that of an older woman married to one she does not love."

Other forms of "recreation"—that hated term which signifies, for the fundamentalists, an attempt to divert the mind from the moral values—have their share in this chapter. Foremost is the nightclub industry, which prospered as a result of the growing tourism from puritanical oil states (encouraged by the demise of Beirut). This is a case where moral protest is linked with an economic one: criticism of an unbridled "open-door policy" bent on maximization of foreign-currency income by every means. The "commerce in the human body," bordering on, or even incorporating, high-class prostitution, is rendered all the more obnoxious to the True Believers, as alcoholic beverages can be sold in the same tourist precincts. This "cancerous growth" is bound to spread to the indigenous society as well through those natives who are associated with the tourist trade or with foreigners.[7]

Religion does figure in the Syrian and Egyptian mass media, but significantly enough, it is a religion made of externals, of gestures shorn of values: prayer, fast, pilgrimage. This is particularly evident in the context and manner of their presentation. The call for the daily prayer comes over television and radio in the middle of entertainment programs (whether belly-dancing or a love scene) with no introductory and concluding presentation designed to separate the holy from the profane. Koran readings are not only much shorter than they used to be, but are also not reverently separated

from the preceding (and following) pop songs; they are often re-
corded "live" in mosques, making them part of show business, complete with the nonaesthetic cries and wailings of ignorant men in
attendance. During the month of Ramadan, while more attention
is given to religious programs, their impact is neutralized by quiz
and prize shows that foster "material obsessions," and by belly-dancing and erotic films. Small wonder that the few, supposedly serious,
religious talk shows deal with technicalities of devotional acts and
seldom with the application of Islam in daily life.[8]

Behind the lamentations and admonitions is a simple truth:
popular culture is incorporating the Islamic world into Marshall
MacLuhan's Global Village.

Education and Its Discontents   A much more systematic in-
                                  troduction of modern culture
is detected in Syrian and Egyptian education. Concerning school
curricula, the radicals voice the all-too-expected complaint that the
teaching of science, though not openly critical of religion, is sub-
verting Islam quite efficiently, precisely by being oblivious to it.
Science offers an alternative explanatory model, supposedly value-
free and objective; it does not even deign to try to reconcile this
model (as, they claim, could be done) with Islam.[9] The implication
is, of course, that by transfer through training, the same approach
will be applied to other spheres. In like vein, the radicals attack the
teaching of philosophy for giving too much place to Western thinkers and above all for having Islamic philosophy represented by rationalistic, Greek-style medieval philosophers such as the Mu'tazila
school, Avicenna and Averroes, branded as deviationists in their own
times. This is deemed a victory for Orientalism and its disciples,
who had tried to trace back a sort of proto-modernist strand in Islam.
Traditional philosophy of the Ash'ari and Ghazzali variety is barely
taught.[10]

Somewhat less expected is the critique of Arab language and
literature studies. Arabic is, after all, the sacred language of Islam,

heavily permeated with its terminology, history, and culture. Yet
the language in question is the classical literary one. Schools and
universities do not do enough to promote it, with the result that
most university graduates cannot speak it properly and prefer the
colloquial or the "middle language" (*wusta*), an amalgam of colloquial dialects, modern vocabulary and syntax, and a debased classical (*fusha*) backdrop. Quite often, it is reported, dissertation
defense—even in departments of Arabic—is held in the colloquial
(*'amiyya*) medium for lack of ability to converse formally in fusha.
The schools, of course, did not unleash this danger, for the mass
media tend toward a growing use of the 'amiyya and wusta, as do
political leaders in assemblies. It is not unusual for an imam in his
Friday sermon to resort to the colloquial whenever at a loss for fusha
terms and structures. Modern literature—increasingly taught in the
schools—is moving in the same direction, toward a language not
far from that of journalism. This so-called contemporary (*mu'asira*)
language is rapidly losing historical—that is, Islamic—connota-
tions.[11]

As for the content of literary studies, it is quite in tune with
ambient popular culture. Not only are junior high school students
taught an ode to Umm Kulthum, "making singing appear as a sublime value," but modern poetry anthologies include works in praise
of physical culture "where struggle is equated with playing football
and happiness with healthy bodies." Other poems praise the beauty
of nature in the pagan manner of pop songs, with no mention of
any values other than self-gratification. Prose is skewed by a heavy
dose of political speeches of the president-of-the-day, part of the
ritual of state worship. No attempt is made to produce separate texts
for boys and girls to foster the values that suit each sex (courage and
endurance, family orientation and chastity, and so on); schools thus
enhance the growing promiscuity typical of mass culture. (The education system, it is lamented, is almost completely integrated at
the elementary and university levels, and is becoming increasingly
so at junior and senior high school levels.) Religious texts tend to

be relegated to "religious culture" classes, and at the university level
there are even cases where Syrian and Egyptian students of Arabic
are no longer required to take courses in Koran and Sunna.[12]

Teaching "religious culture" cannot help matters. Treating it
as a separate topic legitimizes the separation between religion and
daily life, which is much more bothersome for the Muslim radicals
than the more formal separation between religion and state, a danger
they do not consider imminent. Moreover, religious culture is a
"parasitic teaching matter": its time allocation is small; its prestige
low because it is not judged by schools to be a criterion of scholarly
aptitude; the caliber of teachers is low (mostly Arab-language teachers who treat it in an offhand manner); the curriculum is dull,
designed to have students memorize a few sacred texts and learn
some acts of devotion rather than inculcate values. The "religious
vacuum" so many youth suffer from—and which was the most popular topic in a youth essay contest organized recently by the Egyptian
Muslim Brethren—is certainly not being filled by what is judged a
perfunctory endeavor.[13] Not that it would have been an easy task,
for as one teacher remarked to an investigative reporter:

> What if I teach that taking interest is forbidden by the Shari'a
> when our whole economic structure, consecrated by law, is
> based on it? What if I teach Koranic verses on the virtues of
> modest dress when my students see décolleté and miniskirts in
> public places? And what about teaching Islamic doctrine that
> the rich are morally and legally bound to help the poor when
> inequity in income distribution is steadily growing?[14]

Perhaps the most devastating critique is reserved for the teaching of history, in particular that of the caliphate, which could have
been expected to be ideal terrain for religious instruction, basking
as it did in glorious achievements. And yet "Islamic history in
schools is a war against Islam and Belief!" proclaims the headline
of one such critical article, and another: "Why should we distort
our own history?" Most of the blame is laid at the door of Arab
nationalism and its attempt to concoct for itself a genealogy,

thereby—wittingly or not—preempting religion as the prime bond
of solidarity throughout history. An elementary school textbook
reads: "Mu'awiya thus became caliph [in 661] unifying the Arabs
under his leadership," to which a critic retorts, "And what about
the Persian Muslims in the East, the Berbers in the Maghreb?"
Indeed, whenever the term *Muslims* should have been used, the
radicals usually find *Arabs* to have replaced it, "making Islam into
a kind of exclusivist nationalist ideology, a trait of which it is in fact
entirely free." Awkward hadiths (traditions), such as "An Arab has
no precedence over a Persian," are conveniently rendered in textbooks: "None of you shall have precedence over another." The role
of non-Arabs in the development of Islam is minimized and some,
such as the Turks, are given most of the blame for its decadence,
while barely a word is breathed about the vital role played by the
Ottomans in defending and even expanding the borders of *Dar al-
Islam*. Pre-Islamic history is extolled by the pan-Arabists, and its
barbarity ignored. No less "pernicious" is the growing tendency toward supposedly scientific historiography, with Orientalist-style emphasis on natural-rational causation and particular attention to
economics. Thus Muslim motivation in the seventh-century con-
quests is traced back, in large part, to the imbalance between population and resources in Arabia and the attraction of the rich lands
to the north; Muslim victories are attributed more to martial valor
than to religious spirit, and of course no word is uttered about transcendental causes. Here, God does not intervene or push people to
act or impinge upon the form and results of their acts.[15]

Equally disquieting for the fundamentalists are present-day tendencies toward nation-state solidarity, especially in the case of post-
1973 Egypt with its stress on the Pharaonic past. "One geopolitical
solidarity (Pan-Arab) is replaced by another (Egyptian) to the detri-
ment of the wider and all-embracing Islamic one."[16]

The intrinsic relationship between all aspects of modernity is
brought forward by a literary critic: "This pagan Pharaonic approach . . . ends up by calling to make our country a sort of inter-

national hotel to which guests flock from the world over in order to indulge in luxury and pleasures"; the territorial nationalism and cultural openness called for are but a variation of the old infatuation with European culture designed "to extricate our society from the hold of the Shari'a, make it accept usury, corruption, and sexual permissiveness."[17]

Does Modernity Deliver? Last but not least on the list of challenges to religion is economics. The fundamentalists are by no means nostalgic about "Arab socialism," Nasserist or Ba'thist style, committed as they are to the principle of private property, suspicious of an all-too-powerful state and hostile to even the slightest tinge of Marxism. Yet they are far from happy with the "open-door policy" of the 1970s. The doors are opened, to begin with, toward Western investment (though this is in large part due, as they sadly concur, to the failure of oil-rich Arabs to live up to the expectations of Muslim solidarity; yet another example of Islamic "eclipse"). First, Western investment means the integration of the Islamic world into the system of the multinationals, which is totally alien to Muslim concepts of interest, insurance, taxation, and so on. If these traditional concepts have had little impact ever since the onset of modernization, they risk complete eradication (not only in reality but also in Muslim hearts and minds), and any chance of their reintroduction may vanish.

Second, investment brings with it a large foreign contingent— experts, tourists, and so on—and the need to cater to their desires (for example, alcoholic beverages, entertainment), which is bound to corrupt the morality of those who work with foreigners and the *nouveaux riches* who emulate them, and, by osmosis, of other sectors as well.

A third argument, intertwined with the above, is the growing acceptance of an individualistic and hedonistic lifestyle abetted by an increasingly aggressive commercial publicity, inspired by the lat-

est Madison Avenue gimmicks in line with the underlying ethos of
infitah ("open door"), which makes economic growth a cherished
goal and a rise in the standard of living its hoped-for inevitable
concomitant.[18] The appeal of religious values is overshadowed by
the "Pepsi-Cola, Seven-Up . . . fast-food and bright-dress culture,"
laments one writer.[19] He aptly notes that regardless of its moral
defects, consumerism is at odds with the pre-take-off stage of the
Middle Eastern economy, creating new needs and raising expectations that the economy cannot deliver. This is indeed the strongest
argument, in terms of popular appeal, advanced by the radicals.
"Instead of industrial and agricultural growth . . . we have a rise in
imports of luxury goods."[20] Demagoguery aside, it is true that the
much heralded take-off has not yet happened, while inflation has
soared, and income distribution has become more inequitable (and
more prominent as conspicuous consumption is not discouraged as
it was in the 1960s). Basic problems such as housing and public
transport are as acute as ever, or perhaps even more so because of
expectations raised by the October war, the policy enunciated, and
by commercial publicity.

Unlike the antimodernist upsurge in the West in the 1960s,
which was materially gratified but sought spiritual satisfaction, this
is a reaction against a modernity that does not deliver even on its
material promises. It creates a gap—or cognitive dissonance, if you
will—between Western-style consumerist expectations and "Fourth
World" production and per capita income. No wonder that this is
one of the major sources of recruitment to the motley revivalist
groups in Syria and Egypt, especially from among urban youth who
have internalized much of the modernist ethos only to find their
mobility blocked by exiguous occupation opportunities (outside a
mammoth bureaucracy plagued by latent unemployment).

Yet it would be untrue to say that the Muslim militants see
modernity's failure to deliver merely as an opportunity to prove that
in the face of a bankrupt "imported solution" Islam is the sole viable
way out. For one thing, the majority of urban youth have had their

"base instincts" (in Muslim parlance) released by modernity, and remain committed to its ethos, though by now unsatiated and envious. Their energies are desperately bent on finding their own individual satisfaction either within the loopholes of the system, or by selling themselves to its magnates, or by withdrawing and joining the brain drain. The difficulty in avoiding the commercial ethos is indicated by the fact that the fundamentalist press itself carries lavish-colored publicity on glossy paper for men's underwear, crockery, cars, candies, and high-rise apartments. Moreover, economic problems—no less than consumerist hopes—help erode traditional values. Crowded public transport encourages promiscuity and makes the proposed solution of separate buses for women (or at least for female students) more improbable than ever; urban women tend more to go to work to supplement the family budget (impoverished by inflation and by newly acquired needs), thus aggravating the problems created by the modern career-oriented educational system; and, women who quit the home for the job market acquire in turn new and depraved needs (from dress and hairstyles to sexual mores), develop assertiveness, and may even go so far as to join the nascent women's liberation movement.[21]

The housing shortage and the spiraling cost of the bridal dowry force many young people to postpone marriage (thus diminishing prospective natality) or to renounce it altogether—yet another severe blow to the family, that essential vehicle for transmitting Islamic education. Family planning may even become an attractive solution for the harassed urban middle- and lower-middle class. A reader's letter protesting the official attempts to promote sterilization alleged: "They try to convince you that the only way out is this operation, but do not breathe a word about the failure of their economic and social reforms or about the egotism of the rich who refuse to help the poor. They just rehash the theme that our land cannot feed new mouths."[22]

Can Islam Cope?   Can Islam cope with these challenges? The fundamentalist verdict is clear cut: not in the present state of the Islamic establishment. One should either restructure it entirely or operate outside its system (which they do). It is the establishment, by its timidity, servility, and false religiosity which, more than any other factor, is responsible for making it appear as though "prayer, fast, and pilgrimage are all there is to Islam."[23] Truly enough, the Islamic establishment is a governmental institution: the waqf is managed by a ministry; religious jurists, imams of mosques, preachers, and so on, are all civil servants; al-Azhar is a state university; members of the Superior Council for Islamic Affairs are government-appointed. Not only do the militants deplore this state of affairs, but they claim that, first, the subservience of the Islamic establishment should be traced back to a long and ignominious historical tradition of the "Age of Decadence" (fourteenth to nineteenth century). Second, and more important, the establishment does not even try to exercise whatever powers it has in order to have an impact on society. In a manner reminiscent of Khomeini's attacks on the "palace ulama," they take religious dignitaries to task for not giving much backing to legislative initiatives for application of the Shari'a on matters like divorce, alcoholic drinks, apostasy from Islam, criminal punishment, and so on.

Furthermore, the dignitaries are even said to turn a blind eye when their subordinates justify innovation (bid'a), such as family planning, usurious interest, replacing the four shar'i schools by one, rapprochement with the Shi'a. The value of the programs of religious studies in the nontheological faculties of al-Azhar (introduced by government decree in 1961) is quite doubtful and this university even fails to promote the fusha in the literary departments. As for its quarterly Majallat al-Azhar, "it is in one wadi and life is in another," preferring as it does to deal with safe and innocuous questions: details of ritual, purely academic exegesis, historical nostalgia, and apologetics. The same holds for the Academy of Islamic Research, operating under the auspices of al-Azhar University, where controversial socioeconomic issues are taboo. An establishment unable to impose norms of modest dress even on Waqf Ministry employees, dares not try to outlaw commercially distributed tape

cassettes of antireligious jokes and plays, and above all, books red-
olent of "ideological imperialism" (*ghazw fikri*, that is, the materi-
alist-individualist ethos).[24]

Could it be otherwise, as long as the religious leadership is
government-appointed and not elected by their peers? "What is lacking are ulama free of chains of office, function, and dependence,
ulama who cannot be hired and fired at will, and are economically
independent, hence impervious to pressures."[25] For the effectiveness
of the establishment, as representing a system of moral values, is
the major victim of such (real or potential) pressures; it results in
modes of behavior ranging from sycophantic eulogies of the ruler to
supplying information to the security services.[26] At the grass roots,
the situation is no better. Investigative reporters cull testimonies and
complaints that imams and preachers behave as the civil servants
they are, seeing as their role the execution of their superiors' orders.
Apprehensive of exceeding their mandate, they steer clear of community life and find refuge in teaching meaningless rituals of devotion and rarefied sacred texts. The low pay and low prestige of the
imams foster negative selection and poor intellectual caliber.[27]

Islam thus comes out badly bruised from the encounter with
modernity. The latter does not advance at the pace of a Japan, a
Russia, or a China, but advances all the same. One fundamentalist
found that state of siege epitomized by the fact that "work hours
hamper people from praying during the daytime (for lack of special
time slots for it) and entertainment programs divert them from it at
night." Yet another saw it subsumed by the rhythm of life cadenced
by the civil (Gregorian) calendar rather than by the *hijri* one.[28]

Ordeal and Discord   The inevitable result is a state of *mihna
wa-fitna* ("ordeal and discord"); Islam is
virtually absent "in a society where true-blue Muslims are the most
marginal of the marginal . . . living outside the framework of time
and major events."[29] The faithful of Islam are thus "the Party of
Allah pitched in battle against the Party of the Devil" (this is the

title of a book by a young engineer, who is in a modern profession that, as we shall see, has contributed much to the rise of Islamic radicalism).[30]

The picture that emerges is not one which scholars studying Islamic society would tend to refute. Modernity has indeed made important gains, especially in recent decades. Islam, although more resilient than other traditional cultures, has seen its position greatly eroded. It is true that the radicals are given, at times, to conspiratorial explanations, seeing everywhere the hidden hand of the CIA, USIA, KGB, and so forth.[31] By and large, however, theirs is not the case of "paranoid style in politics." The dangers they point to are quite real.

Prophecies of doom and gloom are not easily transformed, however, into calls for action. They could well be a recipe for despair and resignation. How do the Muslim radicals combine pessimism and activism? What are the historical circumstances which made that combination work and spread? To answer these questions one has to enquire into the genesis of the radical phenomenon and delve into the intellectual and social history of the 1950s and 1960s. For while the new Muslim radicalism gained recognition and clout in the 1970s, its physiognomy has actually been shaped during the preceding two decades.

CHAPTER TWO

Barbarity and Nationalism

No to Jihad?   During the last decade a spate of memoirs told
the story of Nasser's political jails. In one of them
a former inmate recounts:

> In May 1967, during the crisis weeks preceding the Six-
> Day War, the authorities tried to enlist the support of the po-
> litical prisoners to the jihad against Israel. Some [Muslim
> Brethren] inmates of the notorious Abu Za'bal prison camp
> resolved to voice their unreserved support and even published
> a wall newspaper to that effect.
>
> Yet a group of young inmates, led by Sheikh 'Ali Abduh
> Isma'il, argued that the State is infidel and so is whoever sup-
> ports it. Israel and Nasser were both, for them, but two varia-
> tions of tyranny, both totally inimical to Islam; they fight each
> other for worldly reasons but "in infidelity they are just one
> bunch." Reported to camp authorities by stool pigeons, Isma'il
> and his followers were thrown into solitary confinement, to live
> on dry bread and a little water. They refused, however, to
> renounce their views and were later to be remanded to ordinary
> cells where they kept to themselves, praying in their own group,
> refusing to have anything to do with Muslim Brethren who
> aided the anti-Israel jihad, and thereby establishing the first cell
> of the Takfir wa-Hijra (the major terrorist organization of the
> 1970s).[1]

The frame of mind of these and other inmates is highlighted by letters sent in late May from the Military Prison by a Muslim Brother:

> There is a lot of talk about war. Yet who is it who is going to fight? Those who prostrate themselves before idols, those who worship other deities than Allah? . . . Verily, God is not about to succor in battle people who have forsaken Him. . . . Can He bestow victory upon people who have been fighting Him, His religion, and His true believers, massacring and torturing them, inflicting upon them imprisonment and humiliation? . . . Don't you know, dear Mother, that those [i.e., the Muslim Brethren] who had defeated Israel in 1948 were thrown into jail in 1955, a year before Israel attacked us, and were thrown there once again in 1966, a year prior to another eventual Israeli incursion? . . . Doesn't that indicate, dear Mother, treason and collusion?

And in a letter to his wife:

> It is inconceivable that those who abolished the religious courts (in 1957)—with the purpose that no legal recourse would be made to the Shari'a—that they would win this war. And do you think that those who "developed" al-Azhar into a secular type university (in 1961) in order that it deviate from its original mission and dilute the substance of its teaching, that such people could triumph? . . . Can those who massacred Muslims in Yemen by napalm bombs and poison gas . . . and allied themselves with infidel Russia . . . have the upper hand?[2]

No wonder that the June 1967 debacle was greeted in the prison camps with a mixture of shock and gloating. "This was no surprise to us," wrote one, "for how can a ruler governing his people with a whip triumph on the battlefield? . . . dignity is trampled underfoot, hypocrisy and cowardice reign supreme." And after the June 9 and 10 demonstrations, which called upon Nasser not to abdicate: "How shameful it is for their leader (za'im) to remain in power after he had admitted his responsibility for the debacle. Why had he not prepared for that war which he said he had expected?" A third prisoner adds: "Soldiers were supposed to obey orders and fight for the slogans and for the za'im. . . . Yet under fire all evaporated. Neither slogans nor the za'im could be of any help. The soldier remained alone and had to save his own skin."[3]

Such reactions are cast into relief when read against the long-term commitment of the Muslim Brethren (hereafter MB) to the Palestinian cause since the 1930s, culminating in their massive participation in the 1948 War and violent opposition to the 1949 Armistice Agreement (as a result of which they were driven underground for the first time). In the mid-1950s, when they were persecuted by Nasser, their erstwhile ally, one of the major accusations they hurled against him was that he had neglected the question of Palestinians and was in effect preparing the terrain for a tacit rapprochement by stages with Israel.[4]

The contrast comes into an even sharper focus when set against the behavior of the MB prisoners during the Suez War. By mid-1956 the prison-camp authorities were trying to brainwash the inmates and also to sow dissension in their ranks by offering parole to all those ready to sign telegrams of support to the regime. Quite a few inmates were persuaded by ideological arguments and/or attracted by the release offer. A hard core refused to sign despite all the promises, the theological admonitions by secret police "Islamic experts," the harassments, and the torture. Yet when the war broke out in October, reminisces one of the hard core:

> We presented prison authorities with the request—to be transmitted to Nasser's government—to allow us to volunteer to fight the aggressors. We solemnly pledged that those of us who would survive, having done their duty on the battlefield, would go back to prison. We further suggested that a special battalion of MB prisoners would be set under special command. A list of names of volunteers was appended to the request and the whole dossier was relayed by the camp commander to the powers-that-be.[5]

In the context of the present chapter, it is immaterial that the government—having for a moment accepted the request—finally rejected it. What is important is the state of mind of the prisoners two years after the onset of Nasser's crackdown upon their organization. By 1967 the picture was entirely different. Nor was the Abu Za'bal case an isolated episode; it rather ushered in a brand new attitude among Muslim radicals toward the anti-Israel jihad predicated upon a reordering of priorities. The Islamic Liberation party (which tried to instigate a coup d'etat in Egypt in 1974) would even argue that the fight for the liberation of Sinai cannot be considered a jihad, for its aim is not the establishment upon earth of a unified Muslim state. Well before Sadat's peace initiative, this and other groups made desertion from the "infidel" Egyptian army one of their major slogans. Shukri Mustafa ('Abduh Isma'il's successor as leader of the Takfir group) responded thus to his judges' question as to what his followers would do if Israel attacked Egypt: "If the Jews or others come, our movement should not take part in combat in the ranks of the Egyptian army. We would rather escape to a safe place. . . . For by no means can the Arab-Jewish conflict be considered an Islamic warfare."[6]

Even the Syrian MB, who miss no opportunity to remind President Assad of his responsibility for the loss of the Golan Heights and the crushing of the Palestinian resistance in Lebanon, adhere to the same order of priorities. Their military commander in Aleppo, Husni 'Abbu, had the following exchange with the tribunal in his 1979 trial:

Q. Don't your terrorist actions serve Israel?

A. They serve Islam and the Muslims and not Israel. What we want is to rid this country of impiety.

Q. Why don't you fight against Israel?

A. Only when we shall have finished purging our country of godlessness shall we turn against Israel.[7]

The most comprehensive exposition of the rationale for this

stand can be found in the book written by 'Abd al-Salam Faraj, ideologue of the jihad group which assassinated Sadat:

> There are some who say that the jihad effort should concentrate nowadays upon the liberation of Jerusalem. It is true that the liberation of the Holy Land is a legal precept binding upon every Muslim . . . but let us emphasize that the fight against the enemy nearest to you has precedence over the fight against the enemy farther away. All the more so as the former is not only corrupted but a lackey of imperialism as well. . . . In all Muslim countries the enemy has the reins of power. The enemy is the present rulers. It is hence, a most imperative obligation to fight these rulers. This Islamic jihad requires today the blood and sweat of each Muslim.[8]

The events at Abu Za'bal in May 1967 are, then, a sort of milestone illustrating the transformation of MB radical thought during the late 1950s and early 1960s, which was to spawn the new breed of Islamic radicalism so prominent today. Indeed the New Radicalism is essentially a product of the experience of the 1950s and the 1960s. By 1964/65 it would already have a fully developed ideology and acquire a foothold in Egyptian society. Its presence would begin to be felt in the realm of politics. The shock waves of the 1967 defeat would spread those ideas from Egypt to Syria, Lebanon, and Jordan, elaborating their substance in the process somewhat further.

Post-1973 events—the euphoria generated by the Ramadan War, the social dislocations created in Arab have-not countries by the oil price upheaval—would sow these ideas in other Arab countries and gain them wider social acceptance in the core area of the Middle East. They would add precious little, however, to the contents of the radical ideology. To elucidate the genesis of the New Radicalism, in the context of the 1950s and the 1960s, is not only a matter of setting the record straight in terms of chronology. It may also shed some light upon the nature of the phenomenon—as a reaction to Nasserism and Ba'thism in their prime and at the beginning of their decline.

The New Jahiliyya   In the beginning was the idea, or rather set of ideas, which Sayyid Qutb, a modernist literary critic turned MB activist, has been working on since the late 1940s. The importance of the ideological dimension of the new radicalism is attested to by a Lebanese disciple: "One cannot account for the first Muslim Empire unless one takes into consideration the prophecy of Muhammad: the groundwork for the French Revolution was laid by Rousseau, Voltaire, and Montesquieu; the Communist Revolution realized the plans set by Marx, Engels, and Lenin; Nazism grew out of a soil labored by Hegel, Fichte, and Nietzsche. The same holds true for us as well."[9]

This self-image was mirrored by the perceptions of the powers-that-be with regard to the movement. Having never underestimated the ideological appeal of the MB in the 1940s and the early 1950s, they gave an even heavier weight to this aspect in their fight against the new incarnation of the MB. It is a measure of how seriously the Egyptian government took these ideas, that the mentors of radical groups (Qutb in 1966, Salih Siriya in 1975, Shukri Mustafa and 'Abd al-'Aziz Bakri in 1978, 'Abd al-Salam Faraj in 1982) would be sent to the gallows in the company of those members involved in actual terrorist activity. Brainwashing of inmates, minute collection and analysis of intelligence data on radical writings, massive propaganda campaigns, including theological debates (not only in the print media but also on TV), continued and developed under Nasser, Sadat, and Mubarak—all further attest to the preoccupation with the ideological challenge. It was a battle of sorts for hearts and minds, of youth in particular.[10]

Prefiguring the profile of future radical leaders, Sayyid Qutb was modern-educated (a literature major at Cairo University). He made his mark as a modernist literary critic in the 1930s and 1940s. His brand of antimodernism would be, hence, that of someone who came to know modernity and then decided to turn his back, and not that of an al-Azhar sheikh looking at it from outside. (Among other Egyptian radical leaders, Siriya had a Ph.D. in science education; Mustafa was an agronomist and Faraj an engineer; in Syria, Marwan Hadid and 'Adnan 'Uqla were engineers and 'Ali Bayanuni a lawyer; Muhammad 'Ali Dannawi of Lebanon was also a lawyer.)

Qutb was more directly exposed to modern civilization during a two-year stay in the United States (1948–50), which was indeed the formative experience that converted him to fundamentalism. Upon his return he joined the MB, where he would soon head the Propaganda Section. Prior to his arrest during the 1965 crackdown, he had produced a number of writings that carried further afield the basic tenets of the MB, but as yet in a haphazard and half-developed manner. These new ideas owed much of their original inspiration to Indian Muslim thinkers.

Frederick Jackson Turner's "Frontier Theory" would seem to be valid for Islam as well. Time and time again throughout Muslim history, movements of return to pristine values of that civilization originated in the frontier lands (the Almohads of Saharan North Africa in the twelfth century, the "moral rearmament" of the Seljukid Iranian heartland in the eleventh century, and so on). This may well be the reason why the renaissance that was to inspire Qutb took place in another Muslim frontier country—India.

This renaissance had its origin in the theory of "Modern Jahiliyya" (that is, modernity as the New Barbarity) developed in India since 1939 by Maulana Maudoodi. He was the first Muslim thinker to arrive at a sweeping condemnation of modernity and its incompatibility with Islam, and to formulate a definition of the danger it constituted. The conclusion toward which Rashid Rida and other fundamentalists were slowly and hesitantly moving during the 1930s—that a compromise between modernity and Islam, vaguely

hoped for till then, could not occur—was stated forcefully by Maudoodi.

Maudoodi's major works—*Jihad in Islam, Islam and Jahiliyya,
The Principles of Islamic Government*—began to be translated from
Urdu and English into Arabic only in the 1950s; the major agent
of transmission was his disciple Abu-l-Hasan 'Ali Nadvi, the future
rector of the Islamic Academy of Lucknow. A famous scholar in his
own right (notably on the Ibn Taymiyya legal school), Nadvi had
always taken a deep interest in the Arab world, which he considered
the heart of Islam. The book he wrote in Arabic, *What Did the
World Lose Due to the Decline of Islam?* expounded Maudoodi's
Modern Jahiliyya doctrine and has been a resounding success ever
since its publication in 1950. The mood of dejection and soul-
searching following the First Palestine War created a receptive atmosphere. When the author visited the Middle East in 1951, he
was given a triumphant welcome from statesmen (for example, King
Abdallah, who was well acquainted with the book) and major thinkers (Ahmad Amin, Lutfi al-Sayyid), as well as students and members
of various Muslim associations. When he met Sayyid Qutb (who
had already read his book) in Cairo, they found their ideas to be in
close affinity.[11] Qutb's ideas seem to have developed along parallel
lines, especially during his years in the United States (which he
came to loathe). Yet there is no doubt that 'Ali Nadvi's influence
helped crystallize the still amorphous ideas of Sayyid Qutb's *The
Struggle between Islam and Capitalism* (1952), the fruit of his own
American sojourn, into the more mature form of his Koranic exegesis (ca. 1953) where the concept of a modern jahiliyya makes its
first appearance in his work (and where 'Ali Nadvi and Maulana
Maudoodi are also quoted at length). What is this concept? In this
exegesis, *In the Shadow of the Koran*, Qutb wrote:

> Jahiliyya (barbarity) signifies the domination (*hakimiyya*) of
> man over man, or rather the subservience to man rather than

to Allah. It denotes rejection of the divinity of God and the adulation of mortals. In this sense, jahiliyya is not just a specific historical period (referring to the era preceding the advent of Islam), but a state of affairs. Such a state of human affairs existed in the past, exists today, and may exist in the future, taking the form of jahiliyya, that mirror-image and sworn enemy of Islam. In any time and place human beings face that clear-cut choice: either to observe the Law of Allah in its entirety, or to apply laws laid down by man of one sort or another. In the latter case, they are in a state of jahiliyya. Man is at the crossroads and that is the choice: Islam or jahiliyya. Modern-style jahiliyya in the industrialized societies of Europe and America is essentially similar to the old-time jahiliyya in pagan and nomadic Arabia. For in both systems, man is under the dominion of man rather than of Allah.[12]

Is this just a matter of laws and legislation? No, the jahiliyya denotes, for Qutb, a polity legitimized by man-made criteria, such as the sovereignty of the people (rather than by divine grace), as well as a man-centered system of values and social mores (for example, materialism, hedonism). Philosophical explanatory models—built on science alone with no place in their universe for God—are the apex, or perhaps nadir, of that jahiliyya.

When one looks at Western societies, says Qutb in this and his other writings, one sees the future—and it does not work. This is the future awaiting Muslim societies: unbridled individualism, dissolution, depravity, leading to moral and social decline. A vast array of examples is marshaled to prove his point: from the writings of Western cultural critics (Arnold Toynbee, Alexis Carrel), to current affairs of the 1950s (such as the scandals in Britain over Christine Keeler and John Profumo, the Burgess and Maclean affair). As the world grows smaller, the danger of "culturally poisoning" the Islamic lands becomes more imminent. Hence the violence of tone and urgency of his message to his fellow Muslims who were tempted and even brainwashed by Western ideas, mostly through the agency of other Muslims, and on a scale and at a pace unprecedented in the history of Islam. "This is the most dangerous jahiliyya which has ever menaced our faith," Qutb writes in his most popular book, *Signposts on the Road* (1964). "For everything around is jahiliyya; perceptions and beliefs, manners and morals, culture, art and literature, laws and regulations, including a good part of what we consider Islamic culture."

In order to "throw off the yoke of jahiliyya," society must undergo a radical change, beginning with its very moral foundations where "numerous man-made idols—from agnosticism to capitalism—hold sway." Domination (hakimiyya) should be reverted to Allah alone, namely to Islam, that holistic system He conferred upon men. An all-out offensive, a jihad, should be waged against modernity so that this moral rearmament could take place. The ultimate objective is to reestablish the Kingdom of God upon earth, "which does not signify that the hakimiyya shall be in the hands of men of religion as in the medieval West" (or, for that matter, among the Shi'ites—Khomeini would not have approved of Sayyid Qutb). "No," says Qutb, "the goal is that the Shari'a will reign supreme," Shari'a not just in the narrow sense of a code of laws, but in a wider one of "the all-embracing way of life, laid down by Allah for the Muslims—from values to customs and social norms, which all in all shape human life."

Does, then, Sayyid Qutb's rejection of modernity entail hostility toward technology and science? No, their instrumental worth is unquestionable, and he even admits the need for basic research, "provided it does not lead one to stray from the path of religion." Hence the need for maximum caution with regard to those fields (biology, astrophysics, and so on) that are liable to have a spillover effect upon major religious tenets. Borrowing ideas from non-Muslims is illicit here, and one should double-check with regard to the religious authenticity of even Muslim scientists.[13]

Qutb's ideas matured during his nine years in prison. The prison experience was to be, in effect, crucial in the making of most of the other New Radicals as well. In the nucleus of each group one finds people who had served time in political prison camps, and tales of their experience played an important role in the indoctrination of new recruits.

Qutb nurtured his ideas first on his own, continuing to write the Koranic commentary, *In the Shadow of the Koran*, then further developed them from the late 1950s on in conversations with fellow MB inmate Yusuf Hawwash, who became a close friend (and his future deputy in the resurrected clandestine MB). Very few of their fellow prisoners were apprised of these ideas at this stage, but they were elaborated upon in long letters to Qutb's brother and sister, both former religious activists. Those letters contained the essence of eight of the twelve chapters of his epoch-making book *Ma'alim fi-l-Tariq* (*Signposts on the Road*), which was to be published in November 1964, a few months after his release from prison (the other four chapters were taken from his Koranic commentary). Well before the publication of *Signposts* the ideas filtered out beyond the Qutb family circle and attracted the attention of a group of MB militants of the middle generation (mostly in their thirties; Qutb was almost sixty years old), some of them former inmates of Nasser's prisons. The latter, who had been trying since the late 1950s to reestablish the MB in order to take vengeance on the regime, asked permission to read these letters. Requested by his family, Qutb granted this request. By the time of his release from jail, quite a number of former MB activists and younger recruits (mostly students and young professionals in their twenties) had been converted to his ideas.[14] Their original quest for revenge was transformed and given an intellectual edge it did not otherwise possess. In age and class (lower-middle to middle), the characteristics of this group fitted in with those of the membership of old MB, yet education was more upscale and more distinctly modern. This was an audience of the same type as its mentor.[15]

By the time of the police crackdown upon the group in August 1965, the overall number did not exceed 250 (much like that of the

Takfir group in 1977), but smaller than the Jihad Organization of 1981). The number involved and the nature of the terrorist acts planned (but only half-prepared) were perhaps less disconcerting for the authorities than the new message borne by the group.

In preparing for the show trial (which was to result in the execution of Qutb and two others and in harsh prison sentences), the secret police carried out in-depth interrogations of Qutb and his votaries on ideological matters. The transcript provides ample evidence that these were done with as much attention to detail as interrogations on operational aspects. The prosecution produced a whole dossier—a veritable *explication de texte*—analyzing *Signposts* as well as Muhammad Qutb's (Sayyid's brother) book *The Jahiliyya of the Twentieth Century* (also published in Arabic in 1964), which elaborated on the same set of ideas. This dossier was to serve as a linchpin of the act of accusation and of the prosecutor's speeches.

The core of Sayyid Qutb's ideas thus consists in a total rejection of modernity—following in this his Indian teachers Maudoodi and Nadvi—since modernity represents the negation of God's sovereignty (hakimiyya) in all fields of life and relegation of religion to the dustbin of history. Thence the sense of virtual despair which permeates his writings: Islam in this century is in the process of losing its grip over society, the world is passing it by; a new Age of Barbarity (jahiliyya) is in the making, similar in nature to one that preceded the rise of Islam in the Arabian Peninsula; it is thus high time for Islam to take the offensive before it is too late. This brooding cultural pessimism centered not only on external challenges—Maudoodi elaborated the main body of his thinking under British rule— but also on internal ones, that is, modern, usually Western, ideas and modes of behavior spread by native converts. Sayyid Qutb, entering the arena as the age of direct colonial rule was drawing to a close, concentrated on the internal challenges alone. His understanding of them deepened and was greatly transformed as the challenges began to come, not from a corrupt monarchy and upper class with a history of collaboration with imperialism and blatant infatuation with Western culture, but from the newly established revolutionary republic, with its impeccable anti-imperialist credentials, close contacts with the MB, and a heavily lower-middle-class origin and all that this intimated in terms of deep attachment to traditional Islam.

Qutb would conclude that the threat was worse and more insidious than at any point in Islamic history, coming as it did from within the citadel and through the agency of ostensibly faithful believers. A sense of almost forlorn urgency ensued—hope against hope. Consequently, he had to develop, for the first time in the history of mainstream Sunnism, a full-blown justification for a revolt against the powers-that-be.

I shall come back later (in Chapter 4) to this revolutionary theory, a sort of Muslim *Vindiciae Contra Tyrannos*. What interests me most in the present context is the nature of new Muslim tyranny (or modern jahiliyya) the radicals were grappling with. In a way, in his quality as an observer on the fringe, Qutb might perhaps also help us better understand the Nasserist phenomenon. And even if he does not, it is his and his followers' perception of the new jahiliyya, whether in Egypt or Syria or Iraq, which lies at the fountainhead of the New Radicalism. This vision accounts for the alienation and the total rejection of the home-grown, nationalist military regimes, as illustrated by the episode with which I introduced this chapter.

Farewell to Pan-Arabism   Nowhere are the alienation and rejection better highlighted than in the New Radicals' attitude toward Pan-Arab nationalism. We have already broached this issue in the first chapter, when dealing with the mature form this negative attitude was to take in the 1970s, and it is now time to elucidate its origins.

The old Muslim radicals have been close allies of Arabism since the 1930s, subscribing to the notion of the Arabs' special role in Islam, as the group destined to lead it—and to the concomitant view that Arab unity is a necessary and practical stepping-stone on the road to Islamic unity.[16] But the MB were not unaware of the existence of a secularist brand of Pan-Arabism where Islam was relegated to a position of one among many cultural-historical components and where major emphasis was put on language. Yet as long as most proponents of secular Arabism remained sufficiently vague in their formulations, and as long as the overriding goal was to chase out the British and the French colonial rulers, the MB fitted well into the nationalist fold, its alliance with the less religiously oriented nationalists cemented on the battlefields of Palestine and the Suez Canal.

The MB espousal of Pan-Arabism stood in stark contrast to that of the Egyptian religious establishment, which had opposed Pan-Arabism ever since the late 1920s. This was either because the ulama viewed it as a competitor of Pan-Islam or because (much like Egyptian-centered nationalism) it was a Western import. It is quite illuminating that when the major proponent of secular Pan-Arabism, Sati' al-Husri, would collect his polemical essays of the 1930s and the early 1940s, his arrows would be directed not merely against the (secularist) proponents of non-Arab—that is, Syrian, Egyptian, Lebanese—particularistic nationalism, but also against the rector of al-Azhar, Sheikh Mustafa al-Maraghi, who in a famous 1938 essay dismissed the goal of Arab unity as racist. (It should be noted that even Pan-Islamists from outside the religious establishment, such as Shakib Arslan, warned that Pan-Arabism is bound to cut the ground from under the feet of Islam.)[17]

By 1952, however, when al-Husri published his *Arabism between Its Supporters and Its Critics*, he would find such critics only among the adepts of particularistic nationalism (*iqlimiyya*). The religious establishment had in the meantime been converted to Pan-Arabism, whether out of conviction—under the combined impact of the mystique of the Arab League (founded in 1945) and the First Palestine War—or just slavishly following in the footsteps of the Egyptian, and Iraqi, monarchies. When the Egyptian Revolutionary

regime switched, in 1954, to wholehearted Pan-Arabism, the ulama
would be quick to join in the chorus.

As for the MB, until their clash with Nasser, and well beyond,
they would continue to profess allegiance to Pan-Arabism. Even a
purist like Sayyid Qutb would write in January 1953:

> Some of us prefer to assemble around the banner of Ar-
> abism. I do not object to this being a middle-range, transitional
> goal for unification, on the road to a unity of a wider scope.
> There is, then, no serious contradiction between Arab nation-
> alism and Pan-Islam as long as we understand Arabism as a
> mere stage. The whole Land of the Arabs falls within the scope
> of the Abode of Islam. And whenever we liberate an Arab
> territory, we set free a patch of the Islamic homeland, an or-
> ganic part of the Islamic body; we would use it eventually to
> liberate the rest of this one and indivisible Abode.[18]

Less than a decade later, in one of those letters from prison,
further developed in *Signposts*, he has to say something completely
different:

> The Prophet Muhammad was no doubt capable of setting
> forth a movement of Pan-Arab nationalism in order to unify
> the strife-riven tribes of Arabia. He was well nigh able of en-
> dowing his movement with a nationalist orientation in order to
> liberate [Arab] lands usurped by the Byzantines in the north
> and the Persians in the south.
>
> Yet Allah, the Omnipotent and Omniscient, did not in-
> struct His Messenger to go in that direction. He only told him
> to preach that there is no God but Allah. Why? Because Allah
> knew that there was no sense in liberating the land from a
> Byzantine or a Persian tyrant in order to put it in the hands of
> an Arab tyrant. Any tyrant is still a tyrant. The land is to God
> and should be liberated to serve Him alone. . . . Men should
> become His servants and none other. . . . All domination (hak-
> imiyya) should be in the hands of Allah, all law (Shari'a) His
> only. The sole collective identity Islam offers is that of the

Faith, where Arabs, Byzantines, Persians, and other nations and colors are equal under God's banner.

Pan-Arabism is, thence, flatly rejected as incompatible with Islam:

> The homeland (*watan*) a Muslim should cherish and defend is not a mere piece of land; the collective identity he is known by is not that of a regime. . . . Neither is the banner he should glory in and die for that of a nation (*qawm*). . . . His jihad is solely geared to protect the religion of Allah and His Shari'a and to save the Abode of Islam and no other territory. . . . Any land that combats the Faith, hampers Muslims from practicing their religion, or does not apply the Shari'a, becomes ipso facto part of the Abode of War (*Dar al-Harb*). It should be combatted even if one's own kith and kin, national group, capital and commerce are to be found there. . . . A Muslim's homeland is any land governed by the laws of Islam. Islam is the only identity worthy of man. . . . Any other group identity . . . is a jahili identity of the type humanity has known during its periods of spiritual decadence.[19]

The divorce with Pan-Arabism is thus definite, all ties to be severed, all former alliances between it and Islam null and void. No wonder that the Egyptian regime made these and other like-minded passages the centerpiece of its case against Qutb. For it was one of major ideas, with the help of which he conferred upon the reestablished MB underground a sense of purpose it had lacked. Though officially the leader of the organization, Qutb seems to have been only haphazardly involved in such mundane matters as training, arms acquisition, and the planning of operations. His ideological ascendancy was, however, uncontested; the challenge to Pan-Arabism was at its core.[20]

The report of secret police on the case dissects the *Signposts* in order to prove the accused's "rejection of Pan-Arab nationalism." So does the special report of the Legislative Commission of the People's Assembly and the Act of Accusation. The regime understood only too well Qutb's direct swipe at Pan-Arabism's claim that the Arabs are God's Chosen People (*khayr umma*), a claim supposedly predicated upon the Koran (II, 110). Qutb, an authority on Koranic exegesis, pointedly quotes this verse to prove that "God's real chosen people is the Muslim community (*umma*) regardless of ethnic, racial, or territorial affiliation of its members. For didn't the first group of Muslims comprise an Arab, Abu Bakr, an Ethiopian, Bilal, a Byzantine, Suhayb, and a Persian, Salman?"[21]

Nor did Qutb himself evade the issue during his police interrogation:

> Q. What is your opinion of patriotism [*wataniyya*, "particularistic nationalism"]?
>
> A. Patriotism should consist in bonds to the Faith, not to a piece of land. The present, territorial, sense given to this term should thus be greatly stretched.
>
> Q. What do you think of Pan-Arab *qawmiyya*?
>
> A. To my mind, this is a type of ideology that had exhausted its role in universal history. The whole world coalesces today in large ideological formations predicated upon doctrines and beliefs. Striving toward Islamic unity is, hence, much more in tune with the spirit of the times we live in.[22]

The Nagging Doubts   Viewed against the backdrop of MB history, the divorce with Pan-Arabism seems abrupt and sudden. It would seem somewhat less so when placed in the intellectual context of the times. Uneasiness with regard to the turn taken by Arab nationalism under the military regimes can be detected in some religious quarters from the late 1950s onward. While the Azharites threw aside past reservations and embraced Arabism fervently, a major independent thinker, Muhammad al-Ghazzali (a former member of the Egyptian MB who left them in 1953), complained that in fighting for Arabism he had to accommodate strange and domineering bedfellows, the secular nationalists:

> Who are these people? They are neither Arabs nor non-

Arabs; neither Russians nor Americans. They are the worst misfortune that has befallen our land. They grew out of the evil seeds sown by imperialism in our hearts and minds. Yet these very people are flesh of our flesh, they speak our language. All of a sudden they rose to prominence, their voices penetrating every nook and cranny like frogs croaking in the night. One should tear the mask off their faces so that no more will they be able to mislead. They cloak themselves with the false mantle of Pan-Arab nationalism while at the same time they combat that very [Islamic] Faith which is the true mission of Arabism. [23]

Note that Ghazzali does not vituperate against the Pan-Arab idea as such; he rather denies authenticity to a major manifestation thereof. His concept of Arabism is still essentially the one he shared with Sayyid Qutb (and the MB in general) in 1953: Arab unity as a step up the ladder leading to Islamic unity. What accounts for Ghazzali's virulent tone in 1959 is certainly not the souring of the relationship between the regime and the MB (from which he has defected in the meantime). It is just that in the early days of the Egyptian Revolution, Pan-Arabism was not a salient slogan and to the extent that the revolution exhibited suspect tendencies (apart from a growing monopolization of power), it was rather toward Egyptianism, that old secularist bogey of the 1920s and 1930s. It is significant that during the second anniversary of the revolution, three months before the major crackdown upon the MB, Pharaonic *tableaux vivants* figured in the July 23 evening processions.

When Ghazzali wrote the above paragraph in 1959, he was reacting to a totally different situation: Pan-Arabism reigned supreme, yet its spokesmen in the media were secularists of the Husri school ('Ali al-Kharbutli, Ahmad Baha' al-Din, Anis Mansur, Muhammad Mandur, Kamal al-Mallakh) who seemed to enjoy the benediction of the regime, for all the latter's continued lip service to Islam. The Egyptian-Syrian Union was founded in 1958 upon an alliance with an openly secularist party, the Ba'th. Islam came to be a servant of Arabism, a mere historical component of a basically nonreligious ideology. This is, of course, the obverse of Ghazzali's notion of "True Arabism" (the title of a book of his, 1961) as "the vessel of Islam." He cannot accept the view that "Islam is nothing but a feature of the Arab Renaissance produced by that great race in the Middle Ages" or that "in a manner of speaking, Islam sprouts out of the earth, not from heaven, it represents the upsurge of a nation rather than Allah's liberating gift freeing us from backwardness and barbarity."[24] The enemy has been operating from within and using Arab-Muslim modes of discourse with the blessing of the powers-that-be. It is a stocking-footed enemy and, thence, all the more pernicious. The regime is not explicitly castigated, but the secularist paragons are. After the breakup of the United Arab Republic, the author was restrained by no such prudence with regard to Syria and would attack the Ba'th for the same sins.[25]

Fathi Yakan, the major Lebanese disciple of Maudoodi and Qutb and yet another believer in the "Mission of Arab nationalism" (title of a 1958 book of his), expressed there the same fears as to the wrong route lately taken by Pan-Arabism. Yakan still thought a return to an Islamic concept of Arabism was possible. An Iraqi admirer of the MB, Muhammad Mahmud al-Sawwaf, in a lecture delivered in 1964, likewise excoriated what he dubbed the "Arabs über Alles" notion as Nazi-inspired, and he demanded to make religion alone the backbone of Arabism. "We are not opposed to nationalism as such but to nationalism predicated upon birth, ethnic origin, or territory. We are not opposed to a nationalism that glorifies Islam and adopts it as a way of life. We do combat a nationalism shorn of religion, nay even attempting to take the place of Islam." Here al-Sawwaf emphasizes the sorest point: "Don't some nationalists say that an Arab Muslim has two religions, Islam and nationalism, and a Christian Arab has two, Christianity and nationalism? Arab nationalism is allegedly their sole common denominator. . . . What a blasphemy!" Moreover, the author is deeply troubled by the efficacy of Pan-Arabism as a surrogate religion: "Young Muslims are sincerely attracted to this type of nationalism . . . ready to fight other Muslims for their new creed. Many of them disdain going to the mosque and scorn reciting the Koran lest they be branded reactionary."[26]

Nationalism and Its Discontents

Al-Sawwaf was by no means overstating his case. Not only a propagandist such as al-Kharbutli made the Prophet Muhammad into the "Messenger of Arabism" (title of his 1959 book), but even a prominent novelist such as Mahmud Taymur argued that "every age has its own sacred prophethood and Arabism is the prophethood of the present age in Arab society; its mission being to unite our forces, tap our capabilities. Arab writers should become the apostles of this veracious prophecy." A Lebanese Nasserist would go so far as to claim that "the Arab cause should be for the believing Arab what belief in Allah is for the Muslim," and the Kuwaiti monthly al-'Arabi declared in like vein (January 1959) that "Arab unity must be for the Arabs everywhere what the unity of God is for the faithful of Islam."[27] The harshest diagnosis about the transformation of Pan-Arabism into a civil religion would be voiced in Saudi Arabia, there perhaps more in glee than in dismay, during the years of the Arab Cold War. One might take with a grain of salt Saudi professed attachment to "true [Islamic-based] Arabism"; this could be no more than a necessary ploy in the polemics against Nasser, given the fact the Pan-Arabism's hold over intelligentsia and masses alike was still strong (albeit already weakened by the breakup of the United Arab Republic [UAR] and the Yemen War). However, Saudi writers were not out of tune with the mood in Islamic circles elsewhere in the early 1960s when they claimed that "the propagandists of Pan-Arabism renege on Islam and seek to dislodge it as religion and polity." That type of "nationalism hell-bent on erasing the very name of Islam from Arab Renaissance today" was, by their lights, the major culprit for the disruption of Arab solidarity.[28]

Sayyid Qutb's evolution during the 1950s and early 1960s thus roughly parallels that of other Muslim thinkers, many of whom used to believe in the alliance between Arabism and Islam, but who had not been exposed to the same prison experience as he had been. Perhaps the most striking parallel is between his evolution and that of Abu-l-Hasan 'Ali Nadvi, that Indian Muslim thinker, who had always been a great believer in the special role of the Arabs in Islam, and who wrote in Arabic extensively and maintained close contacts with the MB from the late 1940s on. When he met Sayyid Qutb during a 1951 visit to Egypt, they discovered, as we have seen, a great intellectual affinity predicated upon mutual admiration for Maudoodi's ideas (which Nadvi had been instrumental in introducing into the Arab East). [29]

By the early 1960s—though based in faraway Lucknow, India (and certainly cut off from his imprisoned Egyptian friend)—this marginal, yet perspicacious observer, grew dismayed by the conversion of Arabism into a surrogate religion by Nasserism and even more so by the Ba'th. In a series of articles and lectures (two of the latter delivered in Saudi Arabia) he sounded desperate warnings to his Arab friends not to embark upon this slippery and jahili path. The tone of his Arabic was milder than that of other polemicists, yet the message was clear enough. "The nationalists are sincere and serious; they have been driven into these erroneous theories merely by excess of zeal, by a desire to glorify the Arab cause. Unwittingly perhaps, they become the agents of destructive Western ideas, helping their religion out of the Arab arena by building up a national movement devoid of an Islamic dimension." For him, as well as for some Arab writers, the fact that so many Christian Arabs (beginning with Michel Aflaq) were so prominent in Arab nationalism was a reason for alarm, whereas "the whole future of these minorities hinges upon the spread of secular nationalism and its replacing Islam; only thus can they reach positions of power and authority in the Arab world and cut the Arabs off from the Islamic world with which these Christians share neither beliefs and feelings nor history." Nadvi could find comfort only in the fact that Pan-Arabism seemed to have made real inroads above all among the intelligentsia: "The masses are still deeply attached to Islam."[30] But the doubt persisted: for how long?

The reverse of the monopolization of Pan-Arabism by the secularists—with the backing of the military regimes (as epitomized in Nasser's 1962 Charter)—was the abdication of the Islamic establishment. The majority of the ulama came to be converted to the Pan-Arab cause rather late and retained the zeal of new converts. While the secularists brushed Islam aside or at the very least minimized it, the ulama tended to identify Islam and Arabism completely, the latter virtually absorbing the former. Some would vie in fervor with the secularists, speaking about a new chapter in the history of Arabism and Islam opened by the 1952 Revolution, in which both would perform their mission to spread justice for the sake of all humanity.[31] An even more excessive formulation is to be found in an article by Ahmad Hasan al-Zayyat, editor in chief of *Majallat al-Azhar* (1963). Not withstanding the breakup of the UAR, he wrote, "The unity established by Muhammad was comprehensive because it was founded upon the bonds of belief, and such bonds, however long-lasting, must ultimately weaken or be transformed. The unity established by Saladin was partial and short-lived, grounded as it was in the personality of that sultan, a mere mortal. As for the unity built by Nasser, it is enduring and capable of further growth, based as it is on socialism in the realm of economics, on freedom of opinion, and on democracy in the realm of politics. These three components constitute a solid guarantee for this union against the danger of exploitation, tyranny, weak rule or corruption."[32]

"Progressive" ulama were perhaps less opportunistic but no less zealous. Muhammad Khalfallah celebrated the fact that language-based Arab nationalism had a religious component, and he prognosticated that Arabism was bound to spread further and achieve hegemony and unity. "The practicality of Islamic unity is, on the contrary, very doubtful,"[33] he alleged. Few and far between were

the voices who criticized such excesses; their tone (unless they came
from Saudi Arabia) was circumspect, their approach roundabout.
Quite atypical was the Egyptian Mahmud 'Abd al-Wahhab Fayid—
significantly enough, not one of the higher ulama—who dared challenge al-Zayyat. Fayid accused him of trying to "turn people away
from the mission of Muhammad," pointing out how under King
Faruq, al-Zayyat used to sing the praises of Islam (as better than
democracy, more just than socialism).[34]

Fayid was a particularly courageous individual who had proved
his mettle when calling for the resignation of Sheikh al-Azhar in
1957 for failing to protest against the abolition of Shari'a courts. At
that date he seemed to enjoy some half-open support, and al-Azhar
students accompanied him to the railway station when he was ban-
ished from Cairo to a teaching post in Upper Egypt. If such support
was forthcoming at all in 1963, it was at best tacit.

Severing the Gordian Knot   Even Fayid, however, still viewed
                                   Arabism as a step up the road to
Islamic unity. Here we grasp the exact significance of Sayyid Qutb's
quantum leap. Sharing the doubts nurtured by some Muslim thinkers on the marriage between Islam and Pan-Arabism, he moved
ahead and took the decisive step calling for a divorce. Qutb came
to perceive the secularization of Arabism not as the regrettable (and
still reversible) victory of one tendency within the movement over
the other, but as an inevitable outcome. As nationalism was a European invention imported to the Middle East, it was bound to ally
itself with that other import, secularism; all the more so, as European nationalism was essentially secularist, bred out of a culture
where religion and state were different entities. The implicit contradiction between nationalism and Islam was blurred during the
anticolonialist struggle, for they had a common enemy. In the postcolonial age, especially with the demise of "collaborationist" monarchies and the rise of nationalist-dominated regimes, the head-on
clash was ineluctable. That secularism now had powerful allies

within Middle Eastern societies—allies who seemed dedicated to the welfare of those societies—made their danger even worse. One had, thus, to move from the struggle against outside enemies to combat enemies within; from alliance with nationalism—or efforts to modify its character—to open warfare.

It is not entirely clear whether Qutb was inspired on this chapter by Maudoodi, who had been a fierce opponent of Indian nationalism in the late 1930s and in the 1940s. He fought with particular vehemence the secularist "Muslim nationalism" of Jinnah, "ensnared by the false idol" of a nationalism anchored in territory, language, and economic interests. Nationalism, for Maudoodi, must inevitably bolster up "jahili fanaticism" and bring misfortune upon humanity. It can in no way be compatible with religion. This was true in the Arabian Peninsula in the seventh century; it is still true today, when "Muslims, blindly emulating the West, glorify in their Arabhood, Egyptianhood, Turkishness, and so forth."

Maudoodi's collected writings on this issue would first be translated into Arabic only in 1967,[35] yet Qutb could have gleaned references to these views interspersed in his other books, which were available in Arabic. That he does not refer to Maudoodi at all on this topic must be due not only to the paucity of such references but also to the fact that the relationship of Arabism to Islam was much more complex than its relationship with Indian or Pakistani nationalism. Islam was born in Arabia, its message defined as the ultimate version of monotheism in "the most eloquent language," Arabic. It was Arab tribes the Prophet united; it was these very tribes who spread the Faith beyond the peninsula and established the empire, all whose caliphs (till the early sixteenth century) were Arabs. Not only prayer but the main body of Islamic intellectual production—law, theology, mysticism, philosophy, and science—had always been conducted in Arabic. The relationship between Arabism and Islam was too close, too intricate for even most modern-day secularists to call for outright separation (especially when they wanted to mobilize the masses). No wonder that radical Islam, of

the old MB variety, saw nationalism—interpreted by their own
lights, of course—as an ally of Islam. Indeed even Nadvi, who
propagated Maudoodi's ideas in the Arab world, thought (and continued to do so well into the 1970s) that an exception should be
made for Arabism, as the sole variety of nationalism which is not
diametrically opposed to Islam and can even be made its auxiliary.

Hitherto influenced by Nadvi, Sayyid Qutb saw his own thinking transformed during the 1950s. He came to inaugurate a new
brand of Islamic radicalism, reacting not to the twilight of colonial
rule but to the postindependence age—by calling for the severance
of that Gordian knot tying together Arabism and Islam.

The New Tyranny   What motivated Qutb to call for a clean
                       slate? What made such a break with the MB
past attractive for radicals in the 1960s and 1970s? Both for him and
for his followers the prison years were the crucial, formative experience. Not only did incarceration and brutal torture breed hatred,
desire for revenge, and alienation, the experience forced them to
face up to the realities of the new nationalist, military-controlled
state: a state characterized by sincere and combative anti-imperial-
ism—hence not to be impugned as "collaborationist" as the old
upper-class rulers used to be. The elite of this state was plebeian in
origin and thus able to address the masses in their own idiom; it was
military in profession with all that this implies in terms of relative
efficiency, cult of order, and penchant for ruthlessness. Consequently, it dawned upon the radicals that not only does the danger
to Islam come from within, it now comes in a manner so effective,
so insidious, and seemingly hard to fault.

The scale and efficiency of the 1954/55 Nasserist crackdown
on the MB, the dismantling of subsequent attempts to reorganize,
the manipulation of public opinion against the MB—all this must
have intimated to the latter that the rules of the game were being
rewritten by the new powers-that-be and that these redoubtable adversaries could play hard and fast.

At the outset, the MB found it difficult to comprehend the new circumstances. It is typical that, as late as summer 1954 when they obtained secret police documents dealing with repressive measures planned against them, their leadership did very little about it. The October 1954 mass arrests and the 1955 show trials set off a reconsideration of strategies. New conceptions were slowly fleshing out.

This was particularly true of Brethren thrown in jail or running for their lives. Thus MB leader Hasan 'Ashmawi, living clandestinely in various Egyptian localities during the mid-1950s, recounts in his memoirs his feelings of almost total isolation, cut off as he was from his support base, and with the rest of the membership falling one after the other into cleverly set traps. He notes the fear the ever-present intelligence services spread among the previously sympathetic populace, and the ease with which the common people were converted to support the regime by propaganda campaigns, plebiscites, referenda, and other "distortions of democracy."[36] Ironically, in this as in other MB writings, a measure of nostalgia creeps in for the good old days of the relatively liberal monarchy, which was more respectful of legality, less efficient in intelligence gathering and in repression. This (admittedly partial) democracy had now been converted into a blatant tyranny. "Former rulers used to maltreat their adversaries, but not until the revolutionary regime have we seen rulers who bring the wife and children of an opponent and torture them in his presence," notes a prisoner. "Democratic life which had allowed for a freedom of political activity was definitely done away with," decries another Egyptian. "The present regimes are animated by vicious hatred of Islam. No ideological dialogue with them is possible, for their sole answer is recourse to repression."[37]

In the same vein the Syrian radicals lament the passing of the old-time judiciary, which "used to be the mainstay of society and the pride of the nation. Judges had been above reproach. They had been held to high standards in ethics and scholarship and had administered justice to all, regardless of social position, even if they had to rule against the powers-that-be. Yet under the [Ba'th] tyranny this venerable institution—much like others—was eaten up by rot. The judiciary and the judges lost their immunity. Opportunists, ignorant diploma holders, greedy individuals, and other time-servers were appointed to the bench. The common people learned that their pleas were of no avail unless they were ready to grease the palms of those who sit in judgment. The guardians of the law became robbers."[38] This brings another spokesman of the Syrian underground to paint a much harsher and broader historical canvas:

> How miserable you are, oh Syria! The Mongols invaded you, followed by the French, killing, devastating and spoliating. Then a worse disaster befell you: the Alawites infiltrated the [Ba'th] regime and started to shed blood, sieze property, and violate taboos. Paralyzed by stupefaction, the nation's power of resistance was sapped; little by little the Syrians resigned themselves to the new state of affairs, and the oppressors firmly sat in the saddle, treating the population arbitrarily.[39]

The abuse of due process, the manipulation of the legislative system (through retroactive laws) and of the judiciary, are common complaints in letters from prison and in memoirs. Massacres like the one perpetrated in the Torra jail in June 1957 and in the Cairo suburb of Kardasa, an MB redoubt, in August 1964, added poignancy to the emerging awareness of a new reality. What made this reality even more revulsive—yet efficient—was the democratic and revolutionary garb it was cloaked in.

Sayyid Qutb, showing the court the marks of torture on his body, would wryly remark, "The principles of the revolution have indeed been applied to us, Muslim Brethren, in jail." During his police interrogation he rested his case upon the regime's trampling on legality. "A government which is not beholden to any law ceases to be a legitimate government." The prime examples he cited were the mass arrests in 1954, "which gave us an inkling of things to come," as well as the outlawing of the MB, though all it had done was to "carry out the religious injunction of preaching." Fighting such a regime, he declared, was a measure of self-defense.[40]

"I am writing to you," says another prisoner in a letter, "from the fearful Bastille of Egypt, from that sinful military prison. The whole of Egypt is imprisoned. . . . I was arrested despite my immunity as a judge, without an order of arrest. . . . My sole crime being my critique of the nonapplication of the Shari'a." And on his jailers: "This is the scum which rules Egypt. What a strange sight they are! Their minds are in their bellies and in their hands." As for his prosecutors, they "departed from its old traditions, threw aside law and facts, and concentrated during the trial upon insults and curses." (Judges like General Digawi, president of the military court, indeed conducted themselves in manifest hostility to the defendants, subjected them to rituals of degradation and disregarded procedural rules.) No wonder that songs composed in prison camps promised Nasser the same fate as dictators such as Mussolini and Shishakli.[41]

A Syrian disciple of Sayyid Qutb, Sa'id Hawwa, would try, toward 1970, to explain the way the exercise of power changed under the military elites: "All over the Islamic world the officers' corps is the most depraved social group. This is particularly true for the upper echelons, which are full of traitors, drunkards, fornicators, non-Muslims, and heretics. All that is due above all to methods of officers' selection. Those in charge of admission to military schools are the vilest elements of the corps and they reject virtually all candidates who are religious-minded; their criteria are, as a rule, imbued with the values of the materialistic jahiliyya." The overall judgment of Hawwa—who was to become the major thinker of the New Radicalism in Syria—does not differ significantly from the one preferred long after the event, by Salah al-Din al-Bitar, founder of the Ba'th and erstwhile ally of the army officers (before being demoted, exiled, and ultimately assassinated), as well as from that of Sami al-Jundi, another prominent, and later disillusioned Ba'th leader.[42]

The brutality of the Ba'th regime in dealing with religious

dissent (in 1964, 1965, and 1967), which far exceeded that of Nasser—lent credence to Hawwa's words. Developments under President Assad, who seized power after Hawwa's book was written, would only further bolster his case, especially the arrests, torture, and massacres of MB sympathizers from 1976 onward. No other elite "in Syrian history ever since independence," said a clandestine MB tract, "had such a monopoly, such a tight grip on all power centers." Another tract reviles the "despotism of the repressive apparatus"; "Thousands are in prison, many of whom die under torture—from electrical shock to severe beating. All suffer deliberate degradation. Those who do not die see their property sequestrated and are deprived of the right to legal defense."[43]

Observing these developments from Tripoli, Lebanon, Fathi Yakan would thus sum them up in early 1967: "The Islamic movement faces now a grave challenge. Leadership in Muslim countries fell into the hands of dictatorial rulers who treat the true believers most harshly—torturing and massacring them, making their wives into widows. . . . Simply put, an open season has been declared on Islam. . . . Our enemies have recourse to all the destructive and immoral means available. On top of the repressive measures they launch propaganda campaigns in the service of the new jahiliyya, spreading false accusations against our militants."[44]

When such a military state controls not only all instruments of coercion but also all instruments of persuasion and can infuse the latter with a mass-mobilizing content—personality cult of the za'im and the "religion of Arabism"—the danger it constitutes to Islam is greatly enhanced.

"There are Muslims," writes Hawwa, "who become enamored of this or that political leader and give him their all-out support, come hell or high water. They allege that the leader is working in the service of his nation or that he is a man of genius, a great historical figure or a sublime hero, and so forth." Hawwa thus came to share Qutb's conclusion—divorce with nationalism is the only remedy. "Should a Muslim embrace national goals whatever their nature?" he asks rhetorically, "or should Islam constitute the supreme goal of our umma? Didn't the Prophet emigrate from his own homeland? For if we are not ready to follow his example, why wouldn't it be licit for a Muslim to embrace the nationalism of an infidel country (Dar al-Harb)?[45]

The rise of the new military state is, for Hawwa, a major cause for the decline of Islam. "Islam has lost hold over real life. Its political regime is a shambles, its concept of the community of the believers (umma) was replaced by [Pan-Arab] nationalism (qawmiyya); its notion of a judicial system was scuttled, its laws relegated to oblivion, its concepts of executive power shunted aside by the barbarity of the jahiliyya.

Combating the state and its nationalistic credo is thus the spearhead of what Hawwa dubs the "Second Islamic Revolution" (the First being the anticolonialist struggle, which ended with independence). This revolution should be directed "against internal, endogenous currents of opinion which are tributaries of powerful worldwide undercurrents," such as secularism and consumerism.[46]

Of all these currents, Hawwa considers nationalism the most dangerous. In a more recent work of his (1979), he sums up the danger with the formula: Arabism as secular religion. "Affiliation to a nationality as such is quite a natural phenomenon. But what is objectionable is that when asked 'What is your creed?' one answers: 'Arab.' For that Arab should rather say that he is Muslim or Christian or Jewish. Ethnic affiliation must have no impact upon the contents of one's beliefs, perceptions, and mores. This grave error ends up making nationalism a substitute for Islam."[47]

Similar ideas had been nourished for some years by another Syrian, Marwan Hadid, who as a student in Egypt (1956–64) seems to have been in contact with Qutb's admirers among former political detainees. Their critique of the military rulers (and of the old-style MB) inspired him to establish in his home country, upon his return, a radical splinter group, Kata'ib Muhammad (Phalanges of Muhammad). It is Hawwa, however, who endowed the group with an ideological coherence, which would later propel it—under Hadid's operational leadership—into armed resistance.

The *Manifesto of the Islamic Revolution in Syria* (1980)— which Hawwa had a hand in drafting—singles out the "Pan-Arab parties" (notably, the Ba'th) as the major force "conducting at present an open warfare against the Islamic movement and pulling its weight in order to banish Islam's protagonists from public life." The *Manifesto*—as well as the *Charter of the Syrian Islamic Front* (1981)—is ready to envision Arab unity, or the unification of any two Arab countries, as a stepping-stone toward Islamic unity; but it refuses to accept Arabism as the major component of Islam. In its definition of Islamic identity the *Manifesto* reduces Arabism to a purely linguistic factor; it is only one of six factors, or strands (together with creed, law, history, territory, and mores) which, interwoven, make up the fabric of Islam.[48]

Fathi Yakan who, already in 1958, had had his doubts about the turn Pan-Arabism had taken, was swayed by Qutb and came, by 1970, to roughly the same views, albeit formulated in a milder manner; the *Jama'a Islamiyya* (Muslim Association) he had founded in 1964 would become their vehicle:

> Pan-Arabism had undergone a dangerous and far-reaching metamorphosis caused by its own intellectual vacuity. Lacking in philosophical contents, it has seen this intellectual vacuum filled in by foreign, materialistic ideas. . . . This would not have happened had we kept the close relationship which had existed in the past between Arabism and Islam, when it has been maintained that Arabism is just body and Islam its soul. The disintegration of this protective alliance explains how the citadel of Arabism could be seized from within. . . . Arabism lost its distinct personality. The umbilical cord linking it to its past was cut off.[49]

Although Yakan still hoped perhaps to have Arabism revert one day to its old self, he knew that at present—and for the foreseeable future—it was all-out war between Pan-Arabism and Islam. Later

Lebanese movements, more radical than the Jama'a, such as *al-Tawhid al-Islami* (Islamic Unification), were to take up vigorously this theme of cutting Arabism down to size ("it consists of language alone") and flatly reject all types of nationalism. "Pan-Arabism," said their leader Sa'id Sha'ban in a November 1983 interview, "has been tried, but did not foster any coming together. Territorial nationalism has been experimented with in Lebanon and brought us nothing but destruction and devastation. Therefore we call upon one and all: come back and worship Allah, your Lord."[50]

Turning Inward   It is the farewell to Pan-Arabism and the concentration upon the "jahiliyya within" that account for the change of attitude toward the Arab-Israeli conflict. They well explain the gloating of the radicals in 1967 at the misfortune of the regime, the shock—for there certainly was one even among MB prisoners—related to what the defeat did to the people (still judged as capable of being redeemed) and to territories of *Dar al-Islam*. The struggle for their reconquest figured, however, very low on the radicals' order of priorities.

That such attitudes could persist, as we have seen, well through the 1970s and the early 1980s, is all the more remarkable as many of the young recruits who flocked to the militant Islamic student associations (Jama'at) and to terrorist groups, did so as a result of soul-searching set off by the trauma of June 1967.[51] Though haunted by the defeat, those new disciples learned to see in it nothing but a symptom; it is the root cause of the illness they had to strike at.

The Israeli challenge was real, at times quite exasperating (though the New Radicals, like many of the older generation, would combine hatred with a grudging respect toward Israel, held as an edifying example of a state built upon religion).[52] But however infuriating the "Zionist entity" was, it could never overshadow the internal challenges.

One catches a glimpse of the problematics involved there with Sayyid Qutb. In his consultations with the five ringleaders of the

MB underground in May 1965, he opposed certain types of terrorist activity with the argument that blowing up major economic installations may unwittingly serve the cause of "Zionist evil designs to weaken Egypt." In spite of his objections, the meeting decided to proceed with planning and training for such acts—though in scaled-down form—for they were still deemed vital to help the revolutionaries seize power and forestall repression (by knocking out electrical plants and communication systems).[53]

To the extent that Qutb's followers would continue to entertain such misgivings, they would be greatly alleviated by subsequent experiences in prison; prisons such as the military jail in Cairo, whose commander, a notoriously sadistic torturer, would tell the inmates in 1966: "You know my opinion of you . . . you deserve to be annihilated . . . for you constitute a worse danger to this country than the Jews."[54] The prison experience would indeed figure as a major factor not only in the making of the first generation of New Radicals but also in the indoctrination of new recruits. Episodes such as the one just quoted must have helped reinforce the argument for a reordering of priorities.

The attitude toward Pan-Arabism among the radicals of the 1970s and the 1980s encapsulates this evolution. Here is how a booklet published by the Muslim Students' Association in al-Minya University (Upper Egypt) comments on the meaning of jihad: "This religion is not a call for the liberation of the Arab man, nor is it a special mission for the sole Arab. It is universal, its scope is the whole earth. . . . It is destined to liberate all humanity from man's domination upon man." And the Muslim Students' Association at Cairo University—in a book that elsewhere exudes hatred toward Israel—proclaims: "Our prime goal is the 'realization of a free Islamic society' . . . a society that is not riven by class struggle nor by chauvinistic qawmiyya."[55]

These views affected the somewhat more moderate MB clustered around monthlies such as *al-Da'wa* and *al-I'tisam* (which resumed publication between 1976 and 1981). The attitude toward

Pan-Arabism there is at best ambiguous (a good movement that went off the tracks), at times frankly hostile. In any case, collaboration with the secularist brand of Pan-Arabism is to be excluded, for, as one writer notes, "it evolved into a surrogate for religious bonds under the impact of a set of ideas which had developed in Europe in a specifically Christian situation."[56] Even in Syria, however much the MB will denounce the regime for losing the Golan Heights "through treason," the frequency and saliency of that charge are eclipsed by sallies against the "apostacy" and "infidelity" of the regime as evidenced in education, laws, nationalizations, and so forth. The ultimate enemy are those false Muslims "who at times cloak themselves with the mantle of Arabism, and at others with the coat of a particularistic (Syrian) nationalism."[57] In either case—much like in Egypt—it was the regime which articulated and disseminated these ideas; it is this "new tyranny" which had to be extirpated, root and branch.

CHAPTER THREE

In Quest of Authenticity

Treason of the Clerics   The New Radicalism thus represents an
evolution of MB radicalism in response
to changing circumstances in the Arab world of the 1950s and 1960s
with the input of a few ideas coming from the Muslim-Indian frontier of Islam, as interpreted by Qutb, Hawwa, Yakan, Dannawi (of
Tripoli, Lebanon), and others.

The imperative of the new situation has been succinctly put by
Yakan: "The demise of parliamentary life and the all-out adhesion
of the military dictatorship to secularism enjoins upon the Islamic
movement to work out a new strategy which will enable it to operate,
develop, and cope with these challenges."[1] The disappearance of
democracy had already been of concern to the MB in early 1953,
and there were inklings of the upsurge of secularism, as we have
seen, by then, with greater certitude from the late 1950s on. Yet it
took some time, and above all the decisive contribution of Sayyid
Qutb, for the new strategy to come into focus.

In seeking to revitalize the movement and to deal with the
challenge of the military, single-party regimes with their ideologies
couched in Islamic lingo, the New Radicals had to begin with a
diagnosis: the MB, the broadest Islamic mass movement in modern
history, lost public support rather quickly, whether from push or
pull, from intimidation or brainwashing by state-controlled media.

That the edifice could crumble so rapidly only served to confirm the deeply embedded cultural pessimism that had always characterized Islamic fundamentalism. Thus the MB of yore was quite preoccupied with "indigenous evils" such as the then-called "Westernization" of schools and laws.[2] Yet even this type of challenge—which in the 1930s and 1940s took second place to fighting the colonial rule—underwent a quantitative and qualitative change in the 1950s and 1960s. The doubling in size of the school system during the first decade of the military regime meant that cohorts of youths (especially in the ever-expanding towns) were exposed to a modern curriculum, including a Pan-Arab version of history. This same version would come to reign supreme in the Syrian school system under Ba'th rule (from 1963 on). Religious instruction shrank in scope and quality in elementary and high school, its place taken by civics and family-planning education. Not only did male teachers come to teach in girls' schools in both countries, but at the university level "promiscuity" was encouraged (colleges being co-ed) and the growing number of female students learned to give precedence to professional aspirations over their duties as homemakers and mothers. Al-Azhar was transformed into a partly secular university (1961), while Egyptian Shar'i courts were incorporated into the civil system (1957). In Syria an effort was made to scuttle the Shari'a Faculty of the University of Damascus by introducing special courses in Ba'th ideology and Arab socialism. Hundreds of religious-minded Syrian schoolteachers were dismissed and elementary and high school textbooks in language and literature were rewritten in a manner to avoid the use of examples taken from the Koran and Hadith. Identity cards issued by the Syrian Ministry of the Interior no longer listed the cardholder's religion. More shocking still were the physical attacks by young Ba'th female militants on traditionalist women, whose veils they tore off in public, the pressures brought to bear by high school principals on their female students to remove the veil "of their own accord," and the alleged moral laxity in Ba'th party women and youth organizations. Such organizations were much more vehemently resented in Syria than in Egypt (where they were much less efficacious), representing as they did a mode of state intervention in civil society, mobilizing two major social groups traditionally subject to special ulama solicitude and guidance.

In both countries, legislation inspired by foreign models—in matters ranging from personal status to banking and nationalization—was produced at an ever-accelerating pace. The Shari'a figured in constitutions at best as one source among many for legislation (and, between 1969 and 1973, it was not even required that the Syrian president be a Muslim).

While in Syria, this backsliding brought about a certain ulama opposition, especially from the lower ranks (in 1964–65 against the curtailing of liberties and the nationalizations, in 1967 against the publication of an atheistic article in the army magazine, in 1973 in order to amend the constitution so as to require the head of state to be a Muslim),[3] almost none was forthcoming in Egypt. This was no surprise for the Muslim radicals, for the MB had always disdained the ulama as a class for having failed to accomplish its historical duty as guardian of the conscience of the Faith, whether out of pusillanimity or opportunism. Al-Azhar was as much execrated by them as the epitome of subservience to the rulers as it was by reformists of the Muhammad 'Abduh school for its dessicated conservatism.[4]

Under Nasser the ulama seemed, however, to have sunk to a new low. "Many are the ulama, men of religion; few of the latter are really men," according to the one radical's epigram. "Before the 1952 Revolution they used to go on pilgrimage to the mansion of the British ambassador to ask for his and the king's blessing; after the Revolution they humbly submitted not only to the dictator, their benefactor, but also to the most junior of his officers," writes another; "they stooped so low that they accepted the tutelage of the Higher Council for Islamic Affairs, presided over by an army captain. It was he who even headed the religious delegations dispatched abroad. Compare this to the situation under the monarchy where kings (up to and until King Fu'ad) used to kiss the hand of Sheikh of al-Azhar."[5]

Typical of that slavishness was the aforementioned Ahmad Hasan al-Zayyat. As late as May 1952 he sang the praises of King Farouk, "defender of Islam and Arabism, protector of al-Azhar," only to find, soon after, these same virtues in the new rulers and to vilify the deposed king as "a satan who dared transgress the religion of Allah and break all taboos. He would go to Friday prayer from his 'love nest,' still sullied with fornication . . . , he would take a married woman for himself and kill her husband, not to speak of pocketing bribes and stealing from the Treasury." In Syria the radicals would point out another sycophant from among the higher ulama, a minister of waqf who compared the entry of the Syrian president into the Omayyad Mosque in Damascus with the seventh-century conquest of this city by Islam.[6]

Nahj al-Islam, the Damascus counterpart of *Majallat al-Azhar*, sang paeans to "the president [Assad], combatant of the Holy War, defender of our sacrosanct religion," due to whom "the spirit of Islam reigns in Syria"; Assad's 'Alawite affiliation was swept under the carpet with the formula of the "five schools" (whereby the 'Alawites, an extreme Shi'ite sect, are added to the four legal schools of Sunni jurisprudence). The magazine even found ways and means of exonerating the attack of female Ba'th militants upon veiled women. The political background of the editor in chief, Muhammad al-Khatib (who also was waqf minister) was quite telling: an MB sympathizer in the 1940s and 1950s, a Nasserist in the early 1960s, he later turned Ba'thist and religious affairs adviser of the president's brother, Rif'at, the regime's security chief.[7]

Despised and hated by the radicals, the religious establishment, these "stockbrokers of Islam," came to be a prime target of the radicals' violence. Two prominent examples are the kidnapping (and subsequent execution) of former Egyptian waqf minister Muhammad al-Dhahabi (1977) and the murder of Sheikh Muhammad al-Misri, director of waqf in Aleppo (1979).[8]

There were, in fact, some manifestations of dissent among the ulama, mostly of the lower ranks. These were particularly daring in Syria, in opposition to nationalizations in the mid-1960s and to the atheistic article of 1967, and on the constitutional question of the religion of the head of state in 1973. In Egypt there was a quiet manifestation of al-Azhar students led by Dr. Muhammad al-Bahi, against the 1957 abolition of Shari'a courts and a similar one against the personal status bill in 1974. More forthcoming were the critique of Arab Socialism by Zaynab al-Ghazzali, head of the Muslim women's association, critique of the nonapplication of the Shari'a by 'Ali Jarisha and the desultory protests of M. A. Fayid. None of all these, except for al-Bahi, could qualify as higher ulama. Even medium- and lower-level ulama, in both countries, would be, on the whole, characterized by sullen silence rather than by dissent (though less so in Syria than in Egypt).[9]

The abdication of the ulama, combined with the ignorance of the masses in religious matters, would go a long way to account for the ease with which the powers-that-be could manipulate Islam to cover many a sin, many an "imported (i.e., modern) idea," a task rendered all the easier by the regime's monopoly over the media. "Things came to such a point," wrote Hawwa, "that somebody can say to the Muslims, 'This is Islam' or 'This does not contradict Islam,' and they would always believe him." A political leader, "however iniquitous and dissolute, however openly he flaunts his transgressions and his neglect of the worship of Allah, would say unto them 'This is Islam,' and they would believe him, even when he endorses the most blatantly jahili idea. What adds to the confusion is that many of those so-called ulama have an erroneous conception of Islam. They are unworthy to instruct the faithful and their legal responsa (fatawa) do quite often more harm than good, making out the illicit to be licit."[10]

The Egyptian group that murdered Sheikh al-Dhahabi in 1977, the Takfir wa-Hijra, went so far in criticizing ulama subservience to the rulers that this was the main argument in favor of its extreme (and hitherto unique) position on the sources of Islamic jurisprudence. According to them, only Koran and Sunna are to be accepted, whereas all laws and injunctions produced after 660 by jurists by means of analogy (*qiyas*) and consensus of experts (*ijma'*) are ipso facto suspect, for the jurists were usually more attuned to the needs of the powers-that-be than to the goals of the Faith. Independent legal judgment (*ijtihad*) can, hence, be applied in selecting and rejecting rules and opinions engendered even during the early centuries of Islam. Such an independent personal judgment is all the more vital as regards legal rules posterior to the supposed "closing of the gates of ijtihad" in the tenth century A.D., for even after that date ulama continued in fact to invoke ijtihad, but that for one aim only: in order to introduce innovations which accommodate the rulers (very recent examples included legal opinions rendering licit interest-bearing treasury bonds and the drinking of beer).[11]

Criticism of the timorous ulama remained one of the most salient radical themes all through the 1970s (see chapter 1). It held a special attraction for the young generation where disillusionment with the religious establishment is rampant. Yusuf al-Qardawi, an Egyptian MB thinker who refused to go along with the Qutb revolutionary school, recounts:

> When I argue with a young extremist and tell him: 'You should get religious knowledge from its holders, i.e., the ulama,' he retorts: 'How can we find men of religion in whose religiosity and expertise we can trust? We see the ulama only in the orbit of the rulers, declaring legal whatever the latter want them to permit, forbidding what they want to outlaw. If the ruler is a socialist they give their blessing to socialism; if he is pro-capitalist they then confer upon capitalism the benediction of Islam.'

Qardawi reports his own half-hearted answer (it is only a matter of higher ulama, among the lower ones one can find virtue, and so on), yet he admits that the state of affairs is indeed as bad as described by the youth. He even cites a true anecdote to substantiate this claim: an important 'alim was invited to a televised debate on "family planning viewed by the Shari'a." The 'alim agreed and said to the producer: "Tell me; is this discussion designed to support family planning or to oppose it, so I should prepare myself accordingly?"[12]

Opinion polls confirm Qardawi's impressions. A recent Egyptian poll shows that while youth are overwhelmingly religious, only 28 percent would like to receive moral guidance from the ulama and 32 percent refuse to do so. It is indicative, indeed, of the radical groups that men of religion are rare in their leadership; they are composed for the most part of university students and modern professionals, autodidacts in religious matters. The 1965 Egyptian organization which had at least one prominent member who (albeit not an 'alim) had a broad religious education, namely, Sayyid Qutb, was in this respect exceptional. More typical was the 1981 Jihad Organization, where only one man of religion figured in the top ranks and served as a rubber-stamp mufti. Of the 123 university students who were members, only 5 studied theology.[13] The situation was only slightly different among the Syrian radicals. Of the 296 members arrested or killed during 1979–81 about whom one has information, 18 were men of religion, and none can be found in the leadership (though one leader, 'Ali Bayanuni, a lawyer, comes from an illustrious ulama family).[14]

The Specter of Ataturk

The fears that deliberate secularization gave birth to are best summed up by the formula Nasser = Ataturk. Sayyid Qutb seems to have been the first to use this diagnosis in his indoctrination sessions, thereby endowing the alienation instinctively felt by the young radicals with both a historical dimension and an ideological depth. During the 1966 trial, one of the defendants, an engineer, spoke of "Ataturk's role in devastating Islam through the abolition of the Caliphate, the transformation of Turkey into a secular state, the abolition [sic] of the Islamic religion and the Arab language and the resuscitation of the Pan-Turanian nationalism." He further affirmed that Nasser was taking exactly the same road "in combating Islam and declaring that the leaders of the 1952 Revolution were nonbelievers." Nasser tries to succeed where Ataturk failed, in introducing a radical transformation of society. Both Nasser and Ataturk are nothing but "agents of the same power, Crusader [Imperialism] and Judaism." When he left the stand and went back to the defendants' cage, Sayyid Qutb embraced him.

This indeed became a stock in trade of radical propaganda dealing with those "twin foreign agents," those "two paradigmatic false historical heroes." The equation would outlive Nasser and be applied to Muslim rulers in the 1970s and 1980s (in Syria: "Assad walks along the path trodden by Ataturk and Nasser"). No metaphor could more sharply express the enormity of "the ordeal Islam has to undergo today" than that recurring invocation of traumatic events of the abolition of the caliphate in 1924, with its implied corollary— the liquidation of the Abbasid Caliphate by the Mongols (1258). The Mongol metaphor, as we shall see, is central to the revolutionary theory as developed by the Sayyid Qutb school. This completes the historical triptych that stands at the center of the movement's demonology: Jahiliyya-Mongols-Ataturk. The latter third is by far the worst because of the "development of the organs of the state in our age: media, security services, educational system, the army, and the like."[15]

Deliberate secularization under Nasser seemed all the more dangerous from the late 1950s on, owing to the close cooperation with the Soviets and particularly since the introduction of Marxist-tinged "Arab Socialism" as epitomized in the 1962 Charter. While social justice and solidarism, and even some version of socialism, were the least objectionable elements in Western culture for a man like Sayyid Qutb,[16] he and his followers—many of whom had spent long hours in the prison camps debating their Communist fellow detainees[17]—were deeply troubled by the growing influence of Marx-

ism and by the prominence of former Communists in the single-
party apparatus in the media. In Syria, where nationalization measures would be somewhat more thoroughgoing than in Egypt, this
would lead the MB to open hostility even to socialist policy, in a
complete break with the positive attitude toward socialism set forth
by Mustafa al-Siba'i, MB leader in the 1950s.[18] This would not
happen in the Egyptian context because nationalization was perceived to be happening, above all, at the expense of the comprador
upper classes and foreign minorities; it is less the act itself than the
mismanagement of the nationalized sector the radicals objected to.
But it is the Communist impact—under the guise of socialism—on
hearts and minds that will preoccupy them most.

The alliance of the Ba'th with the Syrian Communist party in
a National Progressive Front (and Communist participation in government) would have some unsettling effect, coming as it did at a
time when the Syrian relationship with the USSR grew much closer.
In MB demonstrations in northern Syria the recurrent slogan was
"Neither Ba'thist nor Communist; we want the state to be Islamic."[19]

Yet from the late 1960s on the radicals in Syria and Lebanon
would be even more severely jolted by what they tagged the "Leftist-
Marxist-Atheistic" incursion in the realm of ideas. Its harbingers
were the atheistic article published in the Syrian army magazine on
April 25, 1967, and Syrian philosopher Sadiq Jalal al-'Azm's Critique of Religious Thought (Beirut, 1969). True enough, no Syrian
official or semiofficial organ would ever again publish such a blatantly antireligious credo; the Ba'th regime had learned its lesson
from the public outcry (which they had to appease by disavowing
the author and the editor and punishing both). But from time to
time the vigilant MB eyes scanning the press would detect phrases
such as those in an officious youth magazine's (al-Fursan) polemics
against the Saudis: "Let us call upon the Arab rulers to make com-
rade Assad their political qibla [literally: direction of prayer] instead
of kneeling down before the idols of Islam." The radicals' disgust
was all the deeper as by this very time the Syrian president was

making a show of particular attachment to Islam. Textbooks used for teaching "Islamic culture" in schools touted his dedication to the Faith; his security agents were dubbed "the sons of Allah" in the media. The 1973 constitution, though amended under MB-instigated public furor, had also contributed to the legacy of distrust as did the fact that Ba'th ideologues included a Christian, Michel Aflaq, who infused party terminology with faintly Christian terms ("suffering," "sacrifice," "love," "mission") and an 'Alawite, Zaki al-Arsuzi, rumored to have been a great admirer of the pre-Islamic jahiliyya as the Golden Age of the Arabs.[20]

The Ba'th was nevertheless not as efficacious in this domain as the freelance, "New Left" intellectuals of the type exemplified by Sadiq Jalal al-'Azm. Rising to prominence in the years following the Six-Day War, the Arab New Left produced a revisionist historiography and an iconoclastic social critique that called for a cultural revolution designed to liberate the Arabs from the yoke of their (essentially Muslim) past. Beirut, the publishing capital of the Arab world, was the fountain of most books and periodicals carrying this message, despite the efforts of religious circles (ever since their campaign against 'Azm's book) to have the Lebanese censorship intervene. No wonder that Muslim radicals in Lebanon—and later in Syria (where such ideas found their way into school curricula) and Egypt—came to voice deep concern over the spreading "desacralization campaign." Cases in point included the critique of the Arab language—that hallowed vehicle of Islam—"depicting its very virtues as defects" (atomism, flowery style, poverty of abstract terms), and the reinterpretation of certain Islamic extremist heterodox sects (e.g., the ninth- to tenth-century Qarmats) as exemplary social revolutionaries; moreover, orthodox Islam was reinterpreted as refractory to progress. Modernity has thus found a most effective Trojan Horse to penetrate the very citadel of Islam, all the more effective as it can marshal the resources of what for Sa'id Hawwa are the three most nefarious currents, "jahili [i.e., secularist] nationalism, Marxism, and existentialism."[21]

In the conspiratorial outlook typical of a persecuted group, certain acts would acquire symbolic significance in the eyes of the Muslim militants. Thus the fact that Nasser first disclosed the crackdown on the Sayyid Qutb's organization in a talk to Arab students in Moscow, of all places, was viewed as proof of his alliance with communism.[22] The tighter collaboration with Russia after the June war (in Syria's case, persisting to the present) further confirmed such suspicions. As the struggle would be primarily ideological, the major arena became the universities, where the Egyptian MB had a tradition of fighting the Communists going back to the days of the monarchy. The struggle was particularly violent in the late 1960s and early 1970s, at the term of which the Egyptian Muslim militants wrested control of student associations from the "Communist Infidels" and their allies of the New Left. This fight against what were deemed to be open agents of the most blatant variety of secularization will indeed become the recruiting and training ground for Islamic radicals.[23] These will soon have to turn against many a "disguised agent" of foreign ideas, and ultimately even against more subtle, less deliberate forms of secularization.

Media: The Subliminal Message   In fact, one of the most important qualitative changes in the challenges facing Islam during the 1960s was the salience of inadvertent (or subterranean) secularization. This force has indeed been operating in the Middle East for many decades, independent of the consciousness of those involved. It wooed them into de facto indifference to things religious and concentration upon materialism, hedonism—and their concomitant—immediate gratification (be it sensual or economic); a means for all the above is the cult of economic growth. The pace of this undercurrent had quickened in the 1950s and 1960s and its social appeal grew broader. Secularist values seeped into the popular culture through the electronic media in a manner that past conduits—pulp literature, yellow press, theater—had never been able to accomplish in the heavily illiterate Middle

Eastern societies. Film, quite popular as a form of leisure from the 1930s on, had been the harbinger of things to come—in both its foreign and local products—albeit mostly in towns. Movie theaters would indeed undergo an impressive expansion in these decades. But the massive introduction of transistor radios in the 1950s, then television in the early 1960s, tipped the balance. The media could appeal to illiterates, especially women and children, in their very homes.[24]

Preoccupation with the electronic media and their surreptitious, subliminal message had not yet taken in the 1960s the dimensions of the virtual obsession it was to become in the 1970s (with the frenetic spread of color television), as we have seen in chapter 1.[25] Nevertheless, the heightened awareness in radical circles with regard to the formidable danger they constitute is undeniable.

Sayyid Qutb's secret organization would hold that "radio and television, and the kinds of arts they foster and broadcast, conduct an anti-Islamic campaign." The militants, hence, were alleged to have laid down a plan to assassinate a number of Egypt's major popular artists (Umm Kulthum, 'Abd al-Halim Hafiz, Shadiya, Najat al-Saghira) and certain television anchor people and announcers, mostly female. Other plans called for bombs to be set off in movie houses and in theaters.[26]

Following the 1967 debacle, one of the explanations the radicals would offer for it was the corrupting of the moral fiber of society by the media. A prime example cited was the two hundred thousand postcards distributed by the Moral Orientation Section of the Egyptian army to the soldiers, carrying the pictures of five singers (the four mentioned above plus 'Abd al-Wahhab) in order to distract them. The very term *to distract* summed up, for the radicals, the nature of the danger: diverting attention from higher values. "We have thus relied upon the art of entertainment; and when war broke out, the voice of religion was swallowed up by the clamor of the singers." One of Qutb's codefendants who took the al-Azhar exams in prison wrote the following in response to questions on the achievements of the Revolution (exam on "National Culture"): "Establishing theaters and amusement centers, paving roads and building the Corniche [avenue along the Nile] and liberating Woman from her home and garb."[27]

By 1971 Hawwa would lay down as a principal objective of the Islamic movement, "putting the communications media in the hands of dedicated Islamic thinkers so that no element which is unrelated to pure Islam would play any guiding role. No other communications apparatus than that [held by the state]—whether internal or external—would be able to play any such role. Otherwise the Muslim community will not be able to liberate itself from the frivolity that made it lose its glory, honor, firmness, and religiosity."[28]

In adopting this demand as a plank of its program, the Command of the Syrian Revolution later explained, "The confessional ['Alawite] dictatorship exerts itself to reduce the level of culture and make the nation as ignorant as possible, that is, to make a whole nation cherish the values of individualism and of predominance of the Party and be infatuated with all kinds of amusements which distract the mind." Examples abound of MB tracts that wax indignant at Ba'th youth summer camps, immoral entertainment on radio and TV sprinkled with a personality cult of the "heretic tyrant." To drive the point home MB activists would from time to time set fire to movie theaters (especially on Ramadan).[29]

The radicals have learned their lesson: state control of the media is a formidable instrument of power that should be maintained; only the identity of the controller should be changed. A return to the centuries-old autonomy of civil society (where Islam operated) vis-à-vis the state is judged to be nearly impossible, given the technological control devices wielded by the state (not to speak of new organizational mechanisms such as mass movements by age, sex, or trade). Hence, the radicals do not respond to the new challenge by a call to pluralism. The media are not rejected, as evidenced by the fact that, much like their Iranian counterparts, Syrian and Egyptian radicals use tape cassettes to spread their ideas. It is the message of the media that is so troublesome and should be under control.

With the Egyptian Jihad Organization (1981), wresting control of the media became a major argument for the immediate seizure of power; for as long as the present state holds the media under its sway, any Muslim educational campaign is rendered null and void.[30] The pivotal role of this argument can be gauged by its salience in the debates between imprisoned radicals and official theologians (debates later published in the press). Hostility against the media is endemic among militants of the Muslim students' associations who quite often refuse to watch TV as a matter of moral rectitude.[31]

It was Lebanese thinker Muhammad Mahdi Shams al-Din (a Shi'ite, but a kindred spirit to Yakan and Dannawi), who, living in Beirut, the media capital of the Arab world, would set the rationale for what had become by then (1980) an overwhelming preoccupation of Islamic radicals with the media, tools of political and cultural propaganda:

> What renders the ideas of Modern Civilization particularly dangerous are the efficient and scientific methods with which they are diffused. . . . The common man in this day and age is the constant object of a brainwashing which intends to market specific commodities or ideas. It induces in him, through untiring repetition, hopes and fears, and elicits identification with things or thoughts, organizations or trends. Worse than the direct approach is indirect advertising, for it attacks you unawares; mind, feelings, and nerves are subliminally invaded. Unconscious convictions thus develop in us when we are least alert and hence unable to locate the danger and grapple with it. The incessant barrage of ads and slogans pounding upon one's ears and eyes enfeebles the critical faculties and one's freedom of choice becomes very effectively circumscribed indeed.

The similarity between advertising techniques and the propaganda techniques utilized by the powers-that-be is obvious. All this is done through the very same media held in tight grip by the military castes. Shams al-Din continues:

> If we also consider that in many cases this type of ideological marketing operates in an atmosphere of intellectual terror—we see how grave the danger is. For people usually react to intellectual terror in two ways: either they keep silent out of fear for their safety or choose to swim with the sweeping tide of the dictatorship, laying to rest their critical acumen and becoming a mere tape recorder repeating whatever they are told.[32]

Cultural Pessimism   The new military-dominated nation-state has thus dealt a series of heavy blows to an Islamic civilization already greatly weakened by decades of colonization and preceding centuries of slow decline, to the point that one could ask with Qutb's brother, Muhammad, *Are We Still Muslims?* (the title of his 1964 book). This is a much stronger and somewhat different version of the question posed by Shakib Arslan (in the title of his 1939 book): *Why Did the Muslims Become Backward While Others Progressed?*[33]

Preoccupation with decadence is quite characteristic of Islam as it is of other past-oriented, classicist civilizations, but perhaps even more so in the case of Islam, whose founder, Muhammad, has been dubbed—as an article of faith—the Seal of all Revelation. In a way, this cultural pessimism harks back to the crisis surrounding the rise to power of the Omayyads (661), viewed by their opponents as the abrupt end of the Golden Age of the Four Orthodox Caliphs. It was greatly reinforced by the disintegration of the Islamic Empire into successor states (ninth to eleventh centuries), the Crusader and Mongol offensives, and the demise of the Abbasid Caliphate (1258). Ibn Khaldun's inquiry into the causes of the decline of civilization, written more than a century later, is but the most articulate and sophisticated expression of a deeply ingrained cultural trait.

Decadence has certainly been an even more haunting specter for Islam ever since the outset of its modern encounter with the

West. The twentieth century (the fourteenth century of the Islamic era) has been particularly hard on Muslim self-esteem. A civilization that had always viewed itself as destined for leadership suffered one setback after the other at the hands of infidels who now set the pace in all realms of human activity. Thence followed Islam's sense of inadequacy in this new disorienting world, predicated on a sort of cognitive dissonance, to the extent that a theologian would sum it up as the "century of the eclipse of Islam." The old-time radicals of the MB variety had shared in this sense of inadequacy and pessimism. One of their leaders, 'Abd al-Qadir 'Awda (later to be executed), wrote in 1951:

> Muslims everywhere are ignorant of Islam and have deviated from its path, to the point that there is no one town in the whole world where Islam is observed as enjoined by Allah, whether in politics, economics, or social matters. . . . This deviationism brought Muslims to a stage of total neglect of its rules of conduct, setting for themselves rules predicated upon their own fancies and interests. The results were moral decline and depravity, inequity, crimes, and misery.[34]

The diagnosis set by the Maudoodi school, and further developed by Qutb and his disciples, takes this decadence theory several steps further, crossing, in the process, a crucial borderline: it is no more just a question of decline; Islam—particularly under the new military state—has reverted to a stage of jahiliyya that reflects the situation of Arabia prior to A.D. 622. The elites—and other peddlers of modernity—who brought it to that state of affairs, as well as the ruled who tolerate or embrace it, are guilty of apostasy (ridda). This accounts for the marked difference between the type of question posed by Shakib Arslan in 1939 and that raised by Muhammad Qutb twenty-five years later. True, Qutb and many others would diagnose here a long process going back to the Middle Ages (and some extremists among the radicals, such as Shukri Mustafa of the Takfir group would go so far as to claim that ever since the tenth century, Islam

was in a state of jahiliyya). It is argued, however, that the pace of
decline has accelerated exponentially in the present century with
the result that by now "Islam is absent from the stage of life" (Sa'id
Hawwa).[35]

From Pessimism to Activism   If the diagnosis is so bleak, is
                                 there still a remedy? Like other
revolutionaries who begin by taking an unsparing look at reality,
Sayyid Qutb draws not the lesson of fatalism and despair, but rather
of hope against hope. Islam is bound to overcome, he declared in
his 1962 book, *The Future of This Religion*, because modernity is
inherently incapable of quenching man's thirst for spirituality. Yet
such a victory requires a major effort, and that effort should be
undertaken before it is too late, as long as the thirst is still there.
Hawwa would put it in stronger terms: "We should reject the neg-
ativist approach, that counsel of despair which says: 'All is lost; we
can do nothing. Allah should save his religion.' Such Muslims resign themselves to the fait accompli and forget that Allah helps only
those who help themselves."

   The new danger, however mortal it may be, just puts a heavier
(but not unbearable) burden upon the Defenders of the Faith, adds
Fathi Yakan; they should better educate their disciples, prepare
themselves more thoroughly, and plan their action in a more ju-
dicious manner.[36]

   Which is the path to be taken? And in what direction? Sayyid
Qutb rejected what he considered the "utopian fallacy," for there
are no blueprints for the future. He does not deem himself obligated
to paint a detailed picture of an Islamic society functioning and
thriving in the last third of the twentieth century, nor does he think
he should provide a minute scenario leading to its realization:

   Modern jahiliyya puts a heavy psychological pressure upon
   the Faithful of Islam . . . asking them, among other things:
   "Do you have a detailed vision of the Islamic regime you call
   for? What have you prepared for its instauration in terms of

studies or drafts of laws based upon modern principles?" . . .
It is as though all that people lack today in order that the Shari'a
be applied were feasibility studies or legislation proposals. . . .
This is quite a mockery, for these [apostates] pretend that they
accept the domination of Allah and merely need expert jurist
advice on how to put it into practice, in presumed conformity
with the dictates of modernity.[37]

It is, of course, these very dictates and principles that Qutb
challenged, and whereas he had an acutely realistic sense of man's
inability to perceive the future with any precision, he began staking
out his own counterprinciples and broadly outlining the course toward their realization.

In essence, these principles are a call for authenticity. As the
dangers are endogenous, solutions must be sought within the bounds
of Islamic thought and historical experience, and not geared to sat-
isfy exogenous requirements, nor measured by standards alien to this
civilization. That is, one must reject not only modernity in general
but also the apologetics of Modernist Islam, whose proponents (such
as Muhammad 'Abduh) endeavored to salvage whatever they could
from the ruins by arguing that many major elements of Islam are
compatible with modernity (at least if cleverly and "creatively" interpreted).

The Maudoodi dictum, often quoted by Arab fundamentalists,
sums up well this rejection: instead of claiming that Islam is truly
reasonable, one should hold that the true reason is Islamic.[38] The
quest for identity and the liberation from the inferiority complex in
relation to the West is, hence, a sine qua non for turning inward
to find one's own solutions for the crisis. The principal sin of the
Islamic modernists is taken to be their acceptance of Western standards as the ultimate gauges (an argument also used against them
by many Arab thinkers on the Left).

Sayyid Qutb seems to have come by these convictions largely
through direct exposure to the West during his stay in the United

States (1948–50), which he had begun as an Islamic modernist and ended as a fundamentalist. In his major book, he reminisces:

> There is nothing in Islam for us to be ashamed of or defensive about. Yet the present moral defeatism vis-à-vis the Western or the Eastern Bloc, and vis-à-vis the jahiliyya condition we are in, makes some of these so-called Muslims try to find in Islam justification for certain aspects of the jahili civilization or seek in this civilization the rationale for certain Islamic injunctions. . . . During my years in America, some of my fellow Muslims would have recourse to apologetics as though they were defendants on trial. Contrariwise, I took an offensive position, excoriating the Western jahiliyya, be it in its much-acclaimed religious beliefs or in its depraved and dissolute socioeconomic and moral conditions: this Christian idolatry of the Trinity and its notions of sin and redemption which make no sense at all; this Capitalism, predicated as it is on monopoly and interest-taking, money-grubbing, and exploitation; this Individualism which lacks any sense of solidarity and social responsibility other than that laid down by law; that crass and vacuous materialistic perception of life, that animal freedom which is called permissiveness, that slave market dubbed "women's liberation."[39]

It is this very type of modernist apologetics which the military regimes would usurp in order to justify all policies in the name of Islam. Such a manipulation was facilitated not only by ulama obsequiousness and by the ignorance of the populace but also by the fact that the modernists—true in this to the tradition of the ulama— usually shied away from taking any political position.[40]

Authenticity   The Islam that the radicals herald, albeit steeped in cultural pessimism, is evidently activist, preoccupied by politics—or rather by the return of Islam into politics— as much as by moral and social problems. Its outlook is aggressive and authenticity-oriented rather than defensive and apologetic.

The quest for authenticity obviously has some tangible policy implications for the future Muslim society, which is to be built upon the present shambles (Shari'a as the law of the land, purging the media and the school system), but its primary importance lies in establishing firm guidelines whose specific application may vary according to time and space.

Authenticity as the ultimate measure by no means implies slavish imitation of past models. Modern challenges are so complex and revolutionary that one can only look to the Islamic past for inspiration, for a set of core values and ground rules for action. This attitude explains, among other things, Sayyid Qutb's flexible attitude on ijtihad (interpretation of jurisprudence), which departs from the rigid petrification of tenth-century models ("the closing of the gates of ijtihad") common to traditionalist orthodoxy. On this point he is somewhat nearer to the modernists who argued for the "opening of the gates"; the difference being, of course, that the norms of interpretation are, for him, not to be inspired by exogenous criteria. He also intimated that they are not to be applied by just any jurist but by the truly knowledgeable, the leaders of radical Islam (an argument brought to its extreme by Mustafa, the Takfir leader, at a speech in his trial).[41]

On a broader scope this attitude would be best summed by the Cairo Muslim Students' Association in a booklet aptly entitled *Contemporary Reflections on Our Heritage*:

> The return to our heritage does not signify fundamentalism (*salafiyya*) in the sense of rejecting all novelty and resting on the laurels of the past; to the contrary. Any renaissance begins by going back to the heritage, any thought capable of change proceeds from a contemporary reading of the past. Any rejection of the status quo is inspired by a feeling that the present is unworthy of the past of our umma, and by a belief that our community is capable of building a future worthy of her glorious past. . . . We turn to the heritage not in order to bring back the past, for the past cannot be resuscitated, but

rather to seek inspiration in its ever-living values, its eternal ideals.[42]

As could be expected from the historical approach discussed above, past models are looked for, above all, in the early centuries of Islam, especially the age of Muhammad and the Four Orthodox Caliphs (622–61). As for later periods, they are treated with distinct emphasis on internal problems (civil wars, moral decline). The exploits of Islam in combating foreign invasions, such as the Crusades, which inflame the imagination of nationalists and traditionalists alike, are barely treated—a clear indicator of the overall shift of emphasis. For instance, to the extent that the Crusades are discussed, the accent is usually on Islamic disunity as facilitating the task of the invaders or on the ultimate Islamic victory being not only the product of Arab efforts—as Pan-Arabists would have it—but also of Turks, Kurds, and others. As for the Mongols, they are used mostly as an analogy to the present jahiliyya. It is thus not only modernist apologetics but the nationalist apologetics as well that are subjected to severe criticism (shared, here again, by the Arab Left).[43]

The prime example of the search for authenticity in Maudoodi's thought occurred with regard to the holy war. It was in an essay on jihad (1930) that he first staked out his views, refusing to take the usual apologetic stand, that jihad is just a defensive war and hence does not violate the norms of international law. Jihad, claimed Maudoodi, is both offensive and defensive in accordance with the divine injunction to replace domination of man over man by the domination of Allah over all of the globe.

With Sayyid Qutb and Hawwa, this stand will be taken as a major justification for combating the "apostate rulers," whereas the instauration of the jahiliyya creates ipso facto a state of war. The Cairo Muslim Students' Association will indeed interpret in like manner the early wars of Islam as proof that "offense is the best defense," while the Minya Muslim Students' Association will consecrate a booklet to jihad, harping at the lack of any meaningful moral distinction between these two forms of warfare when all that matters is the inherent justice of the cause. Only the "moral defeatism"—a term borrowed from Qutb's vocabulary—of the modernists and other Muslims cowed by the West, could have led them to think in such offensive-defensive categories.[44]

The denunciation of nationalism, discussed above, is yet another example of antiapologetics and the endeavor to be in tune with what is considered the true essence of one's tradition. The critical approach that such an endeavor assumes reminds one, at times, of modern scholarship (however much the radicals execrate it), its methods and findings. Suffice it to compare the articles on "Jihad" and "Crusades" in the New Encyclopedia of Islam to the arguments of Maudoodi and his disciples. This is even more paradoxical than the astounding resemblance with the modus operandi of Arab revisionist historians (liberals and leftists) to which we have already alluded.

The most ambitious product in this domain is 'Abd al-Halim 'Uways' The Later Pages of Our Civilization,[45] which concentrates not only on periods usually forsaken (the middle and late Middle Ages) but most particularly on the question of the rise and fall (especially the fall) of the various successor states that were founded, from Spain to Iran, during the disintegration of the caliphate. The author considers that this constitutes a sharp break with the tradition of modern Islamic historiography "which deals almost exclusively with the glorious chapters of our history, bragging about our heroes and our superiority over Europe. As a result, our history came to be viewed as virtually mythical and epic, as though its major figures were angels and not human beings." The consequences were dire enough: lacking objective knowledge of history the modern Muslim is unable to draw his lessons; and, somewhat paradoxically, because people believe the Islamic past to have been so awe-inspiring they have no sense of historical proportion in analyzing the present, thinking that recent calamities and challenges have no counterparts at all in the preceding thirteen centuries. They are thus driven to exaggerated bouts of despair.

'Uways' basic approach is not sensibly different from that of the leftist revisionist historiography which developed in the Arab world during the last two decades, although on many specific points, such as the revisionists' attempt to present Islamic sectarian movements as social revolutionaries, he disagrees with them sharply. This study of the decline and fall of the successor states leads him to confirm the thesis advanced by Algerian Islamic thinker Malek Bennabi: Colonialism is not the prime source of ills of the Muslim umma; one does not become colonized "unless one has previously become *colonizable*" (to use Bennabi's terms). In the historical cases under the discussion, the Muslims have lost the capacity to build a state on solid foundations and to maintain it over a significant length of time. Among the reasons adduced from the two dozen test-cases are: the search for ethnic (or "nationalist") hegemony of one group over others, dictatorial rule of a person, a family or a military caste who did not know how to keep the unity of the political elite or to preserve the interest of civil society in the elite's survival. The modern analogies are obvious. 'Uways tells a story which is not merely a tale of woe. He underlines the capacity of these successor states to maintain, against heavy military odds, the integrity of the Muslim territory (with the exception of Spain) and even extend it in certain areas (the eleventh-century Seljukids in Asia Minor and the fifteenth-century Ottomans in the Balkans). It is noteworthy that even this positive finding has its iconoclastic value: the villains of the piece who lost Spain are Arabs (further accused of causing dissension by imposing their hegemony on Berbers and Slavs in their kingdoms); the heroes are Turks. The latter aspect fits in with the recent trend in radical (but also conservative) quarters to rehabilitate the Ottoman Empire, so besmirched by Arab nationalism, and to consider it (especially in its prime, the fifteenth to seventeenth centuries) as the last glorious chapter of Islamic history when a viable, organic umma still existed. The linkage to the demonology of Ataturk—the enemy from within, the false Muslim (allegedly of Jewish convert origin) who gave the empire the coup de grace—is self-explanatory. With Ataturk, Muslim authenticity was lost.

Democracy, Socialism, and Minorities   It may be useful to examine the anti-apologetic approach in a few other cases in order to see how sweeping it is. The most illuminating, perhaps, is the issue of democracy. Here the Muslim radicals go one step further than Maudoodi, who exhibits, on this account, some residual modernism, exerting himself to prove that Islam is democratic as evidenced by the institution of *shura* (consultation); a line no different from that of Muhammad 'Abduh or, for that matter, of the MB of yore.[46] Sayyid Qutb was skeptical of that approach already in the early 1950s. In an "open letter" to General Naguib published two weeks after the July 1952 Revolution, he excoriated the constitution of the ancien régime as a vehicle of moral corruption; no purge was possible, he argued, without a "just dictatorship" that would "grant political liberties to the virtuous alone." He further elaborated upon these views in his commentary on the shura chapter of the Koran (sura XLII), where he subjected the text to a rigorous analysis and established that shura embodies the duty of the ruler to consult with at least some of the ruled (usually the elite), within the general context of God-made laws that the ruler must execute. No reference is made, significantly enough, to election of the ruler by the ruled. This set of principles, claimed Qutb, is not related to any particular form of government. From refusal to call Islam democratic, he moved in the 1950s to outright negation: democracy is, as a form of government, already bankrupt in the West; why should it be imported to the Middle East?[47]

Sa'id Hawwa was soon to etch these views in greater relief: "The shura is by no means identical to democracy, and, in certain regards, it is even its exact opposite." The modernists, who cloaked

Islam with a democratic garb, deviated from the authentic meaning
of the shura in the Islamic system of government. Whether they did
so on purpose or not is immaterial: the upshot was that the whole
concept of shura was taken out of the Islamic context. "Democracy
is a Greek term which signifies sovereignty of people, the people
being the source of legitimacy; it is the people who legislate and
rule. As for the shura, it denotes consultation [by the ruler] with a
person or persons with regard to the interpretation of a certain point
of Islamic law. In Islam, the people do not govern themselves by
laws they make on their own, as in a democracy; rather the people
are "governed by a regime and a set of laws imposed by God, which
they cannot change or modify in any case." The concept of majority
rule cannot sit well with an Islamic system of government, "because
Islam would not concur that the majority is sovereign, whatever its
mistakes and errors." In Islam, it is the moral quality and religious
knowledge of the interpreters of the law that make their judgment
acceptable, whatever their number. Indeed, notes Hawwa, one of
the characteristics of the apostasy (ridda) in present-day Islam is that,
much as the term *umma* was transformed from signifying "community based on religious bonds" to denoting "national community," so the concept of shura was emptied of its original contents
and made to mean "democracy, Western style or Eastern style."[48]
Hawwa's words were echoed by MB demonstrators in northern
Syria, who chanted, "Neither Eastern nor Western, we want a Muslim state." Across the border, in Tripoli, Dannawi summed it all
up in a lapidary formula: "The state in Islam obeys Divine Law, not
the people," which he explicates as an emancipatory mechanism—
"liberating the state from subservience to human passions, whims,
and fancies . . . be they of the majority or of the minority."[49]

    More was involved here than outrage at semantic distortions,
not only theory but political realities as well. There is no doubt that
the uses to which "democracy" was put by the Egyptian and Syrian
military regimes—especially the abuse of legality and of the electoral
process—helped give the term a bad name (the same would be true

of Pakistan). Qutb was to denounce this in his interrogation, and other prisoners in their letters and diaries. "This democracy which we imported from the West," writes one Egyptian radical, "became a mere tool in the hands of two groups: plutocrats who used it to bolster the capitalist system [before 1952], and tyrannical rulers who used it as a fig leaf to cover their dictatorship and present it as wholly devoted to serving the interests of the common people. . . . How typical are such rulers of the Arab countries and of the Third World!" "On election time the citizens become puppets, stuffing the ballots with what they are ordered to," wail the Syrian radicals on the eve of elections to the People's Assembly. "Over their heads hover scourges of brutal torturers. Results are predetermined, the competition between candidates is a mere formality. The limits for the citizens' freedom are drastically circumscribed. Real decision-making takes place outside the formal institutions." No wonder that "the People's Assembly does not really discuss questions of war and peace, legislation, etc. Even on the rise of the price of potatoes it just endorses decisions already taken elsewhere."[50]

It is based upon this experience—as well as upon the shura theory—that a former Egyptian student activist would write: "No member of the public is to be able to endorse or to initiate a law which runs counter to the laws of Allah. Such matters fall under the domination of God over man. A free man is one who obeys Allah's rules and orders and worships God alone."[51]

Helped, no doubt, by the Nasserist and Ba'thist abuses, the theories of Qutb and Hawwa had a spillover effect from the radical hard core into the conservative periphery of the fundamentalist movement. Thus the popular Egyptian preacher and television personality Sheikh Sha'rawi declared in a 1982 interview that Islam and democracy are irreconcilable and that the shura does not imply the need to pander to the will of the majority. The interview created quite an uproar. The scandalized responses it drew from modernists as well as from traditionalists—all harping on the same apologetic chord—proved that he had touched a raw nerve and broke a taboo respected not only by these two groups but also by the powers-that-be. The latter had always found the notion of "Islamic democracy" to be very useful, and this was why the single-party weekly *Mayo*, where the polemic took place, espoused a strong stand against Sha'rawi, usually one of its "star" contributors.[52]

Less adamant is the rejection of socialism by the radicals. The reason is obvious: ideals of social justice and equitable distribution of wealth were quite in line with major strands in the Islamic tradition. More recently, they had served as battle cries of the Egyptian MB and as late as 1958 Mustafa al-Siba'i, leader of Syrian MB, would argue in his *Socialism of Islam* that the two notions are compatible, and that the individual's right to ownership is neither sacred nor absolute. Sayyid Qutb, who wrote extensively on Islamic visions of solidarity and social justice from the late 1940s on, shared the same views, but he markedly differs from al-Siba'i in refraining from tagging them with Western symbols and notions. He thus refuses terms such as "Islamic Socialism" or "nationalization" (though he actually agreed to a measure of collective or state ownership of a number of basic services and industries). This was, of course, more than sheer quibbling—such Western terms and symbols stood for what he saw as different concepts, each proceeding from different sets of premises—the one religious, the other secular. However much they may be similar in certain respects, especially in the chapter on solidarism, they are not, and cannot be, compatible in essence.[53]

Much as on the issue of democracy, what was in embryo in the early 1950s would be staked out in full colors in Qutb's 1964 book: "Muhammad could have certainly hoisted a social banner, launched a war upon the privileged and the high-born. He could have set Islam up as a movement aspiring to the social change and redistribution of assets of the rich unto the poor. . . . Yet Allah, in his eternal wisdom, did not instruct the Prophet to take this course. . . . He made him launch only one rallying cry: 'There is no God but Allah!'"[54]

The specific turn taken by Nasserism in the early 1960s (see the 1962 Charter, §73) may account for the stronger stand taken here against socialism: the growing (and disturbing) influence of Marxism and Marxists in Arab Socialism—what its opponents, be they Saudi and Lebanese conservatives or Syrian and Egyptian New Radicals, called "Bolshevized Islam"; "Bolshevized" tendencies which the sycophants of the Egyptian and Syrian religious establishment managed to extol.[55] Socialism turned out to be a dangerous Trojan Horse of secularism, even of atheism, as was evidenced in the resurgence of communism among students. More specifically, the extent of the nationalizations—particularly in Syria—jolted the New Radicals, both because it went beyond all acceptable limits and because it served to bolster an already-too-powerful state. Sadat's economic about-turn would, of course, take the wind out of the Egyptian radicals' sails on this chapter; not so in Syria, where modifications of etatist policy were more modest and the classes hit by it (especially craftsmen and small merchants) much broader.[56] No wonder that these classes were relatively well represented among the Syrian radicals (at least 13 percent of the militants arrested or killed in 1979–81), and even nonmembers quite often obeyed the calls of the Islamic Revolutionary Command and closed shop in sign of protest. The Command's proclamations indeed emphasize the right to private property, and they demand the return of expropriated property, the lifting of "harsh administrative controls on tradespeople," and free export and import of goods (though public ownership of "national resources" such as oil, gas, and minerals is to be maintained).[57]

A final example of the divorce from apologetics regards religious (mostly Christian) minorities in the Islamic world. The modernists had always been eager to point out the long-standing tolerance of Islam toward non-Muslims, defined as Protected Peoples (Ahl al-Dhimma) with their individual and collective rights—including right to worship, judicial autonomy, right to property, security of life and limb—anchored in public law. As for those rights the Dhimmis were deprived of—equality in taxation (they paid extra levies), exclusion from service in the army, access to top civil service jobs, primacy of Muslim over Christian courts—the modernists either denied that these inequalities existed or minimized their importance, or called for further evolution of the Islamic concept of tolerance to comprise the latter, more modern, notions. The MB used to have recourse to the first two approaches, but some of their thinkers (such as Yusuf al-Qardawi) even dabbled in the third. That the MB were keen to follow the reformist lead here is to be attributed to the exigencies of the fight against British and French colonial rulers, where support of local Christians was important.

Once Sa'id Hawwa's "Second Revolution" became the order of the day, that constraint was lifted. Attitudes toward Christians grew harsher, and though by the late 1960s the New Radicals were still far from the fanaticism of their leaflets during the anti-Coptic riots of June 1981, the exacerbation is evident. This was due in part to a more rigorous interpretation of the historical record and to a weakened inclination—inspired by Maudoodi—to make concessions to modern sensibilities: old-type tolerance, as defined by the Shari'a—yes; new (that is, secular-inspired tolerance, predicated on the relativity of all beliefs)—by no means.[58]

Here again the realities of the age had their impact: not only the end of anticolonial struggle but also growing awareness of the deleterious role played by native Christians in introducing modern ideologies to the Arab world (from the incipient Arab nationalism of Butrus al-Bustani and Najib 'Azuri, the socialism of Salama Musa, and the Syrianism of Anton Sa'adeh, to the neo-Pharaonism of men like Louis 'Awad, the secularism of Michel Aflaq, and the Marxism of George Habbash).[59] Rolling back the "local Christian tide" could be done with the help of more restrictive laws. In a way, this was, of course, a logical outgrowth of the application of the Shari'a that the New Radicals called for, which could not allow for exceptions (whether in criminal punishment, prohibition of alcohol, or interdiction of conversion to a non-Muslim religion).

As for the argument that this might create internal strife and break national unity,[60] for one thing the New Radicals cared little about unity at the state or at the all-Arab level; and, for another, they would answer—together with some conservative critics of Pan-Arabism—that non-Muslims constituted a much smaller percentage of the population of the Middle East and North Africa than ethnic minorities. The latter (especially Kurds and Berbers) suffered discrimination under the homogenizing impetus of Pan-Arabism and were, hence, a factor of strife and disunity. Incorporating them into a Muslim state governed by the Shari'a would offset the loss of alienating the non-Muslims. How little the radicals care for the alleged dangers of excluding the Christians of the national community is evidenced in the leaflets distributed during the anti-Coptic riots in the mixed neighborhood of Zawiya al-Hamra' (Cairo, June 1981). The leaflets castigated the mass participation of Muslims in *Shamm al-Nasim* (originally a pre-Islamic Coptic feast, which had become an all-Egyptian spring holiday). This picnic-day outing where popular classes of both religions used to intermingle is taken to be yet another devious mechanism for bringing about the "destruction of Islam in Egypt."[61]

Obviously, there are regional and tactical nuances on the Christian question. In Upper Egypt (where Copts constituted up to two-fifths of the population in some districts), vehement hatred toward them can be discerned in radical circles where the "Coptic danger" loomed as a virtual obsession. This is rarely the case in Lower Egypt (except for several mixed neighborhoods of Cairo). A split along these lines surfaced even in one and the same radical group, the *Jihad*, during its trial (1982). But even in circles less obsessed with the "Coptic danger and arrogance" the tendency is to demarcate Islam from Christianity as evidenced, for instance, in the saliency of theological polemics and of the critique of the ecumenical dialogue espoused by certain Islamic modernists.[62]

In Syria the *Manifesto of the Islamic Revolution*, trying to rally Christian support, promised "civil and legal rights," and "security

of life, limb, and property . . . as laid down in the Koran and the
Sunna," but Sheikh Bayanuni, leader of the Muslim Front—put
the gloss on this promise when he explained that this was predicated
upon acceptance by the Christians (who constitute 15 percent of the
population) of Syria as a Muslim state with the Shari'a as the source
of all legislation (that is, their rights would be those of Ahl al-
Dhimma, non-Muslim "protected" subjects). Sa'id Hawwa stresses
the same precondition to his suggestion—contested by more extremist members—that Christians be allowed access to high positions in
the executive branch, a suggestion, he points out, that does not
contradict Islamic historical experience with the Dhimmis. The only
real innovation he puts forward is the dispensation of those Christians who serve in the army from payment of the humiliating re-
cognitive tax, the jizya.[63]

In Lebanon some (like Fathi Yakan and his Jama'a Islamiyya)
doubt whether an Islamic state, or for that matter a Sunni state (the
Sunnis being less than a quarter of the population), is a realistic
prospect for the near future. They are thus content to work, in the
short range, for a greater Muslim power-sharing. Their long-term
goal remains, however, a state where non-Muslims are subject to
an Islamic constitution predicated on the Shari'a (the only amend-
ment, here again, being the abolition of the jizya). More outspoken
Sunni Lebanese groups forgo such subtleties. Sheikh Sha'ban of the
Tawhid, who claims it is up to the Christians to give the Muslims
guarantees and not the other way around, offers them the Dhimmi
formula; the mujahidun militia branded the Maronites as "new Crusaders" and called for an outright jihad against them.[64]

Farewell to Islamic modernism is thus interwoven with farewell
to Arabism to produce a New Radicalism. Modernism had, of
course, been rejected by the traditionalists ever since the turn of the
century, even as they were influenced by it to some extent (for
instance, in apologetics, and in a grudging acceptance of the ijtihad).
The significance of the New Radicals' stance stems both from its
particular forcefulness and from the fact that these were people well

immersed in the modern world (in terms of their education, profession, etc.) who refused to accept modernist Islam. What one may call their "reactionary modernism"[65] was all the more powerful for their being able to say that they had seen the modernist future (some of them during stays abroad) and that it does not work. Their hand was further strengthened by being able to operate so proficiently the various modern inventions and techniques (from military hardware to tape cassettes). Even the traditionalists always accepted technology in principle—as distinguished from the values it subsumes—but were rarely either conversant or comfortable with it. The radicals, many of whom, as we have seen, were engineers and doctors, would feel no unease or qualms about using modern technologies that could be turned against the rulers, from the use of audial media, to the smuggling and dissemination of ideas (in what is still essentially an oral culture), to terrorism.[66]

The Islamic modernists, with their reflexive admiration of all things modern and their evident ignorance of technology (most of them were from literary backgrounds), were no match for the radicals. Indeed, the efficacy of radical antiapologetics proceeded, in part, from the "technocratic" halo surrounding them. The decline of modernism, evident over the last two decades, may be attributed not only to military debacles, and to the rise of fundamentalist folk religion (see chapter 5), but also to the radical antiapologetics, which put the modernists on the defensive.

Muhammad Mahdi Shams al-Din allows that the modernists had some mitigating circumstances for originally taking the form they did. "The Islamic umma had been suffering [at the end of the last century] from military weakness and material backwardness, ignorance, and illiteracy—all of which eventually contributed to the victory of imperialism. This state of affairs pushed the pioneers of [Islamic Reform] to endeavor to prove that Islam is actually fit to build a community, strong in all respects, capable of being the equal of its colonizers"; its fitness to the task was being judged, of course, by the Western criteria. Yet what could once be justified as part of the quest for self-assertion during the fight against the foreigners is not valid anymore in the postcolonial age. Worse still, it is damaging, all the more so because the new military state employs apologetics to condone its transgressions, keep the masses in virtual ignorance, and preserve their support.[67] Such criticism can be heard on the Left as well, but, of course, with different conclusions as to the path that should be followed after the divorce.[68] For the Islamic "reactionary modernists" the conclusion would be not a cultural revolution—liberating one from the shackles of Islam and the West alike—but rather the rediscovery of authenticity and the return of Islam into the world of politics. Politics now is more important than at any other moment in Islamic history, for the state is more powerful and interventionist than ever. It is no longer content to leave civil society to its own devices. The state encroaches even upon social spheres, which used to be considered beyond its purview— family, education, use of spare time, and so on—and where Islam was accustomed for centuries to shape attitudes and behavior. It is no mere coincidence that such ideas germinated at about the same time in Egypt and Iran, the two Middle Eastern "new states" that first arrived at maturity: by Sayyid Qutb in prison (1959–64) and Khomeini in his Iraqi exile (1965–71). Barred by obstacles of language and sectarian outlook, Khomeini's version of the "politics is the end-all" theology could not penetrate into Sunni lands (but did into the Shi'ite communities in Iraq and, much later, in Saudi Arabia, Kuwait, Oman, and Lebanon). Qutb's version was to exercise a decisive influence in Arab lands. Its primary impact was felt in countries where individuals and groups had already been groping with similar problems—Marwan Hadid upon his return from Egypt to Syria (1964), Fathi Yakan and his followers who established the Jama'a Islamiyya, which split in 1964 from the 'Ibad al-Rahman association over the latter's preoccupation with culture alone and abhorrence of politics.[69] During the late 1960s Hadid's and Yakan's vague gropings were given a firm sense of direction by Qutb's theories and drew inspiration from his martyrdom: the return to politics was to be along the revolutionary path.

CHAPTER FOUR

The Sunni Revolution

Counter-Society   Return to politics is, in fact, the radical panacea. Islam has been banned from politics by
the forces of modernity, spearheaded by the military regimes, and
helped by the age-old pusillanimity of the ulama and the indifference of the modernists (preoccupied as they were by cultural and
social questions). Islam should thus return to the political arena.
Yet how is this panacea to be put into practice?

No single answer is provided to this question. The New Radicals are not a monolith, even when one concentrates, as we do
here, on a number of core countries in the Middle East. Local
variations are quite important whereas the New Radicals accept with
reluctance the realities of that area, that is, its being divided into
nation-states, the latter having proved themselves as viable and effective political entities. While the New Radicals aspire toward
greater unity, they do not pursue the MB ideal of restoration of the
caliphate and resign themselves to operating within the bounds—
and geared to the needs—of their own nation-states. Operational
collaboration between the various national organizations is rather
modest. True, at the ideological level, there is intense exchange and
cross-fertilization, which overflow even to non-Arab Sunni countries
(as evidenced, for instance, by translations of Qutb's work appearing
in Turkey and even in the country that originally inspired him,

Pakistan).[1] It is this ideological dimension that actually makes the New Radicals into a movement. Yet the lack of operational structure is important and accounts for the ideological leeway left to national groups. There is no overall, pan-Islamic, radical leadership. And even within each country different groups have their own way, the decentralization being further enhanced by persecution and repression, which led to the break-up into relatively small groups (with usually a few hundred members). Some radical leaders raised the banner of the reestablishment of the caliphate (such as Siriya and Mustafa in Egypt, Hawwa in Syria), but they see it as a distant ideal, while for the moment one should strive to make one's own state into a Muslim state, most noticeably through the application of the Shari'a.[2]

An ideological justification for this modus operandi would be found in the writings of the fourteenth-century theologian Ibn Taymiyya (who, as shall be seen, was a major influence upon the New Radical political theory). Ibn Taymiyya indeed maintained that the umma does not necessarily need one leader (*imam*) and that when the historical conditions require it, as when there are many Muslim states—which was the case in his time (and presumably now as well)—there could certainly be several imams, provided worthy individuals might be found.[3]

Decentralization often led to sectarian squabbles within the radical ranks, sometimes going to extremes. A case in point is Shukri Mustafa, the Takfir leader, who anathemized all other groups (including Salah Siriya's Islamic Liberation Party) and even declared that Hasan al-Banna, the MB leader (assassinated in 1948) widely respected by almost all radicals, was nothing but an agent of the Free Masons.[4]

Despite the decentralization and the factionalism, certain broad denominators do stand up. The radicals proceed, as we have seen, from a gloomy diagnosis of the malady of Islam, hence the sense of urgency. If urgency does not necessarily lead to violence (though in some groups it would), it does, however, lead to a divorce from—

and almost always to some sort of a revolt against—present Muslim
society and polity. Both attitudes are intermeshed; both are predicated upon the Maudoodi theory that as Islam has reverted to a state
of jahiliyya, true Muslims find themselves in a state of war against
the apostates, and that jihad is but a defensive response to the "war
of annihilation" the apostates conduct against Islam. The true Muslims, the vanguard (tali'a) as Qutb called them, are and must be
set apart within the ambient infidel society as a sort of "counter-
society." As defined by a political ethnographer, a counter-society
is a "microsociety which constitutes a closed society while maintaining some ties with society as a whole. The counter-society must
be capable of being self-enclosed in order to avoid fragmentation or
abdication. It must prevent alien influences from penetrating it, yet
must remain sufficiently open and aggressive to draw from the outside whatever it cannot itself produce. It must pursue the dream of
ultimately becoming a majority. It struggles to demolish the old
society while at the same time hoping to become heir to that society;
radical destruction on the one hand, preservation for the sake of
new order on the other."⁵ Joined to these two major functions is a
third one, the counter-society as model for the society of the future.

A few of the tell-tale names chosen for some of these secret
Muslim societies encapsulate indeed this set of attitudes: in Egypt,
"Society of the Muslims" (Jama'at al-Muslimin, later dubbed by
the authorities Takfir wa-Hijra), "Islamic Liberation" (Tahrir Islami), "Society for Commanding What Is Good and Forbidding the
Reprehensible" (al-Amr bi-l-Ma'ruf wa-l-Nahy 'an al-Munkar),
and Jihad; in Syria, "The Phalanges of Muhammad" (Kata'ib Muhammad), al-Mujahidun; and in Lebanon, "Islamic Unification"
(al-Tawhid al-Islami) and "Soldiers of the Lord" (Jund Allah).

The underlying theme was set forth by Qutb in his statement
at the trial: "We are the umma of the Believers, living within a jahili
society. Nothing relates us to state or to society and we owe no
allegiance to either. As a community of believers we should see
ourselves in a state of war with the state and the society. The territory

we dwell in is Dar al-Harb."[6] Elaborating on this doctrine, Dannawi explained that the exemplary "counter-society" was Muhammad's group of followers in pre-622 Mecca, "a militant microsociety operating in the heart of the jahili society . . . and engaged in battle against the latter; for the barbaric society tends to react harshly using all the means in its disposal: murder and banishment, torture and pressures, ridicule and seduction."[7]

Small wonder that when some of Qutb's votaries (such as 'Ali Abduh Isma'il) began to organize their group in jails during the late 1960s they had recourse to the basic symbols of segregation: refusing to pray with impure imams and choosing to have their group pray on its own. In fact, shunning regular mosques and the company of the "ignorant believers" becomes a distinguishing mark of radical students in the 1970s.[8]

Withdrawal and Revolt   Setting oneself apart is indeed an act of *hijra* (migration) modeled on that of the Prophet in 622 and later enjoined by law upon all Muslims living in Dar al-Harb if they cannot practice their religion. For the New Radicals the hijra (be it physical—usually to caves or to the desert—or spiritual, internal exile) is the one end of the gamut of possible responses to the Modern Jahiliyya. This type of counter-society cuts itself off from the evil society, leads a better life, perhaps does some recruiting (if possible), and hopes for better times. This is the attitude of groups such as the "Emotional Seclusion" (*al-'Uzla al-Shu'uriyya*) in Alexandria and the Faramawiyya sect of Upper Egypt (which also rejects modern medicine). It also accounts for the acts of many individuals who desert the army or leave jobs in the government bureaucracy or in the public sector so as to avoid serving the powers-that-be, boycott radio and TV (and compel relatives and neighbors to follow suit), or rely on "holy men" for arbitration in order not to turn to courts of law.[9] This withdrawn, passive attitude is in line with a certain minority streak in the Sunni tradition. If subservience to the authorities was the general rule, there were medieval men of religion who chose to withdraw from any contact with a corrupt state. Some, like the famous mystic Ibn al-Adham, even refused to drink water from public conduits because they might have been paid for from "non-Koranic," that is, illicit, taxes.

Such quietistic groups were never thought by the authorities to be dangerous; the Takfir group during the "withdrawal phase" of its evolution even enjoyed the blessing (perhaps also the help) of the regime, which saw it as absorbing discontent and channeling dissent in a "positive way."[10] Sayyid Qutb, however, was thinking of a more activist brand of counter-society: activism that is kin in spirit to the MB, yet organizationally different—not a mass movement but rather small, self-contained groups of militants encompassing all facets of life of their members. (In the case of the Takfir group, this includes even employment in group-owned economic enterprises; the same group also encourages marriage between members.) The change in the organizational concept was the result of the changing perception of the challenge: jahili society is so powerful, "its influence seeping into every nook and cranny" (Hawwa), that one should set oneself apart the better to preserve one's purity and then use this secure basis to embark upon the recruiting of wayward Muslims and indoctrinate them; as Qutb put it in his conversations with Nadvi in 1951,[11] by drawing growing numbers of the latter and making them into fully fledged militants, conscious members of the vanguard, one attempts to strengthen the "umma of the believers" in terms of quality and quantity.

Hijra in this perspective is just an instrument not a goal, a stage not an end, a sort of *reculer pour mieux sauter*. This would in fact be the itinerary of many a militant such as the future assassin of Sadat, 'Abd al-'Al, whose first station on his spiritual journey was quitting the army and setting himself up as a religious bookseller "in order to avoid contact with coquettish women and with men indifferent to Islam." He would later find his way to the Jihad organization. A more telling example is that of the Takfir group, who began by retreating to caves "so as to flee from the jahiliyya and preserve our heritage and tradition," and were indeed called for a while "People of the Cave" (Ahl al-Kahf), after the famous Koranic tale (sura XVIII, 9ff.). They would soon branch out into aggressive recruiting and education and ultimately have recourse to violence, though some of their members continued to stick to hijra.[12]

The path of the Takfir group illustrates in a way the whole gamut available to radicals: hijra—education—violence. Not all radicals would cross bounds and move from one stage to the other. Some stuck to the hijra; others (like the five ringleaders of the "1965 plot," who later recruited Qutb and Hawwash) began with the idea of violence. Others still believe in education, such as Nadvi[13] and many members of the students' associations. Even among those who did evolve, the thrust was not necessarily toward greater extremism: many veteran MB members (Tilmisani, 'Ashmawi) drew the lesson of the Nasserist repression as signifying that education is the only viable way open. Certain members of the "1965 group" (Jarisha, al-Sisi) came to that conclusion in prison and followed the same path after their liberation in the mid-1970s. Yet much more widespread was evolution in the opposite direction—from belief in education and reform (mostly by law) to violence.

One could not overemphasize, however, that the common denominator for all three stages (or trends) is broader than the differences, the latter relating to the degree of urgency involved and the degree of practicality of this or that cure. Both elements are intertwined. Hijra and violence denote a very bleak assessment of the situation but differ as to whether one could still really change it or whether one should rather retreat and save one's own soul (and perhaps also a few others). The long-term education track is chosen by those who believe that, although well entrenched, jahili society can still be regained for Islam by spreading the Word piecemeal, and that violence is suicidal.

Whereas the hijra was a path taken by very few, we should rather concentrate on education versus violence, both operating—let it be stressed—outside the established structures of state and society. In that respect, the radical proponents of education differ markedly from their conservative counterparts who operate within the system and do not huddle up in counter-societies (see chapter 5). The affinities and contradictions between radical education and reform are best illustrated by Qutb's own itinerary. In 1951 when he exposed his still unwritten views to his Indian visitor, Nadvi, he stressed that ridding society of the jahiliyya would demand a long-haul educational effort. His activity as head of the Propaganda Section of the MB as well as his books, and particularly the Koranic commentary, were part and parcel of that effort, destined to create a "vanguard" of "first three, then ten, and so forth," adding one reformed and repentant Muslim to another. He had thus hoped "over a period of twenty to twenty-five years" to build a substantial force, a critical mass capable of changing the face of society. Let us emphasize that even at that stage he did not believe he could make the Egyptian system work for his cause. The ever more hegemonic state is jahili and thus all attempts to apply this or that Shari'a law, to introduce more religious instruction into the curriculum, to curb the excesses of the media, would be of no avail. The counter-society should be constituted outside the system and carry a "jihad by word," by education.

Qutb did not reject violence, but it is an alternative he leaves moot, either out of prudence and/or as a last resort. His own evolution toward that course of action—"jihad by deed"—seems to have been catalyzed by his prison experience, which spawned the assessment that the new military state is more ruthless and more secularist-minded than he had thought and should be treated accordingly. Time seemed to be running out. It was no more a question of "twenty or twenty-five years." Even then, when he was contacted by the ringleaders upon his release in 1964, he opposed the idea of immediate recourse to violence for pragmatic reasons—the Damocles sword of the security services. He impressed upon them the need for long-term educational endeavor to form cadres and militants while waiting for the opportune moment to strike. In the meantime, some military training was acceptable in anticipation of self-defense against persecution.

The problems involved remind one of those of Communist parties (another type of "counter-societies") in Western Europe, especially during the ebbing of the revolutionary tide of 1919–23 and immediately afterward: Should one call for an insurgency against heavy odds? If yes, when? If not, how can one keep the counter-society from absorbing by osmosis the values of the predominant society without its paying the price of becoming a tiny (and dwindling) sect? Qutb finally succumbed to pressure (or manipulation) by the ringleaders and gave his blessing to intensive military preparations geared up for terrorism, while he still believed in long-term education as well.[14]

The distinction between both courses of action remained for him—as it was to be for his votaries in the coming two decades—essentially pragmatic, not philosophical. This is why most of the disciples would believe in both, albeit in different, and changing, dosages and combinations. Stress on immediate terrorism was (and is still) evident, for instance, in the northern (Aleppo-Hama) branch of the Syrian MB as well as in the Islamic Liberation Party (1974) and the Jihad Organization (1981) in Egypt. The southern (Damascus) Syrian branch and the exiled faction of the Syrian MB put their faith (at least before 1980 when the savage repression persuaded them otherwise) in the long term, as do most of the Egyptian Muslim students' associations, and as the Takfir group did almost until 1977, when it changed course under the threat of persecutions and out of despair at the successes of the Sadat regime. Yet the underlying themes for this plethora of groups were (and are) the same: the jahiliyya and the counter-society concepts and, above all, the belief in the right to revolt against evil Muslim rulers. It is to the radical doctrine on *widerstandrecht* that we must now turn.

The Right to Revolt   This right is not readily acceptable to traditional Sunni political theory, haunted as it was by the trauma of civil war *(fitna)*, of the type that tore the

Islamic community apart in the mid-seventh century. Hence the
predilection of the ulama—later reinforced by material dependence
upon the authorities—for a sort of pessimistic realism: even an evil
ruler is better than anarchy. The idea was well-entrenched long
before ulama became senior civil servants or lived off generous governmental endowments funding their *madrassas* (which would not
happen before the eleventh century). The ulama accepted any Sunni
political authority as long as it did not openly renege on the Faith.
This does not mean that ulama failed to admonish rulers (albeit not
very courageously) on specific deviations; but criticism stopped short
of delegitimation. A bad Sunni ruler was still better than fitna.

An early version of this attitude is that of the Qadi Amir ibn
Shurhabil al-Sha'bi al-Kufi (d. 721) writing under the Omayyads:
"Love for the family of the Prophet without being Shi'ite . . . and
believe that what is good derives from God and what is evil is of
your own making . . . and obey the caliph even if he is a black
slave." The chief *qadi* (judge) of Harun al-Rashid's ninth-century
caliphate, and one of the most eminent jurists, Abu Yusuf, writes
on the same topic in a book (*Kitab al-Kharaj*) where he compares
the responsibility of the caliph before God to that of the shepherd
to the owner of the flock. Like other jurists before him, Abu Yusuf
perceives a wicked ruler as God's punishment to his community.
"Rulers are a scourge through whom God punishes those He decides
to punish. So do not meet God's scourge with hot temper and anger
but with humility and submission."

Even Ibn Hanbal (d. 855), founder of a most rigorous school
of Islamic law, and certainly not a timorous man, had this to say
about resistance: "You should obey the government and not rebel
against it. If the ruler orders something which implies sin against
God (*ma'siya*), you should neither obey nor rebel. Do not support
the fitna (strife), neither by your hand nor by your tongue."[15]

Delegitimation and the right for revolt are thus virtually alien
to Sunnism, which in that respect is markedly different not only

from extreme sects such as the Kharijites who viewed jihad against
all other Muslims (the "false believers") as a paramount goal, but
also from the Shi'a (which englobes about one-tenth of the Muslims
today). The Shi'a, being ever since the death of Caliph 'Ali (661)
a persecuted minority, developed a sort of pessimistic idealism. Unlike Sunni jurists who held that the state, given human nature (and
the decline since the Islamic Golden Age) is bound to be a necessary—and legitimate—evil in some respect, the Shi'a had a vision
of an ideal, legitimate state to be instituted by its leader, the imam,
presently in hiding. All the Muslim (i.e., Sunni) regimes are ipso
facto illegitimate. Most Shi'ites would not choose to revolt, because
the odds were so heavily against them, but they nourished a powerful
sense of reservation vis-à-vis the authorities, sometimes combined
with consciously hypocritical lip service (taqiyya). A minority of
Shi'ites, quite substantial and dangerous at times, would move from
pessimistic idealism to an optimistic brand of the same approach—
the imam's arrival is imminent, God's kingdom is bound to be
brought upon earth by this messiah (mahdi), and one should help
precipitate its descent by armed revolt. Both approaches are, of
course, unacceptable to Sunnis who reject the claims of the House
of 'Ali, while the Kharijites are completely outside of the pale of
the umma (and can, anyhow, be found today only in small enclaves
in Algeria, Tunisia, and Oman).

The task Sayyid Qutb set for himself was to legitimize revolt
in terms of mainstream Sunni thought. He had, in a word, to ban
the specter of fitna. An illustration of the challenge and an inkling
of the way he came to grips with it can be seen in the transcript of
his police interrogation:

Q. Don't you think the establishment of a Muslim military
underground may bring about a fitna or so serious a calamity that Islam may perish?

A. It may well bring about fitna, but the blame should be put
at the door of those who interdict open [MB] activity thus
pushing Muslims to underground action.

Q. Doesn't Islam require that you prevent a fitna before it occurs and forestall the development of conditions leading to it, i.e., that you should refrain from setting up a military underground organization and not give your blessing to its acquiring arms and training its members for an insurgency against the authorities?

A. What is incumbent upon us is to obey the injunctions of our religion; the fitna supposition refers just to a factual state of affairs. If I do my religious duty and a fitna ensues, the burden of responsibility is to be borne by he who had driven me underground and not by myself.

Q. What are the major divergences between the present regime and the one you aspire to?

A. Now the Shari'a is not the sole source of all legislation; I would like it to be installed as such. This is the major divergence, all others are derivative.[16]

The objections of the interrogator are largely those raised by traditional ulama over the centuries. Much the same objections were raised by the moderate wing of the Syrian MB in the polemics conducted by their organ *al-Ra'id* against the radical wing ("the fighting tali'a"). In response the radicals said:

From time to time the question is raised: "Is what happens in Syria a fitna instigated by the MB?" Islamic thought considers that the worst fitna is the absence of an Islamic regime which administers justice. Indeed, is there a more evil fitna than when corruption and injustice reign supreme, when morality declines, family ties dissolve, and youth falls into the trap of purveyors of films and other instruments of depravity? Is there a more calamitous fitna than when the elites are composed of the most immoral individuals, recruited not according to qualifications but by family ties, party membership, and personal interests? . . . The believers must not keep silent in the face of such evil. . . . Fitna is worse than warfare; this is why one should fight those responsible for the former . . . in order to chase tyranny and its henchmen. Shedding their blood will cleanse our country and help institute there the rule of Allah. What happens now in Syria is, consequently, a revolution to extirpate infidelity.[17]

Sayyid Qutb's—and the Syrians'—answers reveal just the tip of the iceberg. The whole intellectual structure—true to purpose—is organized in the manner of the medieval disputation, replete with Koranic verses, Hadiths, with various commentaries on both tightly interwoven and related to the realities of the present. This structure, which makes a powerful argument for revolution in Sunni terms, is—even more than the notion of counter-society—Qutb's major and most lasting contribution. The genius of Qutb consisted in his grounding his argument in the thought of a prominent medieval thinker, Ibn Taymiyya (1268–1328), and of some of his votaries, through an act of "creative interpretation." Though rigorously puritanical, this thinker certainly falls within the limits of Islamic orthodoxy and is considered by common consent to be the greatest theologian of his century. He has since exercised a major but respectable influence (notably on the mid-eighteenth-century Wahhabite movement, which gave birth to Saudi Arabia).

It is this very respectability which makes a "revolutionary version" of Ibn Taymiyya so effective even today in Sunni Islam, far more than the Khomeini gospel, with its distinct Shi'ite flavor.

Ibn Taymiyya: Apostacy and Revolution   Why has the modern twist given to Ibn Taymiyya proven so effective among Muslim militants? Why Taymiyya rather than another medieval theologian? How faithful to the letter—or to the spirit—of his thoughts are Qutb and his ilk? The best way to answer these questions may be by tracing the history of some of Ibn Taymiyya's ideas, as they passed from their medieval context into the contemporary world.

He lived his entire life in the Mamluk sultanate of Egypt and Syria, and sat quite frequently on the defendants' bench in Mamluk courts for involvement in one religious dispute or another. In some cases he was acquitted, in others sent to prison, where he wrote a number of his treatises. He was ultimately to die in the jail of the Damascus citadel, though not before enjoying a few periods of grace and influence under more sympathetic sultans. This mixture of impact and persecution foreshadowed the ambiguity that he elicits today in the religious and the political establishment.

A firebrand he surely was, but hardly a revolutionary. In a manner that one can find among other ulama but with unsurpassed moral courage, intensity, and intellectual vigor, he clamored for a return to the pristine purity of the first four decades of Islam (622–61). His whole endeavor was designed to cleanse Islam of the dross accumulated during centuries of decline: in theology (toward a more literal—his opponents said anthropomorphic—perception of the deity as against pantheistic mystics); in matters of ritual (against pilgrimages to tombs and the cult of Jerusalem); as well as in legal affairs (stricter application of the Shari'a, the Islamic law). This brought him into collision, above all, with the religious establishment—rationalistic theologians, lax judges, Sufis, and dervishes—and only indirectly with the powers-that-be. The latter were, on the whole, indifferent to the theological and ritualistic controversies he aroused. They backed the religious dignitaries, either out of a sense of obligation to these faithful servants or out of the sheer conservatism of a military ruling caste bred upon the simple notions of the Islam of Central Asia (where the Mamluks originated). Only in legal affairs could they feel directly involved—as when illegal taxes and relative leniency toward non-Muslims were denounced, and when the habits of the ruling class (in sexual affairs, wine drinking) could be construed as the real object of Ibn Taymiyya's vituperations.

Nevertheless, the zealous theologian did enjoy at times the protection of a few sultans and emirs (local governors); and not even hostile sultans and emirs accused him of sedition. Nor was there any reason for them to do so. Never did Ibn Taymiyya challenge the legitimacy of any particular sultan, or a fortiori that of the Mamluk regime. He was thus indicted as a "troublemaker," a "slanderer," or "deviant" from theological norms, but never as the harbinger of insurgency.

Small wonder that for more than six centuries Ibn Taymiyya has been the model for revivalists and vigilantes, for fundamentalist reformers, and other apostles of moral rearmament. But how had he come to be dubbed the spiritual father of the Islamic Revolution, Sunni-style? Is it a case of theological misunderstanding or political distortion?

It is significant that these, the better-known pages of his biography and writings, are not what attracted the attention of his modern radical disciples. It was rather his teachings on the question of the Mongols.

The Mongols of Ibn Taymiyya's adulthood were no longer the heathens who conquered all the lands of Islam east of Syria and put an end to the Baghdad Caliphate. By the late thirteenth century, the Mongols had embraced Sunni Islam even as their expansionist drive continued. The ulama of Syria and Egypt were faced with an excruciating dilemma: was war against the Mongols still a jihad or had it become a mere clash between two Sunni states? If the latter, it created a deplorable conflict but not one that called for recourse to Holy War (as would have been the case had the Mongols become Shi'ites). No doubt it was in the interests of the Mamluk rulers to see the war continue to be called a jihad in order to fire the zeal of their soldiers, recruit volunteers, justify new taxes and expropriations required to finance the war effort, and to deter the citizenry from any collaboration with the invaders.

Paradoxically enough, the most effective answer was to come from the pen of an intellectual not known for his docility. Ibn Taymiyya had been preoccupied by the Mongol menace since childhood. At the age of six he had to flee to Damascus with his family when his native city in northeastern Syria was overrun by the Mongol hordes. This "refugee syndrome" may account for his anti-Mongol zeal and his uncharacteristic readiness to issue a legal opinion so much in line with what the Mamluk authorities were seeking. Yet, heaping irony upon paradox, he was to do that in a manner which could one day be turned against the authorities. In his fatwa (responsum to a legal query) on the Mongols, he admitted that they did profess the Islamic credo ("There is no other god than Allah and Muhammad is his Messenger"); they did perform the five daily prayers and observe the fast of Ramadan. But was this enough to make them true Muslims?

According to the letter of law, of the Shari'a, the answer was no doubt positive. The mere performance of the double formula of faith (*Shahadatayn*) would have sufficed. But here Ibn Taymiyya introduced a new criterion. A professed Sunni Muslim ceases to be one when he fails to keep (or in the case of a Muslim ruler, apply) the Shari'a, when he breaks major injunctions concerning life and limb, property, jihad and the status of non-Muslims, the sexual code of behavior, alcoholic prohibition, gambling. The list of injunctions he draws is quite long; and it is not altogether clear how many nonapplied injunctions bring the ruler (or the individual believer) to the point of no return. When does he become an apostate to be combated? This created some degree of obfuscation—which continues to this very day—as to the full import of his fatwa.

In the case of the Mongols—and it was these "deviants" who interested Ibn Taymiyya in the first place—everything was quite clear. His disciple Ibn Kathir (1300–1372/3) best expounded the viewpoint in his own Koranic commentary on the verses "Whoso judgeth not according to what God hath revealed, they are the transgressors. . . . Do they therefore seek after the *Jahiliyya* (pre-Islamic times)?" (V, 33, 48). The exegesis runs as follows:

> [These verses] refer to people who abide by regulations and laws set by men, to fit their own misguided desires and whims, rather than adhering to the Shari'a bestowed upon us by Allah. This was the case with the inhabitants [of Arabia] during the jahiliyya . . . and (today) with the Mongols who follow the *Yasa* code set down by Genghis Khan, which is a conglomeration

of laws, some taken from Jewish, Christian, Muslim, and other legal traditions, and many others decided upon by the whim of the Mongol rulers; the whole amalgam being given priority over the laws of Allah laid down in the Koran and the Sunna. Those who follow such (man-made) laws are infidels and should be combated until they comply with the laws of God.[18]

Thus the Yasa laws of Genghis Khan, brought by his hordes from central Asia, invalidated the Islam of the Mongols, making it into something worse than heresy (such as the Shi'a). Their Islam becomes the polytheism of the jahiliyya—an old, emotion-laden vituperative term that would have an interesting modern career. That Ibn Taymiyya was not only ruling on the special case and was well aware of its general doctrinal significance is clearly elucidated in his treatise on *Public Policy in Islamic Jurisprudence*:

> It has been established from the Book, from the Sunna, and from the general unanimity of the [Muslim] nation that he who forsakes the Law of Islam should be fought, though he may have once pronounced the two formulas of Faith (in Islam). There may be a difference of opinion regarding rebellious groups which neglect a voluntary, but established, piece of worship . . . but there is no uncertainty regarding the duties and prohibitions, which are both explicit and general. He who neglects them should be fought until he agrees to abide (by these duties and prohibitions): to perform the five assigned prayers per day, to pay the *zakat* [alms], to fast during the month of Ramadan, and to undertake pilgrimage to the Ka'ba [at Mecca]. Furthermore they should avoid all forbidden acts, like marriage with sisters, the eating of impure foods (such as pork, cattle that has died or was unlawfully slaughtered, etc.), and the attack on the lives and wealth of the Muslims. Any such trespasser of the Law should be fought, provided that he had a knowledge of the mission of the Prophet, Peace be Upon Him. This knowledge makes him responsible for obeying the orders, the prohibitions, and the permits. If he disobeys these he should then be fought.[19]

The treatise in question belongs to a rare Islamic literary genre—
political theory. Muslim (or to be more precise, Sunni) thinkers
tended to consider this domain the preserve of the authorities. Thus,
even Muslim legal treatises rarely discuss constitutional law. Those
few who ventured into this awesome realm usually wrote essays
justifying the status quo. By the time they began to do so, in the
mid-eleventh century, the status quo usually meant Turkish, or
alien, military rule, rather more arbitrary than the caliphate of early
Islam.

Ibn Taymiyya was one of the few exceptions to this rule—a
thinker who grappled with the realities of power. Moreover, the
passage quoted above is the nearest any premodern theorist in Sunni
Islam ever came to expounding a theory of the right of resistance to
illegitimate power. As we have seen, while the "right to revolt" goes
without saying for the Shi'ites, a perennially persecuted minority,
this was not the case in the dominant, Sunni, brand of Islam.

It is indeed from the well-trod path of Sunni "pessimistic compromise" that Ibn Taymiyya strays. For him, a Sunni ruler becomes
illegitimate if he does not apply a substantial part of the Shari'a.
The illegitimacy is defined in ulama terms: the ruler who neglects
or transgresses Islamic law is ipso facto an infidel, or rather an
apostate, hence the object of jihad. How substantial a part of the
Shari'a must be transgressed in order for the ruler to become a kafir
was not specified. Perhaps this was because in the case of the Mongols, the introduction of their Yasa rules signified such a massive
abdication of the Shari'a as to render this question superfluous.

But the question is of some significance with regard to the
Mamluks. Why did Ibn Taymiyya and his followers not declare any
of the Sultans illegitimate in view of their transgressions in the realm
of taxes, status of non-Muslims, alcohol, and so on? Fear of these
brutal rulers is not an altogether adequate explanation when speaking of a man like Ibn Taymiyya, who was ready to go to jail even
for the abstractions of theological disputes. It seems that for all his
criticism of their actual behavior he still thought the Mamluks had

not crossed the fateful threshold. One of his present-day followers explains: "The ulama of those times could not imagine their rulers deviating from the way of life set by Allah in the systematic and comprehensive manner we witness today. Nor was it conceivable for them that rulers would throw the Shari'a away altogether, conspire against Islam, maltreat Muslims, and form alliances with the Enemies of God, as happens quite often today."[20]

Yet outweighing everything else was the external, foreign-policy consideration. The Abode of Islam was under heavy and unrelenting attack by Mongols and latter-day Crusaders. The Mamluk battalions, dedicated warriors of jihad, were the only effective dam stemming that tide, from the battle of 'Ayn Jalut (1260) onward. This partly exonerated them. Their sins could be criticized but had to be kept in a proper perspective. Their contribution to the defense of Islam could not be forgotten. It is significant that Ibn Taymiyya took an active part, as a sort of medieval *politruk*, in many Mamluk campaigns against the Mongols (as well as against the Armenian kingdom of Asia Minor, an ally of the Crusaders). His follower, Ibn Kathir, was the author of a celebrated treatise extolling the merits of the Holy War, written in the wake of the massive raids of the Cypriot Crusader navy against Alexandria and Tripoli: "All this," comments Hawwa, "created a state of emergency in Dar al-Islam; and thus even the most devoted ulama, . . . be it even a man as audacious and outspoken as Ibn Taymiyya, . . . had no choice but to resign themselves to the fait accompli on many important questions. They did their best, however, to remedy the situation somewhat with their responsa (which had, of course, to take the state of emergency into account)."[21] There were thus clear limits as to what the Ibn Taymiyya school committed itself to do in the realm of politics. But a new seed had been sown.

During the following six centuries, this school, dubbed the Neo-Hanbalites—with its puritanical rigor, emphasis on literal exegesis, and its animosity toward "accretions, innovations, and

dross"—did serve from time to time as the moving spirit of fundamentalist movements in Islam (notably the Wahhabites of Arabia).
All of these movements operated, however, prior to the onset of
modernity in the nineteenth and twentieth centuries. Ibn Taymiyya
was still being used in order to interpret medieval-type phenomena
and deviations with the same old bounds set upon the right of revolt,
all the more so as the Abode of Islam was coming under devastating
military attack by Western colonialist powers.

The modern rediscovery of Ibn Taymiyya and Ibn Kathir—as
well as Ibn Qayyim al-Jawziyya and some lesser lights—was to take
place in twentieth-century Egypt and Muslim India. This was not
due to sheer accident, for these lands were among the first to come
under the impact of the West. Western influence thus had time to
penetrate the local culture. Many were alarmed by what they considered the undermining of Islam from within and despaired of coming to terms with that alien culture without forfeiting their ancient
identity—and they found in the Ibn Taymiyya doctrine a kind of
inspired solution. The analogy of the Mongols and the concept of
pre-Islamic jahiliyya would be reinterpreted to suit the new state
of affairs.

Commenting on the Koranic verse quoted above (V, 44:
"Whoso judgeth not . . ."), Rashid Rida, a Syrian thinker living in
Egypt (1866–1935), wrote in his *al-Manar Exegesis* that it applies
"to those Muslim [rulers] who introduce novel laws today and forsake the Shari'a enjoined upon them by God. . . . They thus abolish supposedly 'distasteful' penalties such as cutting off the hands of
thieves or stoning adulterers and prostitutes. They replace them by
man-made laws and penalties. He who does that has undeniably
become an infidel."

The reference to European laws introduced in Egypt is obvious,
and further on the author mentions explicitly the imposition of
British laws in India. Coming to the "Jahiliyya verse" (V, 48), he
applies it to the "geographical Muslims of our age," those ostensible

Muslims who belong to the faith by virtue of living in a Muslim land and keeping certain rituals, yet who "set laws of their own making and free themselves from the discipline of the laws of Allah."

Rashid Rida adheres to the letter of the Koranic verse, and he deals merely with the introduction of foreign laws (even though the modern Western challenge was operating on a much wider front). Moreover, he stops short of declaring jihad against the Westernized Muslims and especially against Westernizing rulers. Yet the Ibn Taymiyya renaissance had begun—namely, the application of his doctrine to the new challenges facing the Islamic lands—this time, above all, from within. A challenge had arisen which was somewhat analogous to that of Greek philosophy and the Mongol Yasa laws Ibn Taymiyya combated six hundred years ago; but it was broader and much more pervasive, impinging not only upon elites (as in the case of Greek philosophy) or new converts to Islam (as the Mongols and some Mamluk sultans). The expanding educational system and the mass media created a menace that hovered over all Muslims, especially city dwellers: creeping secularization, whether deliberate or inadvertent.

It is at this juncture that Sayyid Qutb's original contribution intervened. The paragraph quoted above about jahiliyya's being "not just a specific historical period" and holding sway in Arab societies today, is actually taken from his commentary on these very verses (V, 44, 48) in *In the Shadow of the Koran.* He was actually trying to work Maudoodi's ideas into the Ibn Taymiyya framework.[22]

That the jahiliyya theory was articulated within the parameters of the thought of a prominent medieval theologian endowed it with an aura of Sunni respectability it may not otherwise have acquired. Naturally, then, one finds the key Koranic verses (V, 44–48) quoted often by radicals in the 1970s.[23] Ibn Taymiyya could never be banned by the baffled authorities, even though Sayyid Qutb's writings would be (from September 1965 on). As late as six months before the assassination of Sadat the semiofficial Egyptian weekly *Mayo* would single out Ibn Taymiyya as the most pervasive and deleterious influence upon Egyptian youth. From him they learned that "violence and seizure of power are justified by Islamic law and tradition"—and that fellow Muslims, even Sunnis (orthodox, that is, not Shi'ite heretics), could become the target of a "holy war in the cause of Allah." No wonder, *Mayo* concluded, that the proliferating Muslim associations at the universities, where Ibn Taymiyya's views prevail, have been spawning various terrorist groups.[24] Nevertheless, the weekly did not call for outlawing these fourteenth-century writings. Rather, much like the prosecutor at Qutb's trial,[25] it would strive to prove that they had been misinterpreted.

Mayo's premonitions were to be proved correct. The major ideological statement of the Sadat assassins is to be found in a book entitled *The Absent Precept*, printed in a clandestine edition of five hundred copies. Its author was a twenty-seven-year-old engineer, 'Abd al-Salam Faraj, the moving spirit of the group. He was to be tried and executed. The text of the verdict, appropriately enough, devotes ample space to discussing—and refuting—Faraj's ideas.

The Absent Precept (the precept in question being the jihad, for whose revival the book calls) draws heavily upon the writings of Ibn Taymiyya as well as of a number of his disciples, indulging in a detailed exegesis of his arguments in order to show how they apply today, 653 years after his death. The book was read, commented, and meditated upon by almost all the conspirators already brought to trial as well as by many other members of the Jihad Organization. At least three of Sadat's four assassins also did extensive reading on their own in the works of the Ibn Taymiyya school.[26] The trauma did not alter the policy of the regime: Faraj's "willfully distorting" interpretation was "exposed" by the new mass-circulation weekly, *al-Liwa' al-Islami* put out by the regime to combat extremism. References to the key verses (Koran, V, 44, 48) had already abounded in press reports on the activities imputed to Muslim activists jailed during the month preceding Anwar Sadat's assassination. It was no mere coincidence that a long exegesis of these verses was featured in the two issues of *Minbar al-Islam* (organ of the

Ministry of Religious Affairs) published in the wake of the assassination. The brunt of its official argument was that the verses actually
concern Muhammad's polemics against Jews and Christians (on the
one hand) and Arab pagans (on the other). Current politics are not
mentioned, but the warning is clear: Beware of those who manipulate the Holy Writ.[27]

Yet Ibn Taymiyya still remained untouchable, though the editors of *Mayo* have since suggested that it was a mistake to put him
in wide circulation; limited editions for scholars could have circumscribed the danger. Both the aggressive attention given to the twentieth-century versions of his ideas, and the respect in which he
himself is still held, attest to the effectiveness of the choice of Ibn
Taymiyya by Qutb as the vehicle of the revolution Sunni-style.

The Syrian radicals faced a rather simpler case, for, as paragons
of a disinherited majority (the 60 percent of the population who are
Sunnis), they could accuse the Ba'th regime of being plainly heretic
because it is dominated by 'Alawites. Yet even the Syrians had
recourse to the Neo-Hanbalite concepts of apostasy and jihad.[28]
Their organ, *al-Nadhir*, tags Assad's army "the cohorts of Hulagu"
(the Mongol conqueror of Baghdad in 1258); his security agents are
"the Mongols" or "band of apostates" and the president is "the enemy of Allah" (the very title conferred by Sadat's assassins upon their
target). This self-styled organization of mujahidun wages a "holy
war to put an end to the jahiliyya." The 1980 *Manifesto to the
Islamic Revolution* depicts an upsurge of "jahili fanaticism and anti-
Islamic ideas and mores menacing to inundate Muslim society."
The rationale for the armed resistance is specifically anchored in the
activist (or vigilante) strand in Sunni political thought: "The contemporary Islamic Revolution rejects quietism and the proclivity to
stay aloof of politics and wish to remind the believers . . . that the
will of Allah is accomplished through the agency of man, by effort
exerted in real life."[29]

The (typically Neo-Hanbalite) gibe at the passive and *attentiste* tradition of the ulama is evident. It is further elaborated upon in the writings of Sa'id Hawwa:

> Many an ignoramus sheikh considers opposition to any political regime a sin smacking of Kharijite heresy. One realizes how boorish are such ulama when one considers that if they are right, then Abraham and Moses have sinned in resisting Nimrod and Pharaoh. . . . Any revolt against an illegitimate ruler is justified. Isn't it then right to combat a ruler who does not apply the laws set in the Koran? Isn't it forbidden to flee, even when outnumbered, when the fight is one between Infidelity and the True Faith? Doesn't Allah help those who help themselves?

The root cause of all evil, claims Hawwa,

> is the tendency of so many pious Muslims to run away from any kind of political activity, as though politics is a realm of impurity and turpitude to be shunned by all means. This is a most curious attitude, for it would follow that the believers must resign themselves to the political leadership being always in the hands of miscreants and hypocrites. How can God's Word reign supreme if Muslims do not control the decision-making in the lands of Islam? This brings us to an even more bizarre paradox: many of the pious agree to execute policies laid down by infidel elites, policies liable to end up in the destruction of Islam and/ or in making Muslims into infidels.[30]

It is this concoction of quietistic passivity, inherent ambivalence toward politics, and pragmatic compromise with the powers-that-be—typical of the majority Sunni political tradition—which Hawwa and his disciples flatly reject. Hence they embrace the activist minority tradition, that of the Neo-Hanbalites. Yet while operating within the basic Neo-Hanbalite premises, Hawwa—like Qutb before him—carries it one step further; what was hitherto a conservative-vigilante tradition is thereby pushed into a revolution-

ary orbit. This step is required by the new situation Islam finds itself
in today under the nominally Muslim regimes. The state is no more
the "watchdog state" of yore which, to all practical purposes, left
civil society alone, to be guided in matters of ethics and faith by the
ulama. The new military state is interventionistic by nature and has
a panoply of efficient means at its disposal. Politics, hence, impinges
upon social life, and only seizure of power (with its monopoly of
coercive and persuasive means) can guarantee the long-term survival
of Islam. MB military commander Husni 'Abbu (who was to be
executed for his role in the 1979 raid on the Aleppo Artillery School)
put it succinctly in his trial: In order to cleanse the country of all
the depravity that works against Islam, the mujahidun should take
over the state and establish a government of their own.[31]

It is true that the brunt of the Syrian radicals' polemics is directed against the "Nusayri ['Alawite] terror state," a state ruled by
an extreme Shi'ite sect whose heresy borders on infidelity due to its
propensity to place the Caliph 'Ali higher than the Prophet Muhammad (perhaps even making the former quasi-divine). That this
sect constitutes barely 11 percent of the population makes its predominance all the more outrageous. Hence the recurrence of the
epithets *ta'ifi* (sectarian, confessional), *batini* (extreme Shi'ite),
mulhid (heretic), and *zindiq* (atheist) to depict the regime, its various
repressive agencies, and individuals—however humble their role—
affiliated with it. President Assad, who makes a point of presenting
the 'Alawites in the media and in the schools' curricula as falling
within the pale of Orthodoxy (eliciting to that effect fatawa from
Syrian and Lebanese religious dignitaries), is dismissed as a "defector
from Islam clad in Muslim garb," who follows the Nusayri dogma,
which makes a virtue of *taqiyya* (dissimulating one's true beliefs in
an adverse situation).

Yet so great is the prestige of Ibn Taymiyya in the radical circles
that even on this chapter they build their argumentation on his
thought. Their major piece of evidence to substantiate the heresy
and depravity of the 'Alawites is Ibn Taymiyya's "fatwa on the Nu-

sayris." The fatwa depicts them as "worse than Jews or Christians,
worse even than pagans," both because of their theology (divinity of
'Ali and his descendants, hatred of the first three caliphs, rejection
of the idea of resurrection, belief in the transmigration of souls) and
of their alleged moral laxity (sexual license, wine drinking). Ibn
Taymiyya's fulminations against their "history of treason to Islam"—
in presumably helping the Crusaders and the Mongols—are quoted
at length and presented as leading inexorably to their collaboration
with the French colonial power and their more recent "alliance with
the Maronite Crusaders." That Ibn Taymiyya's peremptory excom-
munication of the 'Alawites specified, among other things, that they
should not be employed as soldiers on the frontiers of Islam, is made
the centerpiece of the demand to chase them from the Syrian army,
their power base for the past two decades. [32]

Counter-Propaganda   The best testimony to the linkage
and Internal Disputes between Neo-Hanbalism and radical-
                         ism is the strategy the authorities had to
adopt—isolate the radicals by refuting their claim to be part of the
Sunni consensus. This they do first by having establishment theologians, as we have seen, argue that the radical interpretation of Ibn
Taymiyya is "perverted." Second, the authorities dub the radicals
as Kharijites, after that sect which entered into armed dissidence
against the Sunni Caliphate in mid-seventh century, and allege that
all who do not accept their theory of the caliphate are infidels; a
war to the knife should be fought against them. (It should be noted,
in passing, that so strong is the Sunni consensus on the Kharijites
as villains and sectarians that even today only left-wing historians,
who are essentially secularist, depict them as heroes—paragons of
democracy and equality.)[33]

The Kharijite epithet was hurled at the radicals already during
the pretrial interrogation of the 1965 group and then widely disseminated by the ensuing press and ulama campaign against these "conspirators." It would become a stock in trade of future media

campaigns against the "Kharijites of the twentieth century" under Sadat and Mubarak. The Kharijites' "doublefold sin," said one sheikh, had always consisted in claiming the right to "revolt against evil rulers" and in arrogating to themselves the power to declare other Muslims as infidels.[34] One finds the same analogy echoed in the brainwashing sessions in prison as well as in "debates" with captured terrorists in the press, especially since 1977. By early 1983 such staged "debates" on Kharijism and "distorted Neo-Hanbalism" gained maximum exposure, making it to the screens of Egyptian TV.

Critique of the Sayyid Qutb school was by no means limited to the religious establishment and its political masters. As a revolutionary exegesis this Muslim "liberation theology" was quite problematic for the moderate wing of the MB, headed by Hasan al-Hudaybi, who was the superintendent-general of the MB since 1950. The MB had known some waves of dissidence, in impatience with the gradualism of Hasan al-Banna (which did not, however, exclude violence). The most important of these waves were the Shabab Muhammad, who split from the MB in 1939/40. Similar tensions could be detected in the early 1950s between the military apparatus and the political leadership, presided over by Hudaybi, which was circumspect and inherently respectful of legality.[35] Yet divergences were mostly about tactics; none of these dissidents ever developed an alternative strategy the way Qutb did; nor a fortiori did any of the past dissenters pose a fully blown ideological challenge; a challenge rendered, in Qutb's case, all the more formidable by his vast erudition and alluring style.

Hudaybi (who was in prison until 1955, then under house arrest) was finally released in 1961. He seems to have been only vaguely aware of Qutb's ideological evolution and of the activities of the 1965 group. But when the "conspiracy" was exposed in summer 1965, he was arrested again as a preventive measure together with others of his ilk. Dismayed both by the blow to his already much weakened MB and by the ideological challenge the new underground represented, Hudaybi started campaigning against it in prison. He was further prodded to do so by the spread of the new ideology among veteran prisoners—elated by the sudden resurgence of the MB from the ashes—as well as among former MB activists thrown there again with him for "preventive detention" and, hence, shaken out of their belief that one could work within the (presumably tempered) Nasserist regime. Prisoners who were not plainly attracted were in utter disarray, disheartened by the new persecutions yet unable to come up with a cogent answer to the disciples of Qutb. The questions they raised had their parallels among activists who remained at large. Hudaybi, who was made even more cautious by his advanced age (late seventies) and by what he took to be the lesson of the 1954/55 repression, tried to dissipate the doubts in a series of letters sent from prison, where he sums up a response to his fellow inmates' questions.

The debates continued to rage among prisoners—witness the May 1967 episode—and Hudaybi wrote in 1969 a fuller version of his camp's arguments during these polemics, aptly entitled *Propagandists, Not Judges*.[36] It is not given to man, who does not see to the heart, to judge the veracity of another Muslim's faith, nor to declare him to be an apostate unless he had openly reneged on the credo. Judgment as to whether major sins committed exclude a Muslim from the umma, says Hudaybi, should be left to God alone. Collective judgment over the whole of the umma is even more contrary to the tenets of Islam. Hurling the epithet jahili upon Muslim societies today is thus absurd, all the more so as jahiliyya (and, hence, the hijra) is an historical phenomenon, and not an ever-recurrent human condition.

This was by no means a call for apathy. True Muslims should be active as propagandists, preaching, admonishing, and trying to bring people back to the Right Path. They are not entitled, however, to sit in judgment on the presumed apostacy of fellow Muslims nor to execute such verdicts. Coercion is no solution. As for the educational endeavor, it should be carried out within the system and not by a separate Muslim counter-society, for no human being can have the presumption of declaring himself (and his votaries) to be the sole veritable believers. To do so is to fall into the Kharijite trap.

Hudaybi remained ambiguous on the question of how bad Islam's situation really was. This was not the case of another fundamentalist thinker, Muhammad al-Bahi, whom we have already encountered both as a proponent of the "eclipse of Islam" in the twentieth century and as a moderately courageous critic of Nasser's abolition of the Shari'a courts. Although he shares the cultural pessimism of the radicals and the notion that modernity is tantamount to a new Age of Barbarity, al-Bahi refuses to arrogate for himself (or for anyone else) the right to judge individual Muslims as infidels. Jahiliyya is for him—as it was for Maudoodi—an abstract term, a characterization of a system of beliefs and a *Zeitgeist*, not the judicial ground for inculpation, which should be based on specific actions. Moreover, even in his overview of the state of Islam he does not consider it so completely lost as to warrant taking exceptional measures. [37]

This is, broadly speaking, also the view of former MB leader, 'Umar Tilimsani, who, mellowed by age and tempered by long years in prison, took this position in his monthly *al-Da'wa* (which reappeared from 1976 to 1981) as well as in his appearances in the media following the Sadat assassination.

Al-Bahi and Tilimsani were already in their sixties when the jahiliyya-ridda debate began among fundamentalists in prisons and at large. Yet one should not jump to the conclusion that a sharp generational cleavage underlay these polemics (which is not to deny that some generational elements were involved). Many former MB lower-level and younger activists (such as Yusuf al-Qardawi and Salim 'Ali al-Bahasnawi) shared Hudaybi's apprehensions and/or the distinction made by al-Bahi. Indeed the prison experience—whether lived through or observed—could push people to extreme caution as well as to terrorism, a phenomenon one could observe outside Egypt as well. Even several members of Qutb's own group (such as

'Abdallah al-Sisi and Jabir Rizq) and, later, some Takfir group members (including its founder, 'Ali Abduh Isma'il), were converted to the "No Judgment" theory during their prison years.[38] This theory, in its al-Bahi interpretation (which, englobing elements of Sayyid Qutb's thought, was particularly effective in these circles), received in 1975 a substantial momentum when Qutb's brother, Muhammad, then living in Saudi Arabia, gave it his blessing.[39] Upon their release, such converted prisoners would take an active part in fierce ongoing debates in the 1970s. Successful brainwashing by the authorities could have been involved in their case, and certainly played a role in the repentance of Jihad group members trumpeted every now and then by the Egyptian media.[40]

The regime was quick to grasp the usefulness of the internal debate among fundamentalists and gave it maximum coverage, both in order to deepen the chasms and "recuperate" the conservatives, and in order to bolster their argument that the radicals are actually sectarian, outside the pale. The moderate critics of Qutb were given ample latitude by the censorship to air their views in books and articles, and from the late seventies (and especially after the assassination of Sadat) their articulate and popular spokesmen, Tilimsani and Sheikh Sha'rawi, were often solicited for interviews on these matters in the semiofficial press. The major publishing house of the former MB, Dar al-Ansar, which occupies the middle ground between radicalism and conservatism, could thus launch a series of books under the heading Don't Follow This Path dedicated to this polemic. It is characteristic that the first book in the series was The Kharijites: Historical Origins of the Problem of the Takfir of Muslims. The Kharijites are chastized there both for declaring other believers to be infidel (takfir) and for quitting the umma and turning against it. Whoever shares these views today is an objective ally of the enemies of Islam.[41] Indeed, in the denial of the right to judge others to be apostates as well as in the practical conclusions that follow suit, these fundamentalist critics of Qutb join the argumentation of the Muslim establishment, whose most effective and vociferous proponent was former Waqf Minister Sheikh al-Dhahabi—so effective indeed that the Takfir group saw him as major adversary and would abduct (and finally execute) him. Yet when one reads his *Problems of the Call for the Faith*,[42] certain differences between him and the moderate (or conservative) fundamentalists do emerge.

Dhahabi, while admitting that the situation of Islam is bad, lays emphasis on outside dangers (missionaries, Orientalists, Communists) as much as, or even more than, upon internal problems; in his assessment of the latter he never lays the blame on the authorities (except with regard to insufficient funds for religious education), and he is much more sanguine on the chances for reform by law (application of the Shari'a).

The conservative fundamentalists, however, are caught in a bind. As we shall have occasion to deal with them in greater length in chapter 5, suffice it here to outline their predicament. The conservative outlook on the state of Islam is bleaker, though shying away, either for reasons of principle or out of prudence, from declaring it to be jahiliyya. They concentrate on internal challenges (on all of which, except for Pan-Arabism, they share the radical assessment). While they may entertain some hopes for reform by the state, they have been disappointed by the slow pace and are, hence, less than enthusiastic on this account. What is the alternative they have to offer? Long-term educational effort within the system, destined to bring about popular pressure upon the authorities to conform to Islam (of the type which succeeded in delaying, then modifying, the Personal Status Bill in 1974–79). While criticizing the regime and doubting its commitment to Islamic reform so touted by Dhahabi and his fellow higher ulama, the conservatives—many of whom are lower ulama—reject emigration out of the umma and recourse to violence. These tracks, says al-Sisi, are "but a manifestation of despondency and despair," which he attributes to the horrors of torture and massacre, which "induced [among MB inmates] loathing and hatred toward the criminal rulers of that time." The upshot was what he calls "tendency to escapism"—violence as a sort of *fuite en avant*. Though a former political prisoner himself (1965–74), al-Sisi, and others of his ilk, maintain that real activism should be both clear-eyed and long of breath.[43]

Recourse to Violence   This rapid survey of the jahiliyya controversy serves to highlight the radical position, especially their view that the distinction between educational effort and violence is immaterial. Both are cures to a terrible malady, both are predicated upon a "five minutes to midnight" evaluation of the state of Islam. Consequently, the educational effort, as the radicals envision it, differs from the one the conservatives call for: it should be much more intensive and, above all, operated by a counter-society beyond the pale of the "infidel society" and immune to osmosis by the latter. These conditions were not met by the MB of yore, which as a mass movement could not maintain the purity in doctrine and behavior, the tightly knit structure, and the single-minded dedication, all posited by the radicals as sine qua non. It is true that the MB accepted the legitimacy of violence as early as 1938 and established a separate (and secret) military organization around 1942. Yet this was violence to be directed above all against outsiders (the British), hence the hesitations in the early 1950s when an internal enemy, the Free Officers' regime, came to loom almost as large. Moreover, the "military branch" was never an authentic "counter-society" either in concept or in realization. It was but a specialized arm of a centralized hierarchical mass-movement present everywhere in Egyptian society and operating within its framework. *Hizb al-Tahrir*, an MB offshoot operating in Syria, Lebanon, and Jordan since the 1950s, was likewise rejected for trying to play the political game, establish coalitions with semi-apostates, and setting detailed programs for reform when what society needed was radical transformation.[44]

The model offered by the Qutb school of thought was markedly distinct and was much more akin to that of the Iranian Fida'iyun al-Islam—a plethora of autonomous, relatively small, counter-societies, operating within each nation-state. Small wonder that Nav-vab Safavi, the Fida'iyun leader (executed in 1956) is set by Yakan and by Dannawi as the prime example of modern jihad.[45]

The mujahidun in Syria consisted of a number of radical groups which, from 1964 on, split from the official MB organization; an organization led, as in Egypt, by the legalistic-minded successor ('Isam al-'Attar) of its founder (Mustafa al-Siba'i). Foremost among these groups was the Kata'ib Muhammad, which was transformed into a military organization—"Fighting Vanguard," al-Tali'a al-Muqatila (1974–75)—by its leader, Marwan Hadid, as he despaired of mass demonstrations and strikes as a means of combating the regime. While the Egyptian groups enjoyed complete autonomy Hadid's group (led successively after his death in prison in 1976 by Salim Muhammad and 'Adnan 'Uqla, who were also to be killed, and now by 'Adnan Sa'd al-Din) succeeded to impose a measure of dominance on all extremist groups in the center and north of the country and in 1980 over the old and moderate organization cen-tered in Damascus (under Muwaffaq Da'bul and the exiled 'Isam al-'Attar). The same process, on a much smaller scale, took place in Tripoli, Lebanon, where three Islamic groups were united in Sheikh Sha'ban's Tawhid in 1982–83. All these attempts at unifi-cation or at least coordination (and even in Egypt the student as-sociations had a rather loose liaison framework), never went beyond their respective state boundaries. The nation-state was accepted as the operational framework, a sort of grudging recognition of the success and viability of this "Western-imported" political concept that the radicals so harshly decry. Some ideologues even endeavor to justify this situation in traditional terms. Sa'id Hawwa, for in-stance, quotes at length the hadiths extolling the role of al-Sham (Syria) in the jihad—past (seventh to tenth centuries) and future (in the End of Days) in order to prove the special mission of its modern-day mujahidun.[46]

Jihad evidently denotes justification for recourse to violence,

conceived in this case as a defensive act against the war that the new
military state wages against Islam. The historical model is, of course,
the Ridda Wars of Caliph Abu Bakr against the apostate tribes of
the Arabian Peninsula (632–34). But jihad theory never enjoined
war alone. Economic warfare, counter-propaganda—in brief, any
means of coercion and persuasion—were licit according to circumstances. In the case of apostacy in particular, even Ibn Taymiyya
held that if one could win the hearts and minds of "wayward Muslims" through persuasion, so much the better.

In consequence, when Hawwa and Yakan came to work out a
modern theory of jihad, they infused contemporary elements into
the traditional typology, presenting a gamut of possible actions, from
"jihad by heart" (mental reservation under extreme coercion),
through "jihad by word" (education and propaganda), to "jihad by
hand" (economic and political pressure; insurgency). Recourse to
violence is certainly imperative if there is no other way "to uproot
from the Abode of Islam Shi'ite extremists and other heretics, such
as the Baha'is and Ahmadis, infidel parties like Communists and
ignorant [secular] Pan-Arabists, as well as those who call for separation of religion and state . . . in short, in order to cleanse our
abode from all apostates and render it pure unto the Muslims." Not
only individuals but the state also should be fought, if it is a "deviant
Islamic state, that is when its ruler is unjust, morally depraved,
employs non-Muslims, or incompetent Muslims in his administration, or finally, when the Shari'a is not applied."[47]

Both Yakan and Hawwa claim—whether out of prudence or of
sincerity—that even in dire circumstances it might be useful first to
try to "isolate the nonbelievers" by peaceful means; but there is no
avoiding the implied conclusion that it may well come to a situation
where violence will be the only way out. (Hawwa was indeed to
become in the late 1970s a member of the Syrian Revolutionary
Command, while Yakan's Jama'a Islamiyya set up military units,
dubbed *Mujahidun* or *Jund Allah*, during the Lebanese Civil War.

In his most recent book Yakan even includes, in the chapter on the eventuality of violence, details about the various firearms available "for the defense of Islam.")[48]

An analogous approach was adopted by Sheikh Salah Abu Isma'il, when he appeared in May 1983 in the second trial of the Jihad group. Providing a counter-expertise to that presented by an al-Azhar commission, the Sheikh—who as member of the People's Assembly had been an outspoken critic of Sadat's "religious deviations"—used those deviations in order to refute al-Azhar's arguments about the regime's devotion to Islam. When the Shari'a is in abeyance, he declared, it is the duty of the believers to change the situation "by heart, by word, or by hand."[49]

The crucial point is, consequently, whether the door is left open for recourse to violence in extremis. The conservative (or reformist) wing of the Islamic resurgence is characterized by its refusal to leave it that way. Thus al-Ra'id, an organ of the moderates in the Syrian MB—solemnly opposed "any type of political murder, whether perpetrated by open or secret movements or on behalf of the state." The blame for the rise of the terrorist wing is laid at the door of the "confessional regime, which drives people to violence by its repressive policies." But terrorism is by no means condoned. "One should fight the dictatorship by all legal means . . . in order to establish Islam as a way of life and mode of government with the free consent of the people."[50]

The radical wing justifies violence in terms of their contractual theory of governance. A booklet of the Muslim Students' Association in the University of Cairo argues that already Caliph 'Umar I has laid down that "government forfeits its legitimacy when the ruler usurps even half a meter of cloth. Nobody owes him obedience, be it in jihad against non-Muslims, if he violates the rights of the people or robs the public purse." In underground publications, such as al-Nadhir of the Syrian MB, the Caliphate book of Shukri Mustafa, and the Absent Precept of 'Abd al-Salam Faraj, the call for violence is explicit but still grounded entirely in the same set of arguments.

The code words in both types of radical publication are the same, bearing witness to their underlying unity of vision (not only *jahiliyya* and *ridda*, but also *hakimiyya*, *jihad*, and *tali'a*). Common to both are also the same central texts, in particular Koran, V, 44–48, and the hadith (referred to by Salah Abu Isma'il) which subsumes their revolution theory: "Whoever amongst you who sees something reprehensible should set it aright with his hand; if he cannot do that, let him do it with his tongue; if that is impossible, let him do it with his heart."[51]

As Sayyid Qutb has found out for himself by operating along the same gamut in reverse order, change by peaceful means had become well nigh impossible, given the panoply of coercive and persuasive means at the disposal of the regime in place. The Vanguard, that Republic of the Virtuous Muslims—which had already arrogated to itself the right to interpret the heritage—could no more rely on counter-persuasion. It would have to resort to violent action.

Continuity and Change   In this chapter, as in the preceding two, emphasis was put on the ideological evolution of radicalism in the 1960s, viewed as the turning point; the 1970s and early 1980s figured mostly as prolongation (and, of course, also for the spreading of the gospel to broader strata). This is justified, by our lights, whereas the "generation of the sixties" of the Arab-Muslim resurgence reads like a textbook case illustrating Karl Mannheim and Norman Ryder's theories on the formation of "generational-units" (or "cohorts"), that is, aggregates of individuals who experienced the same event(s) within the same time interval. One witnesses there how the acceleration of social change forces many individuals of roughly the same age-group to reorient their lives with regard to major historical transformations (Nasserism, military state, secularism, end of colonial rule). The "integrative attitudes" and "formative tendencies" that subsume this reorientation impose binding ties upon the members of these peer groups and are catalyzed by common "traumatic episodes" in the 1960s (persecution, prison), which create an "experiential chasm" between them and others of their own age-group. The nucleus of these ideas was evolved and practiced during the preceding decade by older people who were isolated in their own generation (the brothers Qutb and their Indian teachers).[52] The radicals are people who were old enough to live through this experience and young enough not to be committed to family, profession, or way of life. In Egypt the 1950s were thus the period of the "forerunners," the 1960s that of the formation of the New Radical generation. Whereas the Egyptian forerunners—who would play this role for Syria and Lebanon as well—were born during the first decade of the century, the "sixties generation" was made of a nucleus group whose members were born in the late 1920s and early 1930s (the five ringleaders), while at least 70 percent of the membership were under thirty (born in the late 1930s and early 1940s), whose major political experience as adults was with Nasserism.[53]

This generational group was distinct from that of the old MB both by the fact that it barely participated in the anticolonial struggle and in being almost entirely urban (the MB had a substantial rural presence), with a larger contingent of university students and graduates, representing the accelerated urbanization in Egypt and the expansion of secondary and higher education.

Of the principal group of Sayyid Qutb's organization, two-thirds had university education (mostly in the sciences and engineering). In the core groups of Islamic Liberation Party (1974) and of the Takfir (1977) their share was even higher (85 percent). In each of these three cases we have full data for only a core group of several dozens. The Jihad Organization (1981), where we have ample information on 326 members brought to trial, exhibits similar patterns. At least half of the members were university-educated (123 students, 37 in liberal professions). All in all, at least 62 percent had modern education (the latter plus 42 high school students). Of the university students, 68 (55 percent) were in the more modern disciplines—science, engineering, and medicine, where admissions criteria are also the toughest.[54]

In Syria, where the same evolution took place about a decade later—as a reaction to the (post-1963) Ba'th regime—but at a much quicker pace, the same age and professional traits can be discerned. Here again the major catalyst was the prison experience of those (like Marwan Hadid) arrested during the demonstrations of 1964/65, 1967, or 1973. Information gleaned on 296 members arrested or killed during 1979–81, provides us with a virtually identical portrait: almost exclusively urban (barely four fellahin), of whom half were university-educated: 80 students, mostly in engineering, sciences and medicine; 63 in the liberal professions (among whom 26 were engineers and 17 were doctors). Those exposed to modern education (the latter plus 31 high school students and 13 elementary school-teachers) represent at least 63 percent.[55]

The 1960s experience remained the crucially formative moment in the consciousness of those who joined the movement during the next decade, most of whom were born in the 1950s. The 1967 and 1973 wars had much to do with their awakening to the dismal state of Islam; yet the prison experience—that crystallization of the group's unity of thought and action—passed into collective memory through persistent retelling during the indoctrination of new members and became a part of their new identity. The prominent and older militants (Salah Siriya and Shukri Mustafa in Egypt, Marwan Hadid and 'Adnan Sa'd al-Din in Syria) were members of the "sixties generation," as were quite a number of medium-level activists and those of the seminal thinkers who were still active: Hawwa, Dannawi, Yakan, al-Samman.

All this was making for a continuity between the two subcohorts within one and the same generation. Social origin was likewise identical: urban, with a large contingent of peasants who recently moved to town, or of small-townsmen who moved to a metropolis, undergoing the expected dislocation of reference groups that tends to facilitate radicalization; highly educated with a majority in the scientific disciplines, which may explain their attraction to the "reactionary modernism" espoused by the "forerunners." Modernity is thus accepted as an instrument; it is a reality that one can hardly avoid and should rather use (in weaponry, communications). It is mostly among those who withdraw from society (like the Farama-wiya) that science and technology are rejected. Only a single activist group, the Takfir wa-Hijra (which is unique on other accounts as well, such as on ijtihad), exhibits an analogous approach and goes so far as to doubt the value of literacy altogether.[56] But, as argued above, if the majority of the radicals accept modernity's practical contributions, they refuse its values; how to replace them by authentically Islamic ones is their major preoccupation.

While the challenge of the new Arab nation-state, to which they reacted, did remain essentially the same, it was, however, to borrow Raymond Aron's turn of phrase, steadfast and changing. As the 1970s began, there were high hopes in some radical circles. The Egyptian regime, badly bruised by the 1967 debacle, now lost its head. When the news of his death came to the prisons, one political inmate noted in his diary: "I prostrated before Allah and thanked Him."[57] Sadat looked quite promising. "The ruler today begins [all speeches] with a *bismilla* ["In the name of God, the Merciful, the Compassionate"]," writes another prisoner in a letter dated December 1970, "he concludes them with Koranic verses. Our present ruler launches a slogan [the "Institutions' State"] which, if applied, would rectify many a tragedy, and eschew past sins."[58] There certainly was a greater respect for legality in Sadat's Egypt. MB detainees were to be released between 1971 and 1974; two of their monthlies resumed publication; Muslim associations would flourish in the universities (until 1981) with the benediction of the regime, which saw them as battering ram against Marxist influence there. The Shari'a was made (article 2 of the 1971 Constitution) into the "principal source of all legislation" and its gradual application was promised. In some circles the 1973 War made a deep impression, among other reasons because of the distinct religious coloring given to it.[59] In Syria the Assad regime (which replaced Jedid in 1969) also could boast of its 1973 contribution to jihad. Furthermore, a relaxation of the economic etatism and a milder approach to Islam (as evidenced in the 1971 and 1973 amendments to the Constitution: Islamic oath to be taken by the president; only Muslims to be elected to this post; attempts to bring the Alawites into the fold of Sunnism—all combined to endow Assad with a more appealing image.

Inherent doubts and free-floating hostility persisted nevertheless. Not only was the 1973 War challenged by many radicals as giving priority to the wrong combat, but state control was as powerful as ever, though less indiscriminate in coercion. In Syria, Assad's Defense Squadrons were soon to surpass in ruthlessness the rulers of the 1960s, and the alliance with the Soviets was tightened.[60] The regime's monopoly in the media became ever more preoccupying for the fundamentalists of all hues because of the efficacy of television (now in color) which made popular culture and leisure into the most important arena in the fight for the hearts and minds of Muslims. The fare purveyed by the media—hedonism, permissiveness, conspicuous consumption, and greed—was flooding the very citadel of the Islamic social structure, the home. Helping the electronic media to sell the same values was advertising. "Have our streets and squares become the property of advertising agencies?" decries one radical, "Is there no law to defend women's honor and plain good taste against them? . . . Why should public places in all major cities be filled up with immoral advertising that nips children's innocence in the bud. . . . The Satan of Publicity woos our youth, especially girls, with its attractive and colorful pictures."[61] What made publicity particularly powerful was the fact that it was part and parcel of the new Open Door Policy which was seen as geared up to replace the hakimiyya of Allah by a new idol: economic growth at any cost. A "growth economy" entails a large foreign presence (tourists, experts), which contaminates by the example of its way of life. It introduces family planning and it develops a usurious financial system.[62]

Much as in the 1960s, the dangers the radicals pinpointed were not imaginary. And more than ever they were troublesome, because for the most part they were indirect, and hence insidious. There soon emerged, it is true, a number of apples of discord with the regimes-in-place (procrastination in applying the Shari'a, corruption and flagrant neglect of traditional mores among the elites), but it is the indirect dangers that loomed large. Inadvertent, creeping secularization came to be perceived as the predominant danger. The Egyptian and Syrian regimes combated Marxism and shunned Arab Socialism, but the disruptive effects of the New Left continued to be felt among the intelligentsia, its action being rendered particularly vexing with the rise of an Islamic Left, which interpreted this revisionist message in terms hallowed by the Sunni consensus. Moreover, the very insistence of the regimes on economic development in order to be integrated in the world market and profit from the oil-price bonanza, had alarming sociocultural underpinnings. So alarming, in fact, that even conservative fundamentalists who were certainly in the good graces of the regime, grew panicky (see chapter 5). The Syrian and Egyptian nouveaux riches as role models for the young were as preoccupying as the direct atheistic attacks of the 1960s. If Pan-Arabism was dead, the reemergence of Egyptianism with its distinct echoes of the "Mediterranean" or "Pharaonic" mystique of the interwar years brought to the fore yet another secularist Trojan Horse.[63]

Assad's record, especially following the savage repression conducted from 1976 on, became markedly bleak. "The constitution is a sham, referenda a farce and popular organizations a fake," railed the radicals.[64] This accounts for the broadening union between Syrian radicals and conservatives (including many ulama, and not only from lower ranks) against the regime. Sadat's record was mixed. The Azharite establishment could thus argue: "Can one declare a society to be infidel when it can pride itself on having a Muslim metropolis (Cairo), nicknamed the City of a Thousand Minarets? A city in which the voice of a thousand *muezzins* is heard five times a day, glorifying Allah and reciting the credo? Can one declare apostate tens of millions of believers flocking to the mosques? Is it apostate, that society which believes in Allah, in His Holy Book, His angels, His Prophets, and in the Last Judgment; a society that wages the jihad and a regime based upon the Shari'a, as principal source of all legislation, a regime installing shura and equality as enjoined by Islam?"

The set answer to such an argument was given a decade earlier by Hawwa: "Building a mosque in a place where you already have fifty mosques is a work of supererogation. Application of God's law in the whole country is a binding precept. It is such precepts that have been neglected."[65]

The flavor of the ensuing debate in the radicals' ranks about Sadat can be gathered from Abu-l-Khayr's memoir about the Takfir group. "No doubt," it was said in a discussion held in 1976, "that Sadat's regime is a thousand times better for us than Nasser's. Under Nasser we were unable to proclaim openly our views vis-à-vis the jahili society." To which another radical retorted: "There is no real difference between these regimes with regard to goals. The only difference is in the modus operandi. Nasser struck with a heavy hammer in order to forge the social transformation desired by the 1952 Revolution; Sadat represents the stage of consolidation of this endeavor, which was to be covered with a civilian varnish. Nasser's tactics were implacable, destined to stifle the Islamic movement and annihilate it physically. Sadat is stocking-footed and removes obstacles with velvet gloves. Does it matter whether you are hanged with a rough cord or with a silken one? True, Nasser's era was that of revolutionary terror, whereas Sadat's relies upon sovereignty of the law. Yet in both cases the Islamic community is menaced with extinction. This is what counts."[66]

A year after this exchange had taken place, the scales in the

Takfir debate weighed down in favor of the harsher judgment on the regime, leading to the kidnapping of Sheikh al-Dhahabi (July 1977). The Peace Initiative, and the growing persecution of the radicals, accelerated the alienation from the powers-that-be.

Not only Shukri Mustafa, on trial for his life, would declare society to be plagued by jahili vices, but Muslim students' associations would repeat that argument: "Egyptians . . . are not Muslims any more but assimilated and Europeanized." Hence: "Muslim society should be liberated from the jahiliyya." The state is infidel—not unlike the Mongols of yore—as are its national flag (which one should not salute) and its army. The ulama are no better, subservient as they are to their employer, the state, and to majority Sunni traditions.[67] Not without reason, then, would the authorities consider the associations to be the breeding ground of terrorism. In line with the particular preoccupations of the 1970s, stress will be laid on hostility to foreign temporary residents and visitors (be they rich Arabs, or Westerners; or, in the case of Syria, Soviet technicians). The January 1977 Bread Riots in Cairo enunciated this streak with the sacking of the Pyramids' Street night clubs frequented by tourists. More vehement still was the obsession with the media. Refraining from watching television and listening to the radio thus became a norm of the new zealots (including the conspirators of October 6, 1981), often imposed by force on neighbors and fellow students. Films, the press, advertising, and books come in for their share of vituperation.

All through the 1970s, the terrorist groups, as well as the student associations, fought against some of the same medieval "idols" as Ibn Taymiyya: for example, the cult of tombs of holy men, the "arrogance" and undeserved position of the Copts. They would usually do so through sermons, leaflets, and wall newspapers; at times they had recourse to arson and pogroms as well.[68] Yet the main thrust was directed against modern "idols," which replaced those of the ancient jahiliyya, creating a new brand of polytheism. The Ibn Taymiyya message, as reinterpreted by Qutb, thus continued to transmit in cultural code the frustrations and animosities vis-à-vis modernity, and to legitimize in Sunni terms the deeply felt protest against the regime, which upholds its values (through the Open Door Policy, primacy of economic development over war, alliances with the West). Indeed, the reason urban youth flock to the movement lies not only in the idealism and activism of people aged fifteen to thirty, but mainly in the fact that these youths (especially the more educated segments thereof) are the ultimate victims of Egypt's, and Syria's, socioeconomic ills. Feelings of relative deprivation become particularly widespread among the youth of the 1970s, not because of any objective deterioration (on the contrary, the economic situation became slightly better), but because the October war and the Open Door Policy brought about a revolution of rising expectations. The expectations of educated youth, who assumed they had acquired—through education—the keys to modern affluence, grew at an even more rapid pace than in other parts of the urban population. The greater the expectations, the deeper the fall to the abyss of despair when the hopes failed to materialize. Employment perspectives for university graduates are still not bright (except for low-paying jobs in public administration). Housing problems get worse and raise the age of marriage and the percentage of bachelors. Heavily packed public transportation and public housing developments, dirty streets, and the breakdown of the infrastructure deal daily blows to the quality of life. As the bitterness of youth is that of relative deprivation, it is bred not only of the expectations of "people who studied and should enjoy greater social mobility"; it is also the product of comparison with the good life in the West as shown on TV, in movies, and in ads (such as Coca-Cola's dashing "young affluent Americans"—cult figures among Egyptian and Syrian youth). Worse still is the comparison with the privileged segments of Egyptian society (that part of the private sector which works with foreigners, directors of government-owned companies, sundry other "five percenters," so dubbed after their foreign commissions). Not that such a sector did not exist under Nasser, but its size was much smaller and the privileged were not supposed to flaunt their riches; conspicuous consumption and consorting with foreigners in public were banned. Under Sadat's *enrichissez-vous* regime such interdictions were lifted as necessary incentives for economic development. The same holds true—though in a less sharp manner—of the difference between Salah Jedid's economic policy in Syria in the late 1960s and the one followed by his successor Assad during the 1970s. The rise of the New Class of entrepreneurs was particularly resented in the economically and culturally traditionalist towns of central and northern Syria, which indeed became the hotbed of religious extremism.

Radical Islam offers urban youth—its social mobility blocked, its expectations frustrated—a seemingly cogent panacea: a comeback to a puritanical and egalitarian way of life, reducing the social gap by taking from the rich and giving to the poor, lowering the overall level of expectations, and thus limiting tensions and bitterness. Its social criticism is closely interlaced with its moral diatribes. Public transportation is not only slow and tiring but also breeds promiscuity and friction. Housing problems impair the family cell (too tiny apartments, deferring or avoiding marriage) and spread "prostitution and onanism—the twin major ills of our youth." In Syria sociologists spoke in effect of a "real crisis of the institution of marriage," a finding on the whole applicable to Egypt as well, while in Lebanon noneconomic forces—especially the ever-lengthening civil war, operated in the same direction. (It is typical that the response of the Syrian radicals was a call for legislation lowering the age of marriage with state-financed incentives going in tandem.)[69]

No wonder that natives of provincial towns, usually the first in their families to have access to higher education, are so numerous in the movement. These provincials usually moved to a "modern Babylon" like Cairo and Alexandria and suffered a cultural shock. That shock is aggravated by the notion slowly dawning on them that the employment horizon is bleak and bitterness with regard to the Open Door Policy, which "benefits only five percenters and fat

cats," is growing. The resultant spiritual crisis brought such youth
to religion, as sole refuge and solace, and later to religious activism.

It was only befitting that the particular contribution of the "sub-
cohort of the seventies" to the overriding ideology of Sayyid Qutb
is the stress on the "idols" of media and economics: the media create
the dreams, the economic realities crush them.

The most articulate spokesman of this gospel for the youth of
the 1980s was 'Abd al-Salam Faraj. In *The Absent Precept* (1981)
he devoted much space to proving that the Sadat regime was indeed
analogous to the Mongols. Thus a holy war had to be waged against
it without mercy.

> Despite its crucial importance for the future of our Faith, the
> jihad has been neglected, maybe even ignored, by men of re-
> ligion of our age. They know, however, that jihad is the only
> way to reestablish and reenhance the power and the glory of
> Islam, which every true believer desires wholeheartedly. There
> is no doubt the idols upon earth will not be destroyed but by
> the sword—and thus establish the Islamic state and restore the
> caliphate. This is the command of God and each and every
> Muslim should, hence, do his utmost to accomplish this pre-
> cept, having recourse to force if necessary.

The conclusions were drawn in a later chapter:

> There are some who say that the way to follow in order to
> restore the Muslim state is by propaganda, thus creating a basis
> for partisans. Yet this path, for the sake of which some wanted
> to forsake the jihad, cannot lead to the desired goal. An Islamic
> state cannot be reestablished without the struggle of a believing
> minority. . . . And how can one envision propaganda having
> a large success when all means of communication are now in
> the hands of infidels, of the morally depraved, and of the en-
> emies of the Faith? The only viable solution is to work to
> liberate the media from the stranglehold of these so-called Mus-
> lims. Moreover, only victory and the acquisition of power will
> gain us the adherence of the masses. Didn't God say in his

Book (CX, 1–2): "When Allah's succor and triumph cometh thou shalt see mankind entering the religion of Allah by droves"?

There was, of course, a unity of theology and politics or, if you will, theory and practice:

> The question on the agenda today is the following: Do we live in an Islamic state? One of the necessary conditions to make a state Muslim is that it be governed by the laws of Islam. Yet the laws regulating the life of the Muslims are infidel laws—laws conceived by infidels and imposed by them upon Muslims such as Allah said (Koran, V, 44): "*Whoso judgeth not according to what God hath revealed, they are the transgressors.*" Indeed, ever since the abolition of the caliphate in 1924 and the rooting out of Islamic laws and their replacement by laws made by infidels, the situation of Muslims resembles that of the believers under the yoke of the Mongols.
>
> Governments in the Islamic world today are in a state of apostacy. They have nourished at the table of colonialism, be it Crusader, Communist, or Zionist. Of Islam they preserve nothing but its sheer name, although they pray, fast, and pretend to be Muslims. Our Sunna has determined that the apostate be punished more severely than he who had always been an infidel. The apostate must be killed even if he is in no position to fight, while an infidel does not merit death in such a case.

That apostacy—abandoning Islam—is a worse crime than infidelity one may learn from the fatwa of Ibn Taymiyya [on the Mongols]: "Every group of Muslims that transgresses Islamic law . . . must be combated, even when they continue to profess the credo."

There is no point, then, in reformism. Though Faraj (unlike Shukri Mustafa) does not consider the entire society to be already apostate, control by the new and omnipotent state means that the society is in the process of becoming so, and that with the demise of civil society any action from within the system is well nigh impossible.

> There are those who say one must establish an Islamic party modeled on the present political parties. Yet rather than destroying the godless state, such a party would bolster it further and enhance legitimacy through participation in its political life and sitting in parliaments that legislate without reference to Allah. Others still allege that Muslim [activists] should endeavor to occupy decision-making positions . . . so that by dint of having "Islamic engineers," "Islamic doctors," and the like in the upper echelons of government the regime will be transformed into an Islamic one. . . . This is sheer fantasy.[70]

Furthermore, the ubiquitous modern challenge—especially the global village of the media and the pervasive state control—made the withdrawal response less and less tenable, at least for all but tiny groups. Long-term educational efforts, designed to convert society segment by segment to "true Islam," has today even less prospect of success than when Sayyid Qutb began to doubt its efficacy as sole means thirty years ago, before the age of transistor radios, television, and the gigantic growth of the higher educational system. Seizure of power from the hands of "Mongol rulers" like Anwar Sadat and Hafez Assad thus came to be perceived as the only answer to the threat.

CHAPTER FIVE

The Conservative Periphery

By its very nature a counter-society requires a certain periphery, a sort of indeterminate area around it, which enables it to maintain ties with society as a whole and serves as a channel for recruiting sympathizers, and ultimately adherents, with varying degrees of commitment. Students of Communist parties, the quintessential counter-societies, thus endeavored to delineate the "outer circles" made of the readers of the Communist party press, trade-union members, Communist party voters. Unlike the cadres and party members of the "inner circles"—they too with varying degrees of commitment—the periphery inhabitants do not let the Faith (in that case, communism) govern all (or just many) aspects of their life, nor does it have a strong hold over their time. Yet the periphery shares basic beliefs with the hardcore and collaborates with it in various realms of life. It represents the proverbial water where the militant fish can swim.

The importance of the periphery for radical Islam is evident if only because it is part and parcel of a major cultural phenomenon— the massive return to Islam among Arabs, especially town-dwellers, during the last two decades. The roots of this return to Islam (and to religion in general) lie in the crisis of the major ideologies prevailing in the Arab world until the 1960s. Liberalism went bankrupt because of its cynical manipulation by the old parties. Nasserism did not realize the messianic hopes it gave birth to, namely, the unification of the Arab world, and the Syrian-Egyptian union split into its original components in 1961; as for Nasser's accelerated industrialization, predicated on Soviet-style planning and massive nationalizations, it brought only limited growth of gross national product and ended (by 1965–66) in stagnation.

The 1967 War dealt a terrible blow to the reconstructed army, pride and mainstay of the regimes, and upon Arab national honor and self-image. Once again, the Arabs discovered they had not found the panacea for integration in the modern world. A few of the intelligentsia saw Marxism for a while as an answer to the crisis. However, much wider segments of the educated public, of the middle class and, in greater measure, of the lower-middle class and the proletariat, found refuge in Islam. The fellahin have not been mentioned because their Islamic worldview had remained quite traditional. But Arab towns witnessed in the first two-thirds of this century a rapid process of secularization in education, literature, mass media, law, and so forth. This process had certainly encountered many an obstacle, especially at the level of the extended family; it had, no doubt, to fight mass movements, like the MB, which formed in order to block modernization and the "poison of imported ideas." Yet until 1967 the overall development was clearly unidirectional, toward growing secularization. The June war stopped the process and changed its course, bringing in its wake a massive return to Islam, as a faith and as a way of life, a solid ground in a world shaken to its very foundations.

Some interesting quantitative indicators for the return to religion are Egyptian book production and journalism. While under both the monarchy and Nasser the share of religious books was steady, between 8 and 9 percent, it grew incessantly during the 1970s arriving at 19 percent by the end of the decade (by comparison, merely 2 percent of books published in France fall in this category). Arguably the most remarkable success story of Arab journalism in recent years is *al-Liwa' al-Islami*. Launched in July 1981 as a religious supplement to the ruling party's organ *Mayo*, it was transformed in January 1982 into an independent weekly (though put forward by the same party publishing house). Evidently responding to an authentic public need in the period of soul-searching that followed the Sadat assassination, its first independent issue was snatched off the newsstands and continued to be sold out in the coming weeks despite expanding printing. Circulation soon outstripped that of its mother publication *Mayo* and is thought to have reached the 700,000 benchmark. Even if this figure is somewhat "padded," most observers agree that it provides an order of magnitude and also indicates the size of that sector of opinion greatly interested in things religious. In comparison, *al-Da'wa* magazine (banned in September 1981), which appealed to former MB members and their young fundamentalist sympathizers, particularly among the Muslim student associations, had a circulation of about 80,000.[1]

The most popular Egyptian writer in the last thirteen years is Dr. Mustafa Mahmud, a physician who had formerly been a staunch believer in scientific positivism, human engineering, and materialism before converting to religiosity in the late 1960s. His autobiography, *My Itinerary from Doubt to Belief*, is a best-seller of the 1970s, closely followed by a spate of other books (novels, plays, science-fiction, philosophy), all of them singing praises of Islam. Another prophet of the post-1967 generation is Anis Mansur (also known as the editor in chief of the weekly *October* and as former confidant and mouthpiece of Sadat), whose many novels hammer at one major point: the presence of transcendental forces in all facets of human life. The best-seller of 1981 was *The State in Islam* by Khalid Muhammad Khalid, a former secularist famous for his 1950 book *From Here We Begin*, which called for separation of state and religion, and now fully repentant, reneging upon those views and demanding that the state impose Islam as a single code of public behavior.

The reading material of the post-1967 generation in the Middle

East is not the only measure of the cultural phenomenon we are speaking about. No less significant are the crowds of mostly young people, filling the mosques on Fridays and during Ramadan; the proliferation of new mosques upon the urban landscape; tape-cassette recordings of popular preachers like Sheikh Kishk as "hot" items on the market; the return of the veil (for married women); "Islamic dress" (white hood) for an unmarried woman; and the popularity of beards among young males.

While this cultural phenomenon is widespread in all social strata and age-groups, it is particularly prominent among young people of middle-class and lower-middle-class origin, above all among students. The central role played here by the 1967 crisis has been brought forward by a number of field surveys. In one of them, carried out among Muslim terrorists jailed between 1974 and 1977, the interviewers discovered typical stories like that of a twenty-five-year-old who was a secularized high school student during the June war. The defeat put him in a state of shock, not knowing "whither I am heading, whither does Egypt go." He locked himself in his room, crying and wailing for hours. It was only with great pain that his mother persuaded him to return to prayers he had learned as a child, which indeed brought him some peace of mind, as a sort of magic incantation. A friend who came to visit suggested that he come to hear a young and charismatic preacher, speaking the modern idiom. The boy became attracted to that preacher, who opened up to him the treasures of Muslim theology and mysticism. Soon enough he returned to the Faith and began to grow a beard.[2]

The depth of the return to religion is attested by the fact that it engulfed members of the Coptic Church as well, especially from the lower classes, where many who were secularized reverted to the old religion. Ten months after the war a collective mystical experience took place in their midst when the Virgin Mary "made her appearance" in al-Zaytun Church in Cairo. The huge crowds flocking to the Church during her nocturnal apparition comprised not merely Copts but also Muslims. Such mixed crowds continued to

swarm to behold the "photography" of the Virgin "caught" by a
diligent photographer presented to the public by Bishop Samuel.
The Virgin appeared, so it was alleged, "in order to strengthen the
spirit of the Egyptian people, a sign from God that He does not
forsake His people."[3]

This evolution of popular mentalities was accelerated by the
October war—a sure sign that he who returns to religion is granted
victory by Allah. It is not fortuitous that the canal-crossing operation
was code-named *Badr* (after the Prophet Muhammad's first victo-
rious battle over the Infidels of Arabia). The army propaganda ma-
chinery deliberately spread the story that the Prophet in person,
flanked by angels, had crossed the canal with the Egyptian soldiers.
The wide public echo that such symbols and legends enjoyed came
as an unpleasant surprise to secularist circles among the educated
class. As one of them, philosopher Fu'ad Zakariya, remarked ruefully, "fighting Islam is a no-win game. It flourishes after debacles
as well as in the wake of victory."[4]

The existence of the periphery is evident, though it is clear that
it is more amorphous than in Communist parties. How can one go
about sounding its depths, be it for Egypt only? The circles represented by *al-Da'wa* readers (and those of its sister monthlies *al-
I'tisam* and *al-Mukhtar al-Islami*) may stand for an "immediate (or
fundamentalist) periphery," a large part of which actually overlaps
the "counter-society," sharing the jahiliyya diagnosis, strongly ambivalent as regards working within the system, though, as we have
seen, still refusing the recourse to violence. Its members—number-
ing in the tens of thousands as compared to the several thousands
of the hard core—move to and fro between the two spheres. This
"immediate periphery'" had thus already been analyzed to a large
extent in previous chapters (relying in particular on books published
by its publishing houses: *Dar al-Ansar, Dal al-I'tisam*). To stretch
the analogy a bit, it may be likened to Communist party membership—the hardcore being the apparatus—though it is much less
structured and regimented than its Communist "counterpart" (with

the exception perhaps of the Italian Communist party where the line between membership and sympathizers is blurred).

The real periphery—roughly analogous to trade union and front organization members and Communist party voters—should thus be looked for elsewhere. Having an audience in the hundreds of thousands who share its intense interest in things Islamic, *al-Liwa' al-Islami* (henceforward *al-Liwa'*) may perhaps be a good source to scrutinize. It is, needless to say, a semiofficial organ, yet, owing its success to enthusiastic public response, it enjoys a substantial freedom for a journal of that type. It can thus reveal a few things about the preoccupations, mood, and currents among its mass readership. This is particularly true of the reader-letters section and of the one dealing with fatawa (responsa written by a dozen religious experts to readers' queries). A prior selection of letters and queries no doubt takes place, but nevertheless the picture that emerges from whatever is published in these sections is quite enlightening—all the more so when compared with analogous sections in *al-Nur*, the religious weekly of the Liberals, a moderate opposition party, which enjoys some greater leeway; and compared with sermons and fatawa of Sheikh Sha'rawi, a TV "personality" and the most popular preacher in Egypt today, as well as those of another popular preacher, the blind Sheikh Kishk.

Radicals and Conservatives   As one pores over the two conservative weeklies and the writings of the two sheikhs one is bound to be struck by the similarity of their attitudes with those of the radicals on many pivotal issues. This holds, to begin with, for their literalist perception of matters divine. The world inhabited by *al-Liwa'*, *al-Nur*, and their readers is one where the natural and supernatural are inextricably interlaced. A world populated by ghosts, the spirits of the dead, *jinn* (invisible beings) of the harmful and of the helpful varieties; a world haunted by the specter of the Tempting Satan and his demons, where the believer may be succored by holy men and angels and, if need be,

by miracles; a world where communication with the dead (especially
one's relatives) is an everyday occurrence, and where the presence
of the supernatural is deemed quite real, almost palpable.

The Hereafter is so real for *al-Liwa'* and *al-Nur* readers that
one of them even inquires about the fine distinctions between
earthly wine and the wine served to the Just in Paradise. Other
readers ask whether they will be able to recognize their dead parents
when they are resuscitated in the Last Judgment and whether it will
be possible to converse with them (the answer of the ulama is positive, permeated with the same literalist vein). What exactly happens
to the dead from the moment they enter the grave until the Resurrection is the subject of many questions to which the ulama respond in great detail. The procedures and the nature of the Divine
Judgment are queried ("Will cheating on exams be taken into consideration?" asks a student, while others want to know what happens
if good deeds balance out the evil ones).[5]

Given this overriding preoccupation with the afterlife, no wonder the dead are perceived as a real presence exercising a palpable
hold on the living. Frequent visitations to family tombs, vows to the
dead, charity in their name, respect of vows made to the dying, and
other Egyptian folk customs are encouraged. Their underlying rationale is espoused explicitly; "the spirits of the dead feel what happens outside the grave and know when we visit them," writes one
mufti, and yet another discusses the question of how the dead feel
the passage of time.[6]

No less real and influential for the Egyptian believer and his
instructors—especially for Sheikh Sha'rawi—are the jinn of all
kinds. In the current Islamic revival, belief in jinn has even become
fashionable in leftist circles (perhaps for opportunistic reasons), and
their weekly, *Ruz al-Yusuf*, went so far as to publish a story about
a man who married a female jinn. Sometime beforehand such a
marriage had been recognized by a judge in order to decide a certain
legal case. The jinn—especially of the evil variety—preoccupy *al-*

Liwa' readers: What are these invisible beings made of? Can they procreate? (answer: yes); How do evil jinn tempt humans?[7]

This type of realistic religiosity—*realistic* in the medieval sense of the term (the opposite being *nominalistic*)—is the mirror image of that preached by the Islamic modernists, who had endeavored for decades to sublimate and demystify the transcendental presence, for example, by furnishing a psychological explanation for the jinn and for Satan (as incarnation of man's evil urges), endowing miracles with symbolic significance and combating the cult of the dead so typical of popular Islam. Indeed writers and readers in both weeklies reject such rationalist interpretations as *bid'a* ("innovation"), one of the gravest sins. Much like the radicals, these conservatives argue that "the transcendental is not subject to the scrutiny of reason"; it is a "poisonous idea" to probe Paradise, Hell, jinn, damnation, God's attributes and powers, and so forth, with the tools of reason— like historical criticism—as all too many Islamic modernists tried to do.[8] While this is not yet an affirmation of the type of Tertullian's *credo quia absurdum,* it is no doubt nearer to it than to the attempts made already by a few medieval Muslim thinkers and some others in the present century to make religion compatible with reason. One is back in the classical position of the tenth-century theologian al-Ash'ari: what we know about the divine and the supernatural we know *bila kayfa* ("without enquiring how").

Fundamentalism—in the sense of a world view harking back to essential verities of the Faith—thus seems not to be restricted to radical militants alone: it permeates conservative circles as well. If this thesis, which we shall try to test also in fields other than theology, is correct, then it would follow that the pool of potential recruits to radicalism is far broader than that of the "immediate periphery" (Muslim student associations and MB veterans).

The Villain of the Piece In effect, it is not only a literalist, "realistic" religiosity and a rejection of Islamic modernism that make up the shared fundamentalism of the radicals and the conservatives. They are above all united by an intense hatred of the "evil of evils," modernity. Modernity is inherently alien to Islam, consisting as it does of "imported ideas," peddled by Arab secularists, Islamic reformists, and other apostates. *Afkar mustawrada* ("imported ideas") is the ultimate term of opprobrium, an oft-repeated code word, in the jargon of fundamentalists of all hues. Top places on the list of imported ideas are reserved for revolutionary theories of modern science which challenge the premises of traditional religion. Science, argue the fundamentalists, cannot shape human beliefs and values, though it can serve man by coming up with useful inventions. Values relate to the metaphysical world, which science cannot fathom. "Islam and Koran are to science like the brakes to the motor in a car. Science can move humanity but only Islam can give it direction." Thus geology can help us discover minerals but cannot tell us the age of the universe. Darwinism is even more vehemently rejected. Responding to a query by a high school student, an *al-Liwa'* writer says: Man is not descended from the monkey, for, as the Koran has it, we are the descendants of Adam, who was created of clay, "and verily Allah's word for it is more truthful."

Materialism, especially of the Marxist brand, is likewise rejected by all fundamentalists. Worse still, in their eyes, is the impact of materialism on popular culture: conspicuous consumption and the cult of economic growth, hedonism and permissiveness. That this cluster of values occupies most of the place accorded in *al-Liwa'* to modernity and its discontents is only natural. A mass-circulation paper is attentive above all to popular behavior and beliefs. The major conduit of materialistic values to the popular psyche, namely, the mass media, come up for most of the blame. The special importance attached to broadcasting can be gauged from the fact that page two of *al-Liwa'* (page one is the cover) is devoted to TV and radio, which are also the topic of numerous articles and readers' letters elsewhere in the journal. The overall tone is of sharp disapproval. The accusations leveled against TV and radio are the ones that MB organs (*al-Da'wa* and *al-I'tisam*) used to rehash in 1976–81 and that student extremists used to proclaim in their leaflets and in their trials. The danger of TV is thus vividly etched in certain letters to the *al-Liwa'* editor:

> Corrupt TV programs and serials have a deleterious impact upon the mores of children, youth and women; . . . TV lays waste the minds of the young, fostering deviance and criminality and undermining their attachment to religion; . . . it would have been easy for TV to disseminate positive values, but it is still easier for it to propagate destructive ideas. . . . True, there are a few good religious TV programs. Yet what is the use of having sermons broadcast after films full of sex and violence. . . . TV penetrates into the very home of each and every Muslim, transmitting to his children the thought of Satan.[9]

Here is the rub: the pervasiveness of the medium. It reaches even women bound to their homes, and its audio-visual language speaks not only to children but also, as the *al-Liwa'* TV critic ruefully notes, to the 54.2 percent of the adult population that is illiterate.[10]

Catalyzed by the shock that Sadat's assassination produced in the political elite, these criticisms of the fundamentalist press, which enjoyed the blessing of the Islamic establishment, did bear some fruit. *Dallas* and *Loveboat* TV serials—the epitomes of hedonism, permissiveness, and materialism—were finally taken off the air. This was also the fate of their locally produced equivalent, belly-dancing shows. On the whole, censorship under Mubarak operated more harshly in matters pertaining to morals: in a TV documentary about Picasso, certain parts of a nude portrait were covered with a black band; films containing scenes on prostitution were prohibited (even when the film in question was evidently not a "blue" one); video and tape cassettes were subject to close scrutiny (which reached, however, only a part of the "pirate" production). Still the conservatives are discontented: *Dallas*'s J.R. remains a popular cult figure;

the ravages of Arab-language soap operas and tearjerker films, with
their insistence on unrequited love, are considered particularly troublesome. And new menaces cloud the horizon. Thus a reader's letter
to *al-Nur* from a provincial town complains (in late 1983) of a newly
arrived popular fad: youth spend night and day in coffee-shops,
watching video-films (many of which are "pirate" films privately
reproduced and of dubious morality besides). The fact that individuals own about half a million video recorders augurs ill for the
future: the new electronic device, which largely escapes censorship,
is liable to move from "video clubs" to the very homes of the believers, thus propounding the effects of TV.[11]

What should be done about TV? Here radicals and conservatives differ (with most of the MB to be counted, on this issue as well
as on many others, among the conservatives). The radicals see TV
as an "invention of the Devil" arguing with 'Abd al-Salam Faraj,
the ideologist of the Sadat assassins' group, that it cannot be reformed as long as the state controls it. As we have seen, state monopoly of TV and other media, and the wanton destruction of
Muslim religiosity it brings about, served for Faraj as the ultimate
argument for his group's seizure of power. In the meantime, as the
media are in the hands of the authorities, the radicals demand that
their disciples stop listening and watching them and convince others
to join the boycott.

The conservatives, for their part, perceive the media—and by
implication, the state—as capable of reform from within. Participation of a dyed-in-the-wool fundamentalist like Sha'rawi, the master practitioner of the TV talk show, does a lot to further this cause.
It is no surprise that the sheikh himself rejects the view of "those
who forbid TV altogether; TV is licit if one watches it with pure
intentions." The government should be persuaded by protests, articles, sermons, letters, and public-opinion polls to weed out "rotten
programs" and bring in more of the healthier variety during peak
viewing and listening hours.[12] (The same holds true, by the way, of

their demands for strengthening religious instruction in schools, which the radicals had written off completely.) Not all conservatives are that sanguine about the chances of reform. In an *al-Liwa'* round-table discussion, one sheikh related from his personal experience a description of the delay tactics the TV authorities used in order to ward off pressures from religious circles; he refrained, however, from drawing any clear conclusions.[13]

The havoc wreaked in Egyptian souls by TV and radio programs, continues the weekly's litany, is compounded by advertising in these as well as in the other media. They are alleged to encourage crass consumerism, greed, and ostentatious living. Worse still is the advertisers' use of enticing sex symbols. Sex is the major article purveyed by other means of entertainment: dance, theater, movies, cabarets, pulp novels. The fact that entertainers and sportsmen become popular heroes endows "modern idolatry" with flesh-and-blood objects of adulation, a revolting spectacle. Not that the conservatives seek to ban entertainment and sports altogether. Rather, *al-Liwa'* advocates strict use of state censorship and even harsher restrictions on women participating in such activities. As with TV, dissenting voices are sometimes heard, like this reader's letter calling for the boycott of all entertainment, or letters and articles arguing for a ban on performances by females (including vocal music, for, as the ancient Muslim adage has it, "to hear a woman sing is like seeing her naked"). Significantly enough, the dissent expressed comes here from the radical end of the spectrum and not from the modernists of the Muhammad 'Abduh school.[14]

A telling indicator pointing in the same direction is that personalities picked as favorite targets by *al-Liwa'* are all liberal writers (such as Ahmad Baha' al-Din, Hussein Fawzi, Amina al-Sa'id, Yusuf Idris) who call for reducing the role of religion in society and for greater concessions to modernity in order to bring Egypt in tune with the contemporary world, be it in banking, women's work, or legislation. These are the very same concerns that used to preoccupy

al-Da'wa and *al-I'tisam*, as well as the spokesmen of the terrorists;
one of the latter, Shukri Mustafa, devoted almost a whole session
in his trial to a diatribe against some of these "secularist demons."[15]

By and large, the conservatives share the view that Islam in
Egypt has been badly mauled by the forces of modernity, though
they would not concur that total ruin is imminent. While not at
"five minutes to midnight," the situation seems to them and to their
followers bleak enough. A case in point is the type of queries submitted to the muftis: Is it permitted to have dealings with a person
given to blasphemy? What should one do with a son who, though
fasting on Ramadan, does not pray and sometimes drinks alcoholic
beverages? What should a young woman do if her boyfriend is indifferent to religion? What should students (at the American University of Cairo) reply to the vilification of Islam by foreign
classmates? The situation of established religion is a no lesser cause
for complaint: salaries (especially of prayer leaders and preachers)
are low, many mosques are in a dismal state of disrepair, many
communities lack religious functionaries. Higher ulama come in for
their share of criticism: Why do so many of them opt for modern
garb? Why do they sit apart in public ceremonies in major mosques?
This is the tone of most readers' criticism, which *al-Liwa'* journal-
ists, high ulama themselves, fend off as best they can.[16]

The influx of tourists and other foreigners (experts, business-
men) due to the Open Door Policy is yet another cause for alarm,
bringing in its wake the prominence of "immoral dress" in public
places, sale of alcoholic beverages (in hotels and special bars), pornographic postcards, "licentious nightclubs," as well as an inunda-
tion of foreign books, many of them questioning the Faith.

State Reform   If the conservatives are outraged by all these
                    trends, they do not go so far (in their reaction) as
to call for a complete rejection of modernity in Egypt. Nor are they
as eager as the 'Abduh-style reformists to seek out modernity and
bend Islam backward in order to accommodate it. The conservative

is as wary of modernity as the radical, but he is resigned to the need to accept certain elements thereof while surrounding them with as many precautionary bulwarks as possible. At the same time he seeks to eradicate certain modern excesses, trusting here, too, that he will be able to persuade the state to contribute its share in accomplishing this mission. Yet he considers himself as also having a direct role to play: in the mosque, in the school system, in the media (al-Liwa' being a case in point).

In the final analysis, conservative ulama are fully aware (perhaps more so than some of their followers and readers) of the limits of their own power. This is why they pin most of their hopes on state action, as in the two examples cited above: harsher TV censorship, a greater emphasis on religion in the school curriculum. To the extent that import of technology and capital is imperative for the economy, they should be welcome; yet the state should keep them under tight control. Modern banking could be accommodated if the state can find a solution to the legal problem involved, as amended by medieval Muslim jurists and further developed in recent decades, allowing interest on "productive loans."[17]

The linchpin of this reformatory enterprise is the slogan of "application of Muslim law" (tatbiq al-Shari'a), or in its up-to-date, and somewhat pared-down form, "codification of Muslim Law" (taqnin al-Shari'a). Indeed, after a long, drawn-out struggle waged by radicals and conservatives, the Egyptian government, jolted by the Sadat assassination, seemed to relinquish its delay tactics and gave the People's Assembly the green light to work out draft bills incorporating Islamic laws in certain criminal matters (adultery, theft, robbery, wine drinking). The conservatives welcomed these measures with a resounding fanfare, arguing—perhaps in order to allay criticism from radical quarters—that this taqnin is but the first step toward full-fledged "application" (tatbiq) of the Shari'a, which should include review of all existing laws in order to amend or abolish those contradicting it. In the meantime, the journal cheers those judges who have recourse to the Shari'a in deciding moot

legal questions, basing themselves on that article in the Sadat constitution which declared the Shari'a the principal source of all legislation.[18]

Not all *al-Liwa'* articles and readers' letters share these hopes
with regard to the taqnin strategy (*al-Nur* is even more skeptical).
Much like one of his colleagues on TV reform, a leading legal
scholar voiced his apprehension lest the present draft bills be
shelved, as former ones had been under Sadat, and never be enacted
by the Assembly. Other scholars and correspondents wondered
whether, even if enacted by the Assembly, such laws were not too
limited in scope, devoid as they were of any impact on the media,
entertainment, women's dress, nudity at the seashore, and other
major ills that plague Egyptian society. Would it not be better to
have all branches of government submit outright to the Shari'a?[19]
Here again the misgivings, tensions, and internal contradictions in
the conservative stance are evident, all of them due to pressure from
the radicals (who call for immediate application of the Shari'a). This
is readily explicable, for is it not true that the radicals share the same
ideals as the conservatives, only with greater consistency, and freer
from compromise?

Women: Tempted by the Devil   There is no legal matter
                                       where these pressures are
more manifest than with regard to the Personal Status Law, enacted
in 1979 by presidential decree, and not by the People's Assembly,
in order to put an end to five years of delaying maneuvers on the
behalf of fundamentalists of all hues. Once the law was enacted,
the Islamic establishment—for all its reservations, open and tacit—
gave its official sanction. Hence the dilemma facing *al-Liwa'*. It
was duty-bound, on the one hand, to defend a law that deviates
from the Shari'a, and its hallowed game preserve, family law. Indeed, the new law, among others, empowers the wife to initiate
divorce proceedings if the husband has taken a second wife against

her wishes, requires a divorce to take place before a judge, and
endows the wife with wider rights in matters of alimony, custody,
and domicile. On the other hand, the weekly had to take into consideration the powerful opposition to this law not only among radicals but also in the mass following of the conservatives, as evidenced
by the spate of readers' letters it provoked. These letters, far exceeding in number those received on any other topic, were particularly
virulent, many of them coming from divorced males who alleged
they had been victimized by the 1979 law. That the weekly published quite a number of such letters is evidence enough that it
could by no means avoid the subject. Indeed, the very articles defending the law it chose to publish in its earlier issues were rather
lukewarm and apologetic; they were soon followed by others markedly hostile to this piece of legislation, which "runs counter to basic
precepts of Islam," "has already pushed up the divorce rate," and
"is bound to bring about the dissolution of the family in Egypt."

   While not taking an editorial position against the law, al-Liwa'
is as near to the radicals as it safely can be. Feedback from the
readership is but a partial explanation. One should note that most
of the religious establishment was far from happy with the bill when
it was proposed in 1974, and that al-Azhar students took an active
part in demonstrations against it. Moreover, the 1979 law flies in
the face of everything al-Liwa' stands for in matters of family, that
basic cell and last bastion of Muslim society. In line with a position
taken by the traditionalists with special vigor ever since the late
1940s, the family advocated here is patriarchal, the female role being
procreation and care of children. Defenseless and inherently inferior, women need male protection and guidance. One fatwa rules
that a woman neglecting religious practice can be coerced by her
husband to comply, whereas if a husband is guilty of such a lapse
the mufti tells the wife that she can merely plead with her husband
yet has no grounds for divorce. Women, according to Sha'rawi, al-
Nur, and al-Liwa', should be educated and may even go out to

work, but not at the expense of child care and preferably in "professions that behoove their maternal instincts," such as teaching, social work, nursing.[20]

These two rather limited concessions to modernity—which exceed by far what the radicals would agree to—do not signify a lack of concern on the part of the conservatives about the challenges modern life presents to traditional femininity. Such worries are, in fact, the most salient items in the weekly. The "diabolical sexual temptations" of TV and advertising are but one instance. Here is a reader's *cri de coeur*: "On the street, in the bus, at work, everywhere, we encounter immodestly attired women who arouse turmoil in men's souls. How can one avoid them? Is it enough to avert one's eyes?" And another: "If I touched a woman on the bus during Ramadan, does this invalidate my fast?" (Answer: not if it happened inadvertently).[21]

To stem the tide of "indecency" and "promiscuity," the conservatives advocate stern measures: sexual segregation of students in lecture halls, male doctors to treat women only in emergency cases when no female doctor is to be found, unmarried women to be chaperoned (even when in the company of their fiancés), wives to go out only with their husbands' permission, women to be debarred from certain positions of authority (for example, judgeship). They likewise advocate a return to the veil, though they are ambivalent on the stricter "Islamic dress" espoused by the extremist student associations and, needless to say, call for a sparing use of cosmetics. Some folk customs, such as female circumcision, are deplored but—typically—the conservatives do not take an outright stand against them as Sheikh Shaltut, rector of al-Azhar in the 1960s, used to do. And, as could be expected, basic Shari'a principles related to female inferiority are to be respected, such as males' larger share in inheritance; two female witnesses to be counted as one male witness; prayer leadership to be reserved for males.[23]

The only significant area where the conservatives—with the exception of *al-Nur*[23]—do differ from the radicals is family planning.

Al-Liwa' quite faithfully toes the official line, which sees family planning as the cornerstone of the regime's economic strategy. From the outset it published large government-sponsored advertisements extolling the virtues of small families—the picture on the ads showed a traditionally garbed woman with two children—as ensuring female health and beauty as well as family well-being. The ads were followed by fatawa that harped on similar themes ("birth control prevents poverty and ill health"), founded on medieval authorities such as al-Ghazzali, but perhaps interpreted more loosely than the latter had intended. Certain types of birth control (such as sterilization) are flatly rejected and Sha'rawi takes a strong stand against abortion for socioeconomic (but not medical) reasons. On the whole, however, a measure of dissent on the whole issue is permitted in the pages of *al-Liwa'*, smaller, yet as significant as the one allowed on the Personal Status Act. Dissenting readers point out that the government advertisements stand in dire contradiction to the weekly's basic position on the female role in society. Thus, this is yet another case of the radicals acting as the bad conscience of the conservatives, with the latter being well aware of the fact that they are compromising on ideals they share with the former.[24] It is true that on this issue the conservatives do adhere to the modernist view, whether out of sincere belief that flexibility is dictated by the need for economic survival (which is *maslaha*—utility, a principle preached by the modernists) or out of subservience to the authorities. Yet the contradictions involved and the resulting tensions within their ranks are manifest.

The Limits of Tolerance   The sensitivity of the male/female issue stems from the fact that it has always constituted one of the three basic status differences in Muslim society, together with the Muslim/non-Muslim and master/slave cleavages. The last issue having lost most of its relevance today, the attitude toward non-Muslims remains a crucial acid test, all the more so in Egypt, where anti-Coptic slogans have been used effectively by the radicals for the last half-century, and with greater intensity in recent years. Anti-Coptic riots instigated by the extremists in June 1981—and condoned by the MB and the popular Sheikh Kishk—prompted the Sadat crackdown on the opposition (which preceded, and precipitated, his own demise). Given this background, one could expect the conservatives—who, unlike the radicals, accept Egyptian nationalism as fully compatible with Islam—to spearhead the fight against anti-Christian feelings in order to preserve national unity (and, of course, render a service to the powers-that-be). Yet this is not exactly the case.

While anti-Coptic riots and pogroms are condemned—as is any recourse to violence—the conservatives reject the liberals' view that application of the Shari'a will damage national unity. On the contrary, they argue, the imposition of Muslim law on Copts will be beneficial for them (e.g., strict regulations in matters of feminine dress that enhance virtue, or harsh punishment of criminal offenders). Al-Liwa' breathes not a word on whether Shari'a laws discriminating against non-Muslims (barring access to the top government posts and to military service, special taxes, and dress) may have the same beneficial effect; perhaps because such laws are not at present on the parliamentary agenda. Yet it is symptomatic that this weekly does not make any attempt, such as those made by a number of modernists, to reinterpret the Shari'a as endowing non-Muslims with full equality before the law. The basic conservative attitude toward minorities is still that of a medieval type of tolerance, granted as a special favor and not by right, by an inherently superior group to an inherently inferior one. The underlying condescension and suspicion are evident in the fatawa taking a dim view of Muslim males marrying Christian or Jewish women, and that even though the women usually embrace Islam (marriage of non-Muslim males and Muslim women is strictly forbidden). The clinching argument in al-Liwa' diatribes against certain folk customs (visiting tombs on religious holidays, female circumcision) is that these are nothing but ancient Pharaonic customs transmitted by the Copts. Al-Nur even goes so far as to adopt the radical ban on the *Shamm al-Nasim* spring holiday.[25]

One should note that many of the readers' letters on these issues come from Upper Egypt, that hotbed of radicalism, where the percentage of Copts is particularly high. These letters tend to repeat the argument of "Christian arrogance," that is, breaking the consecrated hierarchy where Muslims are on top, and they indulge in conspiratorial theories about Coptic stratagems for a takeover of Egypt. (It is no sheer coincidence that such themes were rampant during the anti-Coptic riots in June 1981 and in the thinking of the Upper Egypt branch of the Jihad group, which called for a holy war against Christians and Sadat alike.) Such pressures from below may have had their part in shaping the conservative stance: a classic case of opinion-molders being influenced by those they were supposed to lead.[26]

Facing the "New Jahiliyya"   The brunt of the argument till now has been on the existence of a broad fundamentalist trend, which encompasses a whole gamut of opinion ranging from al-Azhar scholars and popular preachers, such as the sheikhs Sha'rawi and Kishk, through the MB to the extremist students' associations and actual terrorists. The common denominator of the conservative and the radical facets of this phenomenon is wide and stretches from metaphysics to everyday behavior. Both groups evince the same scripturalist religiosity. Both share an intense suspicion of modernity, a suspicion that does not entail total rejection.

There are, nevertheless, primordial differences between them. The conservatives are great believers in what they call the "social education" process, combined with piecemeal legal and other (for example, media) reforms. While they intend to operate even outside the framework of the state (and/or of the Islamic official apparatus), they see the state as an ally, albeit a misguided and uncertain one that needs to be admonished and goaded incessantly. The radicals despair of the snail's pace of the educational process and of the state and its token reforms. Yet more is involved here than just divergence of opinion about the means to achieve common goals. The two groups differ in their assessment of Egyptian society.

The radicals argue that, to all intents and purposes, modernity has already won the day; society is in a state of jahiliyya or in process of becoming so. For the conservatives, despite the ravages of modernity—outlined already in chapter 1—contemporary Egypt is still essentially Islamic (even in parts of its power structure) and, hence, redeemable.[27]

Mindful of these divergences, which, although smaller than their differences with the modernists, are nonetheless significant, the conservatives insist on fleshing them out in minor, yet telling, issues: endorsing prayer in mosques with tombs (an "innovation" in the eyes of the Neo-Hanbalites); qualified approval—and not outright prohibition—of female dance and song; more flexible attitudes on bank interest; beards, and tentlike female "Muslim dress"—the hallmarks of the radicals—are judged optional; attempts by some radicals to ban all contact between the sexes outside the family enclave are frowned upon.

The conservatives thus perform a useful role for the authorities, which explains why the ruling party would launch and sustain al-Liwa' and why the regime lets al-Nur be published and Sha'rawi preach so frequently on TV. These conservatives combat the more extreme radicals, the terrorists, on their own terms, on their own turf, and on the basis of the same world view. They further maintain a dialogue with the less extreme radicals (jama'at, Muslim students' associations, which do not condone violence, MB), and try, successfully at times, to co-opt them. (A prime example of this process is Muslim MB 'Umar Tilimsani, who has been inching toward a conservative position.)

Yet the success of the conservatives is not devoid of contradictions and dangers. Dialogue, as we have just seen, requires feedback from the readership. This not only requires that, within certain bounds, *al-Liwa'* be ready to serve as a forum for radical views dissenting from its own (for example, media boycott, family planning, female entertainment), but also places these views time and again in a defensive posture. Hence the apologetic tone with regard to its concessions to modernity (e.g., birth control), or when the measures it calls for fail to materialize (amending the Personal Status Act, media purge). As prominent a conservative thinker as Sha'rawi voiced his impatience, for instance, with the slow pace of codifying the Shari'a.[28] As the conservatives share most of the ideals of the radicals and an essential part of their bleak view of the state of Islam, the former thus face a double danger: their very ranks may well be infiltrated by hard-core radicals and/or their own views may gradually become radicalized. To some small extent that has already happened (note their growing criticism of the Personal Status Act). For here is the dilemma: the state which backs the conservatives is also well embarked upon an economic plan based on modernity. Certain conservatives may thus eventually conclude that reforms are slow to come for intrinsic (and not bureaucratic) reasons, that in any case the educational approach they espouse may well be ineffective against the consumerism and hedonism unleashed by the Open Door Policy. The present system would come to be seen as beyond repair, or jahili and infidel.

Two-thirds of the readership of *al-Liwa'* are said to be *shabab* (youth, under thirty). And it is, in fact, for the souls of the young that the journal is fighting. Yet while a portion of this age-group turns to radicalism—one study evaluated the Muslim Associations' membership at one-tenth of the student body, at the most—much more numerous are those who turn to materialism rather than metaphysics, being career-oriented status seekers. In a way, the conservatives are much more disturbed by that huge cohort, with its exponentially rising material expectations, than by the radicals. "This is the elevator generation," says Sheikh Sha'rawi, "where all university graduates crave luxuries like cars, and aspire to become deputy ministers overnight."[29]

This process of inadvertent secularization—to which we have already alluded in chapter 1—clouds many conservative assessments of the state of Islam. For the moment the tone is not alarmist, but there is reason to expect that many conservatives will be drawn one day to despair, possibly to radicalism. It is true that a sort of safety net stands prepared for such an eventuality as the conservative leadership tries to downgrade the level of expectations of its followers: thus codification rather than application of the Shari'a, media reform rather than purge. But what if even these goals fail to materialize while the waves of modernity continue to rise?

In recent years, the public agenda in social and religious matters has been set by the radicals, and that is, in a way, their greatest achievement. In other terms, they have seized the moral high ground, they have achieved cultural hegemony. The conservatives simply follow suit with their diluted version.

How long this version will remain attractive is a moot question. The danger of the conservatives' being won over by the extremists is evident. As Charles Péguy has put it, what began in *mystique* may well end in *politique*.

CHAPTER SIX

Assessment by the Left

The Marginal Observers   All through the preceding chapters,
one could watch how the radicals op-
erate as social commentators, adding insights to our understanding
of the Middle East. They certainly sharpen our perceptions of the
watershed mark in Middle Eastern history set by the establishment
of their major enemy, the military nation-state. They help us to
understand the decline and fall of Pan-Arabism, the "revolution of
rising expectations" in the 1970s, the role of the electronic media.
The constraints under which social scientists conduct research in
the Middle East make their contribution all the more precious,
especially as on some issues (for example, the nature of the new
state) they detected the major characteristics and problems well before outside observers (or even Arab scholars) did.

This very same heuristic device, which one may dub the adversarial method—the use of adversary literature as evidence—may
be helpful in assessing the impact and role of the radicals themselves.
In this context, commentaries of the Arab Left about resurgent Islam
should be of value. Once again, it is a case of marginal observers
throwing a critical look at a major sociopolitical phenomenon; it is
in a way reminiscent of Sayyid Qutb's case against Nasserism in the
1950s and 1960s.

The term *Left* figures here in the broad and somewhat loose sense in which it is used in the Arab world, comprising a gamut from liberal to Marxist. The merit of the left-wing thinkers for our adversarial method is that on the one hand they operate within Arab society, and are thus likely to develop insights and a feel for it that may escape the outsider. On the other hand, they are far removed from the phenomenon discussed, the Islamic resurgence, in terms of basic values, while having no interest in the survival of the social order that the Muslim radicals attack.

The accomplishment of Arab leftist intellectuals as social commentators is, indeed, quite impressive. Observing from the sidelines both nationalism and traditionalism, they have acutely analyzed the weaknesses of nationalist history-writing and mythmaking, the impact of Islam upon political and social behavior even among the supposedly modern strata, and so on.[1] They were among the very first to note the initial rumblings of the Islamic resurgence: the Syrian philosopher Sadiq Jalal al-'Azm perceived as early as 1968/69 the true significance of the "Miracle of the Holy Virgin" in Cairo, and of the insistence upon Jerusalem as a politico-religious symbol for the jihad against Israel—in a word, religion (meaning, above all, Islam) was popular, both at elite and folk levels. In late 1973 and early 1974, Egyptian thinkers detected the same spiritual evolution in their homeland as well.[2]

One should expect, of course, a certain propensity for the pedagogic hyperbole in these leftist writings, for are we not dealing here with committed observers bent upon changing reality and not only understanding it? Yet their intellectual standards are as high as those of Sayyid Qutb and his circle; their examination of this society is hard and sober. In spite (or perhaps just because) of their frankly hostile ideological position, they are, hence, not only worthy adversaries of the radicalism Qutb created, but also helpful observers assessing its impact and role. Moreover, reared as they are in an old left-wing tradition of self-criticism, these intellectuals can offer a candid inside view of the modernist and secularist forces, past and present that could till now be glimpsed only through the prism of their opponents. In the process, they may also shed light on how some secularist thinkers attempt to cope with the challenge of the Islamic revival.

The intellectual temper of the times in liberal and leftist circles can be characterized in one word: malaise. "Writers and thinkers, old and young, become convinced that they are sowing to the wind, and are doing nothing but spinning wheels. They feel, as the Arab proverb has it, that they 'plow the sea' or, in the words of Keats, 'write their names on water.'" It is thus that Tunisian writer Muhammad Masmuli sums up what is considered the irrelevance of intellectual endeavor. In the same alienated vein the Egyptian Amir Iskandar writes:

> Arab intellectuals are used to opening their books and articles with the traditional formula: "In these fateful moments in Arab history . . . it is incumbent upon us," etc. Such fateful moments are indeed many, yet the decision makers, if they happen to read these works at all, pay them no further regard. And as for the small reading public—in an Arab world where illiteracy remains so high—it has read so many words on topical subjects which failed to change matters even a whit, that by now it is eaten up by doubt, if not sheer despair. Words appear to have lost all value, becoming a sort of cheque without cover. Has the intellectual no role to play any more? Has the arena been left to the man of action, or rather to the ruler alone?[3]

The editors of a new periodical launched in summer 1982 introduce it in a distinctly downbeat mood: "A new poetry magazine in a dead time? Time of war and defeats, decadence and frustration? A poetry journal in an uncivilized time? In a nonpoetic time? Isn't this a contradiction in terms? . . . Previous wars created shock waves and brought about many a cultural project, a multitude of manifestoes. But what was their long-term impact in all levels: poetic, literary, political? Didn't they collapse at their first encounter with the real world? . . . Why expect something better now?"[4]

The Lebanese poet Adonis encapsulated that mood in the heading of one of his press articles, "We write, we talk, but what for?" while others are torn between contradictory moods, such as the Egyptian Ghali Shukri, who recently protested against the "slogan of despair," only to announce three months later that "cultural collapse is imminent."[5] And a survey of Egyptian literature during the 1973–83 decade concluded that, in contrast to the previous two decades, writers seem to consider themselves as "internal exiles," a finding confirmed by in-depth interviews.[6]

The reasons for this state of mind are manifold. The intellectuals have witnessed the devaluation of their social role and their progressive replacement by the technocrats, especially since the oil-price revolution. What with runaway inflation harassing the already straitened intelligentsia, no wonder that "many intellectuals, professionals and opinion makers . . . came to believe in the adage that what is good for business is good for the country"; they withdrew from the struggle for their erstwhile ideals, and joined the technocrats, their principles and thoughts now being colored by their private economic interests. Some of those who lack credentials—the passport of the New Class—went back to their studies, laying aside their creative work.[7] The rest, still a majority of the intelligentsia perhaps—while feeling betrayed by their own kin and shoved to the sidelines by the New Mandarins, were further frustrated by the heavy curbs laid by the state on freedom of expression. As Egyptian philosopher Fu'ad Zakariya put it: "the cultural crisis would have been a healthy one had it resulted from a developmental lag between thought and reality (or vice versa); such a lag has been the background for many a creative phase in human history; yet the present Arab crisis proceeds from the stifling of thought and expression by the powers-that-be."

Those intellectuals who "flee abroad from the hell of Arab military and bureaucratic autocracy" are condemned to an even more despairing marginality, as attested by reports from the "illusory paradise" of Paris and London. "To criticize the Arab intellectual is to criticize a weak element, fettered and shackled," muses Zakariya in another article. He is basically a victim and thus more to be pitied than blamed, as he lacks the very opportunities for *trahison des clercs* so common in Europe. "The Arab world," concludes Halim Barakat, "stretches across continents like a huge stranded octopus, drained of its water of life and indignation. Traditional and authoritarian governments have silenced the Arab people."[8]

Lack of freedom of expression is by no means a new phenomenon, yet it has been felt with particular poignancy in the 1970s because of the failure of all the gods, which the modernist intellectuals used to believe in and to share, in part at least, with the "revolutionary" regimes of the 1950s and 1960s.

> The aspiration for critical thought, questioning and reassessing, ended up by creating apologetic and repetitive tools. The quest for [Pan-Arab] unity produced an even greater estrangement, disintegration, and discord between our countries. The quest for secularism fostered virulent confessionalism. The aspiration for socialism created a new class that plunders national wealth and monopolizes power. The cult of state led to enslavement: the state as repressive tool or as prison. . . . The cultural effort did away with the role of culture and of the intellectual alike: culture became a mere weapon of the ruling apparatus and the intellectual a mere servant.

Thus Adonis, and Salah al-Din al-Bitar, the founding father of the Ba'th, would declare a few months before his assassination:

> The Arabs have not created any original idea for the last two hundred years, devoting themselves entirely to copying others. The liberals transplanted Western European liberalism; the Marxists transferred ideas from Eastern Europe; the Nasserists and the Ba'thists, being eclectic, borrowed here and there. . . . Furthermore, the military juntas which seized power were uncouth and uncultured. They pushed aside the only social group capable of leading the Arab renaissance, the intellectuals, who were even more severely handicapped by the absence of basic liberties.

A more nuanced, but in the final analysis more scathing, verdict on Arab thought is pronounced by Egyptian thinker Hasan Hanafi, who finds it crippled almost from its inception by numerous defects—dependence on authority, hypocrisy, no sense of reality, vagueness, respect for social taboos, tendency for personality cults—all of which doomed it to fail. The corrupting influence of outside forces was just a catalyst.[9]

Islam: The Challenge   The most confusing phenomenon the despondent intellectuals had to face was no doubt the growing role of Islam in society and the movement of Islamic resurgence. Particularly disoriented appear the liberal master-thinkers of the post–World War II generations. The Syrian-Lebanese Costi Zurayq expresses profound disappointment at having to witness, after forty years of intellectual endeavor, the danger of theocracy's drawing nearer than ever. Egyptian philosopher Zaki Najib Mahmud reacted even more sharply to the resurgence of the MB:

> I rub my eyes and think I am living through a nightmare or a frivolous comedy. I had to live to see the fundamentalists clamor for cutting off the hands of thieves, for stoning the adulterous and similar penalties which run counter to the spirit of our age! Can they really be serious in calling for a return to the glorious past while using the radio and other modern media which did not exist in that past and were created by the modern spirit?

Looking back at his own life, he notes: "How curious and unfortunate it is that intellectual questions were raised in the 1920s in a more creative and original manner. Thinkers and writers of genius figured then in the intellectual arena while its so-called renovation today makes one wish one could hide oneself."[10]

Such nostalgia for the times when Taha' Husayn subjected the Arab past to rigorous scrutiny and 'Ali 'Abd al-Raziq called for

separating Islam from the state, is not merely the lot of aging philosophers. Many young writers—including Marxists—talk rhapsod-
ically of the period between the wars as "the most flourishing period
of our modern history in terms of freedom of thought and expression." Towering figures of that period are still celebrated by the
modernists today with special fervor; all the more fervently perhaps
as they are the object of vituperation of the MB, who do not stoop
at claiming that Taha' Husayn, for example, had been an agent in
the pay of French intelligence services, which had even found him
a French wife to facilitate his task. There is certainly a measure of
exaggeration in the argument that the "rationalism of . . . 'Ali 'Abd
al-Raziq has become the barbarousness of Mustafa Mahmud," but
it does translate the dismay with which modernist intellectuals view
a climate of opinion, where Mustafa Mahmud's books are best-
sellers. That Mahmud is particularly popular among the young is
all the more disconcerting as it is part and parcel of a wider and
"more repugnant phenomenon where such obscurantists find their
way into the universities, gaining hold over the minds of the new
generations . . . including students in the sciences, engineering, and
agricultural faculties and at medical schools." A prime example is
the booklet distributed in Egypt by religious student associations,
which endeavors to prove that the sun revolves around the earth.
At the lower levels of the educational system the extension of "religious instruction" courses in past years was a further cause of
alarm. No less shattering were other cultural developments the modernists chronicle, such as the debates in the Egyptian People's Assembly on the reinstatement of Muslim penal law and on the
demand to seize the books of Ibn al-'Arabi (a thirteenth-century
mystic) as "antireligious." The modernists also note the violent opposition to very mild changes in Egyptian personal-status law, the
decision of an Egyptian court that accorded legal status to a witch
doctor, the decline of the number of visitors to family-planning
clinics.[11]

These trends are found not only in Egypt, though the most

vivid reactions do come from Egyptian intellectuals, perhaps because the gap between the level of modernity and that of Islamic
revival is wider there than in other Arab countries. Expectations
were higher in Egypt, and the disillusionment of the modernists is
thus the greater. "We still live in the Age of Myth and have not yet
really entered the Age of Reason," laments philosopher Murad
Wahbah (echoing the hopes of another hero of the twenties, agnostic
thinker Isma'il Mazhar).[12]

The resurgence of Islam has preoccupied some Arab thinkers
ever since 1967, yet in a desultory and superficial manner. Even
those who gave it serious attention, such as the Syrian Sadiq Jalal
al-'Azm, tended to explain it away, in the final analysis, as an
overreaction to the military defeat and were confident that the rational and scientific approach would overcome. This was, after all,
the heyday of the Arab New Left—and on a wider canvas, of the
Third World triumphant—with the belief in the "Secular and Democratic State" as a panacea not only for Lebanon and Palestine, but
for the whole Arab world. True, had the leftists—and, a fortiori,
the more moderate rationalists—paid attention to the Algerian experience, their enthusiasm might have been tempered. Algeria,
whence the slogan "Secular and Democratic State" originated during its War of Liberation, had after independence defined faith in
Islam (rather than residence) as the condition for automatic citizenship and proceeded to make the Shari'a the basis for all legislation.
But Algeria was too far away from the centers of Arab intellectual
activity and too closely associated with revolutionary warfare for its
credentials to be scrutinized in detail. Besides, only recently has the
inside story of the Front de Libération Nationale (FLN) been made
public, revealing how the secular slogan launched by the tiny nucleus of leftists has been manipulated for foreign consumption by
the leadership, who, ever since the 1956 Party Congress, covertly
opted for a nonsecular formula as best befitting the mentality of the
Algerian people as well as the predispositions of this very elite.[13]

Arab modernist thought did not become engrossed by Islamic

revivalism before the second half of the 1970s. Cries of alarm were heard, however, immediately after the October war. On the pages of *al-Ahram* (November 18, 1973), Fu'ad Zakariya decried the chorus of voices celebrating Egyptian initial successes in the war as the result of Egypt's return to Islam and/or of the intervention of celestial forces. One of the instances alluded to was the legend, propagated among others by the Army Religious Section, that the Prophet Muhammad in person had crossed the canal with the Egyptian soldiers; it reminds one of that declaration of a Lebanese ulama leader cited by al-'Azm in 1968—that God's angels will assist Arabs as they did in Muhammad's battle against the infidels of Arabia. One thus better understands Zakariya's distress: Is Islam due to surge in the wake of defeat as much as of victory? Two months later, in an article in *al-Katib*, another Egyptian, Salah 'Isa, discussed "Taha' Husayn and the Ordeal of Reason" as a paradigmatic experience; Husayn's failure is, for him, of vital relevance to the present, when rationality is in retreat.

The Watershed: Lebanon   Yet those were solitary voices. The question of Islam's role in society and the role of the fundamentalist movement did not begin to attract attention until 1976 when the impact of the civil war in Lebanon and the rise of the Muslim radicals elsewhere became clear. Modernist thought was prepared to some extent by the early 1970s when it had become far less certain that socioeconomic change or the Revolution (which no longer seemed imminent) could sap the passive resistance of religion. The failure cf the Arab Left to leave its mark on the political scene and numerous field studies on the lingering impact of tradition made this only too clear. There were almost no intimations that the defensive would soon become an offensive.

The impact of the 1975/76 Lebanese Civil War—more immediate, because of its violence, than the creeping and cumulative changes on the cultural scene—can best be perceived in the writings of several thinkers who were preoccupied with the religious question well before that war. In a 1969 dissertation, George Corm was one of those who considered the Lebanese confessional structure to be authentic and endogenic, based on history, culture, the web of social relationships, and education, and it was not to be dismissed as a mere invention of the French mandatory power. He thus realistically evaluated the onerous task of deconfessionalization and warned that "as long as the present system is here, nothing can guarantee that on the occasion of this or that grave event, or outside intervention, the confessional peace will be maintained." Nevertheless he was cautiously optimistic. The rapid economic development in the 1960s seemed to be "working in the direction of an opening up and a readjustment of ideologies and mentalities, spearheaded and catalyzed by the strong leftist current passing through Lebanese youth." Even Islam did not seem to him as impervious to secularization as in the past. On balance, the book wavers between such hopes and the realization of how deeply anchored the confessional system is, joined to the author's thesis that secularization, being a product of Christian culture, cannot be too easily transferred into a region shaped by Islam.

Most of his hopes were shattered by the war. But not so much because the delicate balance was broken; this the author foresaw. What struck him, in a post mortem of the war published in 1978, was, first, the fickleness (even cynicism) with which both sides regarded the slogan of secularism, viewed above all as a tactical weapon: the "Muslim Progressives" calling mostly for deconfessionalization in the realm of political representation (which would hurt the Christians), and the Christians calling their bluff by demanding complete secularization, including the realm of personal-status law, which was unpalatable for most Muslim progressives, let alone for conservative Muslims. Only minuscule leftist groups fought for secularism with any measure of ideological commitment. Second, and more important, was the fact that in their respective enclaves, neither side—and the Palestinians and Syrians as well—tried to depart from the traditional authoritarian mode of government, nor did they begin to institute deconfessionalization. Third, the war on the whole strengthened intercommunity cleavages based on greater residential segregation; it proved the resilience of the confessional structures and brought to the fore religious personalities and organizations.[14]

These observations—corroborated by other analysts (Khalidi, Nasr, Ghaylun, Toubi)—seem to have driven Corm to conclude that the slogan of the secular and democratic state has been dealt a heavy blow. The permeation, even of so-called radicals, by culturally alien ideas such as secularism was a tougher task than formerly gauged. Aspirations had to be scaled down. Much like Khalidi, Corm resigns himself to the continued existence of the confessional political system (with minor changes) and calls for concentrating on the creation of a single system of education and a single judicial system. This semisecularization, "doing away with the mental ghettos," is a distant goal that must be preceded by long-range educational effort, beginning in the ranks of the Left. It may be greatly facilitated, in his view, by the almost inevitable failure of Arab economic modernization to create widespread prosperity and to cut off (rather than increase) dependence upon the West. The crisis ensuing from this might change the nature of religion; but, cautioned Corm on another occasion, it is impossible to know whether that would be in the direction of greater rationality or a heightened penchant for metaphysics.[15]

While Corm passed from muted optimism to muted pessimism, his compatriot Halim Barakat passed from muted optimism to hope against hope. As one who had studied the beliefs and attitudes of university students in the years preceding the war, he was struck by the extent to which confessional identity was still (in 1968) the crucial factor in shaping mentalities, though he found ground for optimism in the growing number who were breaking out of the traditional molds, auguring a passage from a "mosaic society" to a truly pluralistic one. Like Corm, he warned, however, that unless this happened, a violent eruption might bring the whole edifice down.

The war gave the lie to such hopes. What he calls in sociologese "vertical loyalties"—and above all religion—proved to be much stronger than expected. Barakat pushes the analysis one step further than Corm and poses the question on the scale of the Arab world. Given his belief that these loyalties are endogenous, do they not create an almost insurmountable obstacle not only to secularism but also to Arab unity? And is this not particularly true with regard to religion, as Islam is a component of Arabism and is also manipulated by the rulers? Without trying to answer these daunting questions, Barakat passes to a declaration of faith: faith in the inevitability of a secularist-socialist revolution; but, he adds, "is it a dream or an illusion? . . . the choice is, indeed, between dream and nightmare."[16]

A third type of response, from exuberant optimism to hope against hope, is exemplified by Nasif Nassar, a vigorous proponent of the "philosophical liberation" that should bring about the shedding of religion altogether. In *Toward a New Society* (Arabic, 1970) he expresses the belief that the progress of scientific education, combined with industrialization and the decline of rural society, are in the process of undermining the foundations of the confessional system and might even create a serious challenge to religion per se. Nine years later he still calls for "joint coexistence" in one Lebanese society and rejects the compromise formula of "peaceful coexistence" between autonomous communities. But "is this not to indulge in daydreaming?" he asks himself.[17]

These various expressions of pessimism can be discerned in fiction as well. A 1980 collection of stories by Ghada al-Samman deals—in a manner reminiscent of Barakat—with the way dreams of revolution turned into the *Nightmares of Beirut* (the book's title). A survey of other writers finds the recurring themes to be disenchantment with all ideologies, alienation bordering on nihilism, and the incapacity of the heroes of fiction to make rational choices as long as mentalities are besieged by religious establishments. "Religion still fills the consciousness of the masses and serves as the tool of the authorities, the ideology of rulers and revolutionaries alike. All prophets—true and false—have recourse to religious conscience which is supposed to confer legitimacy on both the political and the military. On both sides of the barricade the same kind of sword is wielded."[18]

A different type of response—which foreshadowed developments to come in the wake of the Iranian Revolution—came from the pen of Jérôme Shahin.[19] A Christian leftist, he saw the power of religion as manifested in patterns of wartime behavior (kidnappings, for example), the inconsistency or insincerity of most so-called proponents of secularism, and concluded—not unlike Corm—that this is tantamount to the "bankruptcy of the Arab Left." If the Left wants to remain both Arab and progressive it has to make its peace with religion as a social factor and drop the secular ideal almost altogether. But this does not mean acquiescing to the status quo. Only one religion is to be embraced and that is Islam, the major cultural component of Arabism. It should even be made the state religion while transforming itself into a revolutionary ideology. Such a transformation, argues the author in a sibylline phrase, "will be tantamount to secularization on our own terms." How and why this can be done is not explained. Neither can one look for guidance to the formula the author borrows from Tunisian writer Hisham Djait: "Reform should not be made against religion; it will come by religion, in religion, and independently of religion." But then Djait—who somehow wishes to combine Islam as state religion with separation of the legal system from religion—is writing on a country without non-Muslims. Coming from Lebanon and from a Christian at that, Shahin's idea—however imprecise and confused—is indicative of a state of mind: secularism having failed, the only hope for radical change may lie in the religion of the bulk of the masses which the intellectuals want to lead, that is, Islam.

Iran: Intellectuals-Turned Mystics   Shahin's kind of approach
                                        was due to rise to promi-
nence when the unhoped-for happened and a revolution erupted in
the Middle East. Erupting at a time when progressive intellectuals
resigned themselves to a protracted eclipse of the ideas they cherished, the Iranian Revolution was a most exhilarating surprise. At
a time when the decline of the "political vitality of the masses" was
being lamented, the latter burst upon the scene and revolted. Quite
a few intellectuals were carried away to unbridled waves of enthusiasm. The leading voice was that of Marxist thinker Anwar Abdelmalek. "What is taking place today in the Middle East and what
some call the Islamic Wave is in reality nothing but a wave of
oriental Arab nationalism born of the womb of oriental culture, a
culture made of two circles, the Asiatic one centered around China
and the Afro-Asian one centered on the Arab nation." This second
circle produced "Political Islam." Much like in the colonial period,
Political Islam serves as a major defense mechanism against the
continued onslaught of the West; Khomeini is thus progressive by
definition, as were Muhammad 'Ali, the Urabi and Abdelkrim revolts, the Algerian ulama under the French in the past; in our era
the analogies are: Musaddeq, Nasser, and even Saudi king Faysal
(on the issue of Jerusalem). That checklist of examples barely helps
to clarify the meaning of Political Islam, and neither is it clear how
all this fits in with the author's Marxism. While the emphasis on
the political role of Islam is evident, this is not a new idea, nor is
it evident how the political dimension can be isolated in such a
holistic religion. Yet what is important is once again the state of
mind manifested here. Whatever pertains to Oriental "specificity"
(*khususiyya*), a term Abdelmalek coined in 1974, when he began to
develop in that direction—is ipso facto a positive factor. It is all the
more so when this "specificity" takes measures to forestall "cultural
conquest" by the West. Progressive thought and action should draw
therefrom its very vitality and inspiration.[20]

Other writers followed suit, celebrating the huge potential of

"Islam and Oil," which ushered in a new phase in the age-old East-West struggle. "The illusion of cutting ourselves off from our past was definitively refuted by the Iranian Revolution. There is no progress without holding on to our authenticity. The Arab Liberation Movement has by now learned that there is no revolution unless one passes through Islam, the only factor capable of unifying and driving the masses to action." What the Arab countries need is a "religious revolutionary wave with a strong popular basis, opposing the powers-that-be and championing a distinct nationalist vision."[21]

Much more eloquent than this sample of phrases is the fact that the leading left-wing publishing house *Dar al-Tali'a* (Beirut) hastened to publish Khomeini's *Islamic Government*, which went into a number of printings, and prefaced it with a eulogistic introduction: "Despite the religious characteristics of this revolutionary thought . . . it is essentially a nationalist, contemporary, and modernist ideology. . . . The Islamic mode enables it to win a broad popular basis without losing sight of other objectives." No less incantatory was another Beirut publisher's introduction to the 1979 printing of Munah al-Sulh's *Islam and the Arab Liberation Movement*, which was the forerunner of the Abdelmalek-Shahin syndrome, arguing already in 1973 that in the Arab World—"The vanguard is [Pan-] Arab but the masses are Muslim," hence the revolution should first draw upon the numerous progressive ingredients in Islamic tradition. Iran, writes the publisher, vindicated that view; Islam is not by necessity reactionary and is at present the sole available agent of radical change. Even Sulh's erstwhile main critic, Ilyas Khuri, has by now been converted—not without some misgivings—to the view that Islam is the vehicle for the reentry of the masses upon the political scene and expresses the Oriental spirit fighting the imperialist West.[22]

Leftists and liberals could scoff at those "intellectuals-turned-mystics" and "Marxists who have all of a sudden seen the light and turned in repentance to religion." They could impugn their motives and speak of "political and cultural exploitation of the Iranian Revolution," or (in discussions witnessed by the present writer) of "catering for a *third-worldnik* clientele anxious above all to find ersatz compensation for its inferiority complex vis-à-vis the West."[23] The lack of intellectual rigor and historical grounding of "Political Islam" could be easily demonstrated; all the more so as Anwar Abdelmalek was to revert from time to time to other definitions that emphasized the cultural dimension of Islam. Yet there was no escaping the fact that such views did enjoy an audience by no means negligible, thence the need for sharp rebuttals. The defection of these leftist thinkers—"alienated intellectuals who suddenly found in Political Islam a reason for hope and rapture"—could be perceived as a sort of writing on the wall, especially as they insist on keeping their leftist credentials, thus adding to the confusion.[24]

The challenge of Islamic revivalism could also be minimized, to some extent, by attributing a leading role to the leftist organizations in the Iranian Revolution.[25] But the later vagaries of the revolution made this argument less and less tenable. The mushrooming fundamentalist associations in the Arab countries were likewise traced back by some observers to occult manipulation by the powers-that-be, especially in Egypt. The ambiguous relationship between the MB and the monarchy in the 1930s and 1940s was presented as prefiguring their "shady" relationship with Sadat, who was supposed to be aiding and using them to combat the Left. Such conspiratorial explanations are still quite common, although a growing number of secularist writers came to recognize that the Islamic movement is ready to challenge the government (on the Personal Status Law and the Camp David Accords, for example) and even resort to terrorist activity. Moreover, they came to admit that it is self-propelled, with roots in the demise of the ideologies of the 1950s and the 1960s, the 1967 debacle, and the frustration of hopes pinned upon the oil-price upheaval as the gap between Arab haves and have-nots grew wider.[26] The lack of coherent social thinking both in Iran and among Arab fundamentalists can be rightly pointed out, but it is just a cold comfort. For if the expansion of "irrational and metaphysical ideas" can be adduced to "the masses feeling utter impotence and bewilderment in the face of contradictory realities created under the sway of tyrannical regimes,"[27] why could the Left not profit from this state of affairs? Why did it not strike roots among the urban strata, which were to constitute the power basis of the fundamentalists? Why did the bankruptcy of Nasserism lead the youth back to Islam, that eternal "refuge and bliss" of the populace?

Self-Critique   George Corm, among those who prognosticated the imminent demise of the economic strategy devised by Arab and Iranian technocrats, admits that he was taken by surprise when this led not to the spread of revolutionary ideas but rather to a "relapse to *passéiste* notions." The implication is, of course, that other countries, such as Egypt, where such a crisis of economic development might occur, could behave in a like manner. The review *Dirasat 'Arabiyya* blamed itself for not paying these phenomena much attention in the past, even though for more than a decade "the masses, looking for a way out of the suffocating atmosphere of defeat and disillusionment, found it in the reawakening Islamic movement." Although the editors do not accept that the "religious revolution is the viable alternative," they admit their concern that talk of that nature is becoming increasingly fashionable on the Left. "Much like Western analysts," writes Wadi' Sharara, a Lebanese-Shi'ite sociologist, "we (Arab progressives) did underestimate the role the religious factor can play in anchoring popular resistance in stony soil, in strengthening its bonds with history, culture and local institutions and in enabling the leadership of the resistance to talk to the whole people in one commonly understood langauge." Much like the editorial quoted above, he calls for a reassessment of left-wing perceptions, ideas, and methods in the wake of the Lebanese Civil War, the Iranian Revolution, and the Arab return to Islam as well as of the decline of Pan-Arabism.[28]

Such a reassessment actually evolved well before these calls were made. Its main point related to the role of Islam in society, which during the last decade quite a few leftist thinkers and social scientists have already given serious attention. There even developed a school of revisionist historians who tried to go beyond the existing impact of Islam and trace its origins across fourteen centuries. They did much to remedy the cavalier disregard of past-permeated factors that characterized the leftists in the 1950s and 1960s. As Sharara recalls in the memoir on his Marxist students' group in the 1960s: "The world seemed to us to mirror our own souls. We thought it to be devoid of history and imagined we had none. Who are we? This is a question we never asked ourselves, considering it to be a mere trap laid down by the Forces of Evil. . . . And not for a moment did we doubt that Arab societies began with us a new phase in their history . . . and are on their way to the historical paradise."[29]

This excessive future-orientedness, argues the present self-critique, still remains a major characteristic of leftist and secularist thought. Cultural factors were not given due attention on the assumption that socioeconomic changes move inexorably toward diminishing the role of the past. How facile that assumption was is made evident in the number of recent studies carried out by left-leaning analysts.

A survey of students from eight Arab countries carried out at Kuwait University during 1979–81 found that most respondents, regardless of sex, ranked religion first in their hierarchy of group affiliation, followed by family, nation-state citizenship, national origin (Arab), and political ideology. These students (99 percent of whom were Muslim) ranked high on most indexes of modernity. In another survey dealing with the Arab-Israeli conflict and carried out among Arab nationals living in Kuwait, the following question was asked: "Which is the ideology most appropriate to conducting the conflict?" Among the respondents—all of them university-educated—44 percent of the Egyptians and 33 percent of the Syrians named religion as the most appropriate ideology, and that after three and two decades, respectively, of revolutionary regimes.

A study of the political culture of Egyptian peasants (parents and sons) found religiously inherited attitudes—submissiveness mixed with suspicion toward the powers-that-be, fatalistic explanations of calamity and inequity, mysticism—to be somewhat diminishing, yet still strong, among the young generation; the long educational and media exposure seem to have had only a limited impact. In both age groups the prominent traits of nationalist identity include religiosity and forebearance (*sabr*, a Koranic and Bedouin virtue). Likewise, in a broader survey conducted in ten Arab countries, it was found that everywhere but in Lebanon about 60 percent of the respondents—all of whom had at least secondary education—"emphatically agree" with the statement that the "Islamic dimension is a major component of Pan-Arabism" (their share rising to 70 percent in Egypt). On the average, another 30 percent agreed with some reservations. Out-and-out proponents of secularist nationalism numbered, on balance, less than one-tenth. When asked whether they would prefer Arab unity on an Islamic basis as an immediate goal, leading in a second phase to all-Islamic unity, 36 percent answered positively, and that more than a half century after the demise of Pan-Islamism.

Even among a group expected to be highly prone to change— the Palestinians in Kuwait—immigrants, urbanized, well-educated—while important attitudinal changes were discovered on sensitive issues (family, child rearing, women, education, profession), the realm of religion has been found to be the least amenable to transformation. More than half the respondents to a survey conducted among them declared that religious practice should be enforced by the family (another 12 percent saw the family role here as "orientation"). Marriage with partners of another religion was opposed by 92 percent (as compared to 56 percent who rejected marriage to non-Arabs and 38 percent opposed to marriage to non-Palestinians).[30]

But was it just a case of bad judgment? Did the intellectuals merely underestimate the resilience of Islam? The accusation of fickleness is carried one step further by a few critics who take a hard look at what modernist thought had to say on religion. They find that "ever since the accession (of Arab countries) to independence the intellectuals have observed an anguished silence on the problem of religion.[31] With a few exceptions (Khalid Muhammad Khalid in 1950, Sadiq Jalal al-'Azm in 1968/69, perhaps also Bu 'Ali Yasin in 1970/73), religion actually remains—as Yasin put it—part of the "triple taboo" (with sex and government) regulating Arab behavior. Both respectful and afraid of the sensitivities of the masses they want to mobilize, the intellectuals chose either to ignore Islam altogether or used it to confer legitimacy upon their ideas. Even staunch admirers of Nasserism on the Left now begin to perceive that by resorting to such tactics, Nasserism—as well as the Ba'th—has kept the traditional religious hold over society and culture, which goes a long way toward explaining the easy and immediate resurgence of Islam once a sympathetic regime came to power in 1970.[32] The apologetic approach—which the Left either condoned or actually abetted—is in fact a legacy of the Islamic reformism of the late nineteenth century that present-day critics find to have been not a "creative rationalist religious thought," but merely a defensive mechanism designed to maintain religion intact while paying lip service to modern fads; Islam still awaits its reformation, writes Hanafi, a sine qua non for genuine secularization. The true voices of religious criticism from the early decades of this century (Mazhar, Shumayyil, 'Abd al-Raziq), which the Left used to quote reverently as paragons of enlightenment, are suddenly seen as isolated and embattled individuals with too elitist a following. The Left has much to blame itself for, if "most people still consider secularism as tantamount to a sort of monster of atheism harking from the West in order to tear Arab society to pieces and instill moral depravity in it."[33]

The intellectual (and political) sin of the Left was that of trying to avoid the religious question by alternating silence and vague slogans while not always resisting the temptation to utilize Islam for legitimation. Even such an outspoken proponent of secularism as

Nasif Nassar was very nebulous in his 1970 book-manifesto as to how such a society could be brought about, given the Islamic permeation of all spheres of life. Such a lack of intellectual earnestness would help explain how many left-wingers could so easily compromise their secularist ideals for the sake of alliances with Muslim political formations or, later, enthusiastically embrace Khomeinism.

The superficial, slogan-ridden character of much old-time secularist thought is put in relief by its failure to discuss seriously the minorities question. Here it barely differed from Arab nationalist thought in general, where a recent contents-analysis has discovered that in all its stages this was the last item on the priorities list (its take never exceeding 2 percent of the total effort). George Corm's book, one of the few devoted to that topic, appeared in French and it took eight years—and the Lebanese trauma—to be translated into Arabic (having earlier been published in Serbian). Even after the Lebanese Civil War, few and far between are those like Sa'd al-Din Ibrahim who try to rethink the question.

Ibrahim admits that ethnic and religious minorities (the 15 percent of the Arab world that is either non-Arabic speaking or non-Muslim or both) have an authentic grounding in history and social structure (and are not a sheer product of imperialist manipulation), that they are to some extent excluded from the core of Arabism because of its linkage with Islam, have authentic fears of being submerged, and cannot be really integrated into the core unless a pluralistic vision of Arabism is developed.[34]

But despite Ibrahim's warning—joined by Adonis—that the refusal to take seriously the fears of the non-Muslims is one of the major reasons for the failure of Pan-Arabism, the Ahl al-Dhimma (non-Muslim) question is rarely touched upon by revisionist historians, and quite a few leftist thinkers continue to ascribe recent events, such as the Muslim-Coptic clashes in Upper Egypt, to the machinations of the security services. Had it not been for "a few hotheads on both sides," it is argued, integration would be total and intercommunity peace would reign supreme.[35]

Conscious of their intellectual sins, the liberal and left-wing thinkers are also aware of how few they are. As Rabi'u, a leftist-turned-Khomeinist, observed sarcastically, the hard-core secularists are "voices launching their appeals from faraway places." Indeed a good many of these voices today are heard from exiles and émigrés—in Paris, Lyon, Göttingen, London, and Washington—and not always in the Arab media.[36]

Those operating within the Arab world complain of being cut off from the masses. While their historical revisionism has convinced them that Arabism is not an eternal phenomenon, but a product of the late nineteenth century, they have to concur that "the Arab masses continue to perceive Arabism from an Islamic viewpoint."[37]

The progressives have indeed to face two alternatives which Rabi'u defies them to recognize: "they must either try to take hold of Islam and save it from the reactionaries who exploit it in order to defend their own interests, or be relegated to the marginal role of observers of the historical storms due to be unleashed."[38]

It is precisely this choice that they refuse to make; hence their confusion. As they have shed their past apologetic approach (for example, Islam is rational and inherently secular), they tend to look askance at those who see Islam as the purveyor of the revolution. Most of them perceive the Iranian case to be sui generis, based upon the Shi'ite tradition of implicit or explicit resistance to the powers-that-be and the semiindependent socioeconomic basis of the ulama. It is thus barely applicable to the Arab world with its long tradition of ulama, subservience to Sunni governments and exploitation of religion to legitimize authority and to inculcate fatalism and submissiveness among the masses. "Islam is neither equivalent to the spirit of Arabism nor does it contain an explosive revolutionary potential." The vagaries of the Khomeini experiment reinforce this skepticism.[39]

All that actually boils down to a declaration of what a quantum leap the progressive and secular ideal requires, how out of tune it is not only with present realities but also with the historical traditions underlying them. The revolutionary streaks that revisionist historians discover in the Muslim past (slave revolts, for instance) may be useful didactic tools for the long-range task of educating the masses. But objectively they are quite meager and what is more, they do not exist at all in the collective consciousness, owing to efficient white-washing by court historians. On the secularism issue one could argue with M. Arkoun[40] that in a way it conforms to the realities of post-Muhammadan Islamic history (and contrary to the myths of traditional historiography): secular rulers governed by decree and gave it religious sanction only post factum; the Shari'a was actually operative merely in the domain of personal status and (in part) in commercial law and was utterly debarred from regulating the relationship between branches of government, the transfer of power, government-citizen relations, and foreign policy. This conformity of secularism with objective historical facts could be an interesting point of departure (much like S. Ibrahim on the minorities) for rethinking the whole notion of secularism, but such an argument runs counter to well-entrenched popular perceptions, and the enormity of the reeducation task remains.

The Danger of Born-Again Islam   In the meantime the leftist and liberal intellectuals— shorn of illusions but also of support—have to face up to the fundamentalist challenge. While they may be in sympathy with the latter's opposition to the "American model" (title of a recent book by Zakariya) for development and consumption, and while they may join together in opposition to Arab conservative regimes, their overall reading of the situation is bleak. The Islamic wave is sweeping over every nook and cranny, coloring perceptions across the whole political gamut. The danger is described by Egyptian historian Tariq al-Bishri: "What the political Islamic currents spread is a past-oriented, fundamentalist approach. It is to be feared that we may soon witness a fundamentalist Wafd, fundamentalist Nasserism and so forth."[41] The danger seems all the graver to the Left as it reinforces all the major (and, in their lights, negative) trends that have lately developed in the Arab world.

First and foremost among these trends are the centrifugal tendencies, that is, the rise of the nation-state (*qutriyya*) as a relatively stable, legitimate foundation of political life as well as of group identity. Today even a paragon of Pan-Arabism like Iraq tends to draw upon Babylonian-Assyrian history for national mythology and symbols, and even extreme-left writers in their optimistic moments expect the nation-state to endure for some time and Arab unity to come by stages, especially through growing cooperation on pragmatic issues, a unity that will hopefully end in a confederal structure. Most other Pan-Arabists are far less sanguine. At such a juncture the resurgence of Islamic fundamentalism poses a twofold challenge.

On the one hand, it may well replace Pan-Arabism as a focus for supranational identity. The born-again vitality of Islam and the widespread opinion that Arabism has failed enhance that danger. Even a writer as sympathetic to the Iranian Revolution (and to Islam as a major component of Arabism) as Munah al-Sulh sounds the alarm: "The role of Islam cannot be positive if it is presented as an alternative to a paralyzed Arabism." Such a feeling of impotence pervades even the Left, where many look to Islam as a source of regeneration of Arabism, and it underlies the "Political Islam" eulogies of Abdelmalek and his disciples. A typical spokesman of this mood is a liberal like Ihsan 'Abbas who calls for drawing vitality and inspiration "from Islam, the external concentric circle of Arabism," but not at the price of establishing a religious state; he finally admits that he does not really know how this can be done. That failure of nerve is all the more prevalent beyond the hard nucleus of the true believers in Pan-Arabism. The raw energy of Islam and its much-coveted conduit to the masses strengthen its appeal all the more, and heighten the danger—the source of inspiration turning into an alternative. "Extolling traditionalism poses the risks of producing an Islamic unity rather than an Arab unity," especially as the MB and other revivalists are highly suspicious of Arab nationalism, which they perceive to be yet another nefarious Western import. "Soon enough," writes Ghali Shukri, "they may come to the 'logical' conclusion that Arab nationalism is nothing but a colonialist conspiracy and that the Ottoman Empire was our Golden Age."[42]

On the other hand, the Islamic revival enhances confessional cleavages as already evident in Egypt (with the anti-Coptic propaganda and riots), Sudan (Christians versus Muslims), Algeria (Arabs versus Berbers), Syria (with the anti-'Alawite infidels' coloring given to the opposition), Iraq (Khomeinist Shi'ite resistance to the Sunni elite), and of course Lebanon. The more or less assured place of the minorities in the national community (be it a nation-state), which Arabism helped to bring about, is thus menaced. If the falling apart of the nation-state is not something Pan-Arabists would have tended to lament in the past, they are deeply troubled by it today, as they are by no means the ones who stand to profit from it. The specter of "chauvinistic mini-states"—present-day Lebanon becoming the all-Arab pattern—is not one to warm their hearts. More immediate is the danger that non-Muslims will feel less at home even in the Pan-Arab movement as its Islamic coloration and collaboration with Muslim revivalists tend to grow. A Maronite intellectual recently launched this anguished cry: "I know that the crushing majority of Muslims consider that Arabhood and Islam are one and the same thing, an opinion that most Christians have come to share ever since the Lebanese Civil War, and thus look at Arabs with suspicion and fear. I still cling to the belief that those are two separate things. . . . I still belong to that crazy minority which continues to declare: 'I am a Christian Arab; proud of my Christianity and of my Arabhood alike.' But were the choice between the two to be imposed upon me, I should opt to remain Christian."[43]

The second danger lies in shutting off receptivity to modern culture, as manifested by the modish slogans of "fight against the imperialist onslaught on our minds," "reject imported ideas." The Left and the liberals who draw much of their inspiration from Western philosophies stand to suffer from the ruthless spread of these slogans; and on a broader canvas, the openness to modernist ideas—which has never proved satisfying from their viewpoint—is bound to diminish. Leftists and liberals point out that the essentialist notion underlying such slogans—that there are immutable and authentic characteristics of Arab-Muslim societies to which the latter should remain attuned—is nothing but the mirror-image of the old-time Orientalist concept of an immutable East (or Islam), once cited to account for its backwardness. Clinging to essentialism, revivalist-style, will only maintain—and not undermine—that very backwardness and dependence the imperialists would have liked to preserve.

The essentialism of the ex-leftist paragons of "authenticity" is no different, and perhaps more dangerous, coming as it does from people like Abdelmalek, steeped in Western thought, who can, hence, reject it in a more sophisticated and convincing manner. "The best proof of the fallacy of 'down with imported ideas' slogan is that Arab social life, whether under progressive or conservative regimes, has suffered for many years from the same ills: authoritarianism and paternalism in the professional sphere, the extended family governing male-female relations, lack of democracy, tribalism, confessionalism, etc.; all that behind the thin varnish of modernized political and economic institutions."[44] Many of these ills can be imputed to that supposedly glorious past which is to be resuscitated. No wonder that externalization of guilt goes in tandem with the new essentialism, perhaps even more among the new converts from the Left than among true-blue Muslim radicals. The creativity of Muslim society in the Middle Ages, argues Nasif Nassar, may not have suffered when it fought against the cultural impact of the Crusades, as Islam was then the spearhead of progress; today, when most new ideas are produced outside the Islamic sphere, creativity cannot be regenerated without selective recourse to the West.

Most exasperated by these new trends—an "Islam mobilized rather than reassessed" in the words of Arkoun—are Muslim liberal thinkers. Hasan Hanafi even dared criticize the master thinker in person, Khomeini:

> But for the importance of the emphasis he puts on Islamic identity, of his refusal to let the Muslim personality be dissolved and of his critique of Westernization, it remains nonetheless that when he rejects out of hand everything Western—such as parliamentary institutions, democracy, and liberalism—he leads the Islamic Revolution from action to reaction, from anticolonialism to hostility toward anything Western. He thus dismisses rationalism, the scientific spirit, humanism, in a word, progress.[45]

The last danger is the further reduction of democratic liberties—the decline of which greatly preoccupies the Left—through charismatic authoritarianism of the Khomeini type, which risks reinforcing some related traits of Arab regimes: the cult of the personality, political exploitation of religion, marshaling of the intellectuals to serve the state. The latter menace disturbs liberal and leftist intellectuals all the more as the spread of externalization of guilt and of Islamic apologetics signifies to them that the battle they have been waging for the last two decades has failed. "Instead of a military intellectual we shall have a military cleric," as Adonis put it, "it will be yet another variation of functional thought, subservient to authority, designed to fight the other rather than criticize onself." The narrow-mindedness of military cliques, which Salah al-Din al-Bitar lamented, will be replaced by a similar set of mind, more dangerous perhaps, because it is more consistent and more engrossed with things of the spirit. The danger is all the greater as the educated public at large does not share the preoccupations of the intellectual elite (only 5 percent of the respondents to the ten-countries-survey were particularly sensitive to the lack of democracy).[46]

This sense of failure of past combats, present impotence, and lurking danger goes a long way to account for the despondency among leftist intellectuals. At a deeper level it is a sense of no exit, Islam being so intimately interwoven into Arab life that to escape from it one can only take refuge in a fringe sectarian existence. And yet how to deal with that phenomenon—a relic of the past supposedly condemned to the "dustbin of history," and yet powerful and growing at present—is even less clear to the Left today than a half century ago. Francis Bacon's dictum applies to them topsy-turvy; greater knowledge rendered them powerless and confused. Indeed, these are not easy times for secularist intellectuals in the Middle East.

Conclusion

The jeremiads of the Left—curiously resembling, in counterpoint, those on the Right (chapter 1)—have an evident heuristic value. Even more than the Muslim conservative writings (chapter 5), they testify to the cultural hegemony seized by Radical Islam during the last decade. The radicals set the issues and the terms with which they are discussed. All other social forces have to react to them. While, barring a serious socioeconomic crisis, actual seizure of political power by the radicals remains an elusive prospect—given the repressive efficiency of the nation-state—the seizure of cultural hegemony represents a substantial achievement. The leftist assessment of the dangerous potentialities of born-again radicalism is grounded in a realistic evaluation of the current situation in the Sunni world, even though at times the Left tends to exaggerate (on the subject of centrifugal tendencies within the states, for instance). Foremost among these potentialities is the rise of a selective receptivity to modernism, permeated by a spirit of essentialism (or "Orientalism in reverse," to quote Sadiq Jalal al-'Azm).

Yet the principal merit of leftist observers on the margin is their putting in relief the bedrock of traditionalism, which had withstood the challenge of over two centuries of Westernization, that bedrock upon which the radicalism is founded, even as—dialectically—it also partly rebels against it. By "bedrock of traditionalism" we do

181

not mean mere petrified "survivals." For as an ethnographer would remind us, the mere fact that medieval Islam persisted as a living tradition well into the contemporary era implies that it had to change to some extent over the centuries. "The concept of survival is almost always a confession of defeat before the challenge to find a contemporary sense in anything . . . societies can only be understood in the present as a point of transition between a former and a future state."[1] Nevertheless, the modifications introduced until very recently in medieval modes of thought and behavior were by no means monumental (see chapter 5). In consequence, continuity was far greater than change, so that one may be justified in speaking about a "traditional bedrock." The *bedrock* here relates above all to human fundamentals: attitudes toward life and death, sex, politics, and so on. In these realms Arab liberal and left-wing researchers pioneered discoveries about the resilience of Arab traditional mentalities and patterns of action.

Thus Sayyid 'Uways found out that attitudes toward death are roughly the same among Egyptian intelligentsia and fellahin, based upon a common belief in life after death and the notion of obligation toward deceased relatives and toward saintly and pious people who have died. Egyptian gynecologist Dr. Nawwal al-Sa'adawi drew upon her professional experience to observe that in all key areas (centrality of the issue of virginity, the notion of "honor" and premarital sex, legal status, subservience to males, entering marriage as a market commodity, lack of right to initiate divorce and to get lifelong alimony, lower share in inheritance) the female condition in both urban and rural Egypt is still governed by the Islamic Law and by the social norms it spawned throughout the centuries of total male domination.[2] The major bastion of traditional Islamic values and the principal intermediary between the individual and his social and cultural milieu is the family. Syrian and Palestinian scholars found that the extended family is essentially a microcosm of society and thus its structure and patterns of relationships reflect and uphold the traditional values of the society at large; through its primordial role in child rearing, the family inculcates these values in its young members, preparing them for the social roles. Such values include: authoritarianism based upon age seniority and male sex, overdependence vis-à-vis the social milieu, helplessness as regards the powers-that-be and the lack of personal initiative.[3]

It is little wonder that when a team of Egyptian social scientists (headed by 'Imad al-Din Sultan) tried to gauge the generational gap within the middle classes, it found the gap to be insubstantial. Based on a field survey of a sample of four social groups (high school seniors, university students, and their respective parents), the Sultan team found all four groups were strongly imbued by traditional Islamic values. "It is our finding," wrote Dr. Sultan, "that religious faith is deeply rooted in all sectors of Egyptian society." The overwhelming majority of the respondents—regardless of age, sex, and educational achievement—agreed with statements like "a person cannot live without religion," "everyone must believe in life after death," "civilization is bound to collapse without religion," the latter being a cornerstone of the cultural heritage in which Arab youth, according to 86 to 92 percent of those interviewed, "should take an active interest."

When these attitudes in principle were tested in specific fields, the prevalence of Islamic norms of behavior (above all in interpersonal relations) was manifest. "God created woman to make man's life easier" elicited a high rate of positive response, as did statements such as, "children should be subservient to their families until they marry." Family descent, it was concurred, is the most important criterion in selecting a mate. Only with regard to career orientation and education did traditional norms not gain the upper hand, and a significant value conflict between generations appeared.

If this is the situation among the educated urban elite, that social group most exposed to modern norms, how much more so in the lower ranks of the socioeconomic scale and outside the Cairo metropolis. Egyptian psychologists indeed found that the overall level in less industrialized Arab countries, such as Jordan and Syria, is analogous to that of rural Egypt.[4]

While the ravages of modernity were quite important, it is clear that traditional Islam still held its ground in certain key areas, as one could also see in chapter 5. The revival evident since the mid-1960s, and whose goal had been to stop the erosion, could operate from a solid enough basis, deeply steeped in medieval lore and behavior. This is not to minimize the contribution of the radicals, nor to say that their holding operation did not imply departure from traditionalism in certain spheres. The pivotal departure is the passage from what one may call "passive pessimism" to "activist pessimism," analogous perhaps to differences between Old Right and New Right in turn-of-the-century Europe. "Right" is understood here in the nineteenth-century sense of the term—*les forces de résistance* (as opposed to *les forces du mouvement*).

The New Right in Islam shares the Old Right's gloomy view of a civilization in decadence, but claims that one should take the initiative and work energetically to stem the tide rather than withdraw into the primal social cells and just try to stand fast. This is the philosophical inspiration for the radicals' raising the banner of revolt against "infidel" (modernized) Muslim rulers, in a sharp departure from fourteen centuries of Sunni political theory and practice.

Liberal and leftist thinkers have in fact pointed out that quietism and submission to authority were the principal forces impeding the development of an activist revolutionary mentality in Arab lands. They argued, along with Halim Barakat, that

> religion is an important factor in encouraging [the Arab] to accept rather than confront his situation. The believer is content with his condition, is satisfied with what Allah has alloted to him, and leaves the task of changing the world to the "supreme authority." Man is "powerless in the face of his problems." . . . It has rightly been said that the Arab viewpoint on

relations between Heaven and Earth is that "Heaven has de-
creed, and Earth must obey, since the Creator has commanded
and directed, and his creatures must rejoice in their lot." Con-
tentment, acceptance, and satisfaction are precious qualities to
the believing Arab, through which he becomes a virtuous man.
These qualities are a bulwark against true revolution and they
prevent the Arab from facing up to his powerlessness and attempting to overcome it. The Arab repeats the statements of
the eleventh-century thinker al-Ghazzali that "to maintain silence in the face of Satan throughout one's life is a deed which
embodies no harm," that "the believer most beloved by the
great Allah is the poor man who is content with little."[5]

Another leftist, Nadim al-Bitar, put it even more bluntly:

Ours is a society which defines all its activities and the events
occuring around it through ritual and relationship to God. The
prevailing principle is *peccatis nostris*: if we failed, this is because our relationship with God and other occult forces did not
attain the required level of morality or because the omniscient
and omnipresent God had acted against us for an unknown
reason or because angels and satans stood in our way. Modern
culture is the exact opposite: it believes that there are objective
forces and rules in history and society and that man's freedom
is predicated upon his trying to understand them and act in
accordance. . . . Arab political action is still largely governed—
unconsciously perhaps—by this traditional mystical mentality. . . . It is no coincidence that the major manifestations of
Arab political action are idealistic, moralistic, and messianic . . . [inspired] by a typical Third World cultural pattern:
transcendental, hierarchic, fossilized, and passive.[6]

Yet it was Radical Islam which succeeded where the Left
failed—in developing an activist political philosophy, aiming to in-
duce structural change, though not a change of the type the Left
aspired to. The radicals proved that while maintaining most of the
traditional attitudes—and thus maintaining a powerful attraction for

the masses—they could introduce sufficient modifications to make Islam capable of meeting the challenge of modernity head on and in the most energetic manner. Neither spiritualism nor the traditional vision of history had to be sacrificed, although some modern versions of traditionalism (Arabism, apologetics) would, of course, be liquidated in the process.

It is here, in fact, that one can detect the crucial contribution of Maudoodi and Sayyid Qutb, a contribution based on a triad: the diagnosis—modernity as jahiliyya; the cure—rebellion (first internal, then external); the means for administering that cure—the tali'a (vanguard) of the True Believers organized as a counter-society.

This triple contribution made Islam much more resistant to modernity, in what it perceives to be the deleterious aspects of the latter (the rest, that is, the instrumental aspects, are accepted). The success of the *forces de résistance* is above all evident in the struggle against open (or deliberate) modernization, as one could judge from the complaints of the Left in the previous chapter. Yet what about the eroding effects of the "inadvertent modernization," those forces unleashed by economic development and by the electronic media? For it is this danger, present even before the rise of radical Islam, which looms large today, its evolution having been greatly accelerated over the last decade.

The Muslim radicals themselves consider this to be still a moot question. Whatever their successes in bolstering the resistance, they know that their surreptitious enemies—the subterranean forces operating at the level of popular mentalities—are strong and may even be getting stronger. This is what accounts for their mood of doom and gloom (chapter 1), a mood predicated upon a sober assessment of the world they live in rather than upon moralistic despondency. The radicals would add, of course, that their movement constitutes an autonomous factor in this ongoing struggle and that much depends upon its success to lure the conservatives, who, as we have seen (chapter 5), share most of its analysis but not necessarily its activist approach.

An important linchpin in this context is the revolutionary mystique, deeply immersed in a vision of the Hereafter that characterizes traditional Islam and inspired by an age-old concept of readiness to sacrifice one's life for the jihad, that is, in the service of the umma. The umma is bound to be saved upon earth, the self-immolating individual getting his recompense in the Afterlife. For indeed while Arab radical Islam, that "spiritual right," fits in with the "scripturalist," Shari'a-based model of Islam (suggested by Clifford Geertz),[7] it does tap—here as well—the resources of traditional Islam. Even though the new radicals, much like the MB of yore, are highly critical of the Sufis because of their superstitious accretions and their fatalism, and though they brand a mystic like Ibn al-'Arabi as heretic, they are ready to use the mystical tendencies so prevalent among the masses in order to fan the flames of enthusiasm in their ranks. This is particularly true of the indoctrination of the hardcore, those who may be called upon to sacrifice their own life for the cause.

This aggregate of a "scripturalist" (or "behaviorist") concept of jihad—which is after all enjoined and defined by Muslim law—and the mystique of sacrifice for the sake of a reward in Paradise is nothing new in Muslim history. Ibn Taymiyya himself, a legal scholar who took part in jihad campaigns, is a prime example thereof, together with his disciple Ibn Qayyim al-Jawziyya whose treatise about the Hereafter and the End of Times is very popular among the radicals.

The linking up of both concepts is done through the notion of sacrifice for the community (and not through personalist redemption, based on essence rather than upon acts). But the success of the radicals in resuscitating this alliance is proof of the extent to which they are still tributary to the tradition and its overwhelming preoccupation with the Hereafter (see chapter 5), even as they transcend it in their theory of the right for rebellion. As one reads poems on jihad written by radicals, or letters written by terrorists before going on a suicidal operation or to the scaffold, one notes the combined vision of society as jahili because it neglects the Law, with an exaltation at their own imminent martyrdom.[8] (This linkage is, by the way, even more powerful among radicals in Shi'ite Islam, where the myth of the martyrdom of Hussein has always held center stage.)

In the final analysis the success of radical Islam and its future prospects, depend not only upon what it does but also upon the mistakes and failures of its opponents; this is after all, quite common in politics, that sphere of life that the radicals call upon the Muslims to return to. As we have seen time and time again, the very failure of modernity to deliver upon its promises explains the appeal of the radical message. This is particularly true of Arab have-not countries, where, indeed, the movement is powerful. Of the countries treated in this essay, Egypt and Syria had always belonged in this category, while Lebanon joined it with the 1975/76 civil war. A measurable success of the economic system and/or the lowering of the level of expectations through deliberate acts of the powers-that-be, would no doubt tend to diminish the appeal of the New Radicalism.

One must have remarked that very little was said here about the impact (present or future) of the Iranian Revolution. This is, first, because as "scripturalists" the radicals are keenly aware of the divergences with the Shi'a, a heresy in the eyes of Sunni law (while among mystics of both persuasions interchange and overlapping abound). Second, and most important, the Sunni intellectual tradition and historical experience are very different from those of the Shi'ite lands. Thus legitimacy and the right of revolt pose a lesser and different problem for Shi'ites, who have no use for Sunni contractual theories and consider any regime not ruled by the Imam, the descendant of the Caliph 'Ali or his representative, as ipso facto illegitimate. Although a majority of Iranian theorists did not necessarily draw therefrom any insurrectionary conclusions, a minority did take this leap. Khomeini built upon this minor tradition which had always refused even de facto accommodation. Likewise, Shi'ite men of religion (the mullahs) enjoyed higher prestige than their Sunni counterparts, were less economically dependent upon the authorities and, in Iran at least, had (from the mid-nineteenth century) their own self-imposed hierarchy headed by *marja'-i taqlid* (the most illustrious of the religious doctors). When Khomeini discovered toward 1963 (about the same time as Sayyid Qutb) the need for Muslim activists to go back into the realm of politics, it was only natural for him to think that the revolution (and the postrevolutionary government) must be controlled by men of religion headed by himself as the Great Faqih of the Age and Vicar of the Hidden Imam. All these ideas were foreign for Sunnis who thus could not accept Khomeini's politico-religious authority and his claim to be the leader of a universal Islamic Revolution. It was inevitable that in Arab lands, Indo-Pakistani (that is, Sunni) ideas had always found greater echo than those coming from Iran.

This is not to say that the Iranian Revolution did not elicit sympathy and enthusiasm. Indeed, it served as an inspiring example: the unthinkable can happen, a modern Muslim tyrant may be toppled by the people.[9] The triumph of the Iranian Revolution, said the Syrian MB, "shows that victory requires patience and endurance and that no revolution can win unless it is ready to pay a heavy price in blood, human life, and financial effort." The "exemplary love of martyrdom of the Iranian people" is further extolled.[10]

Beyond this inspirational value there were certainly practical lessons to be learned from the act of seizure of power. Lt. Col. 'Abbud al-Zumur, the military commander of the Jihad group, explained in his trial that he drew from the Iranian events of late 1978 the conclusion that there was no point in trying to recruit members among the armed forces; the revolutionary strategy should rely on a popular uprising (following the physical liquidation of the political elite on the parade stand on October 6, 1981 and the resulting chaos). "Iran taught us that the army and police cannot stand against an insurgency of the masses"; internal scission in their ranks was soon expected to develop with some of them joining the revolution (either for sincere or for opportunistic reasons).[11]

Yet Khomeini's mode of government was never taken as a model and the fratricidal turn taken by the revolution as well as its other vagaries (including the hostages affair, which Arab radicals have seen as contrary to the Shari'a), created a growing disenchantment. Typical is that leader of the Lebanese Jama'a Islamiyya, who declared: "In its early days the Iranian Revolution has broken down the division of the Islamic world into Eastern and Western zones of influence and has shown that Islam can stand between the two superpowers without being committed to either. All Muslims admire this aspect of the Iranian experience. Yet later developments in Iran . . . were grist to the mill of the enemies of Islam, enabling them to distort the image of the Islamic mode of government and of the significance of the establishment of such a regime nowadays."[12]

'Adnan Sa'd al-Din, member of the Syrian Islamic Revolutionary Command, denounced the new Iranian constitution as "undeniably sectarian" (Shi'ite) and noted that "government organs attack good Muslims for rejecting the Shi'a and besmirch the [first three] Orthodox caliphs." That the Teheran regime soon allied itself with the Syrian government rendered worthless all dialogue with it.[13] His Lebanese counterpart, Sheikh Sa'id Sha'ban of Tripoli, locked in pitched battle against the Syrian army, argued that, had the Iranian Revolution said it was ready to take the Koran as program and the traditions of the Prophet as exegetic instrument, he would have supported it. "Instead of declaring Iran to be Shi'ite in doctrine they should have called for Islamic unity and the application of the Shari'a.[14] Khomeini, for Sha'ban, is consequently the enemy of the Faith, and the best way to combat him is for Muslims to close ranks and restore the Koran and Sunna as the governing mechanisms in all domains of life.

It is not surprising that although some members of the Jihad organization which assassinated Sadat did read Khomeini's *Islamic Government*, the blueprint for their revolution was Faraj's *Absent Precept*, inspired as it was by Ibn Taymiyya, a mortal enemy of Mongol infidels and of Shi'ite heretics alike. Sunni Islam, then, has, and will continue to have, to search for its own revolutionary path.

Notes

Preface

1. J. C. Vatin, "Revival in the Maghreb," in A. Dessouki, ed., *Islamic Resurgence in the Arab World* (New York, 1982), pp. 246–47.
2. Except in one case, and for a short time, see S. Ibrahim, "Islamic Militancy as a Social Movement," in Dessouki, ed., *Islamic Resurgence*. For other constraints under which this study was conducted see the same author's article in *al-Ahram al-Iqtisadi*, November 1, 1982.

Chapter 1. The Mood: Doom and Gloom

1. M. al-Bahi, *Mustaqbal al-Islam wa-l-Qarn al-Khamis 'Ashir al-Hijri* (Cairo, 1978).
2. *Al-Muslimun fi Suriya wa-l-Irhab al-Nusayri* (n.p., 1979), hereafter, *al-Irhab al-Nusayri*; S. Hawwa, *Jund Allah*, 2d ed. (Beirut, 1977); S. Hawwa, *Tarbiyatuna al-Ruhiyya* (Beirut, 1979); F. Yakan, *Madha Ya'ni Intima'i li-l-Islam* (Beirut, 1977); F. Yakan, *Al-Mas'ala al-Lubnaniyya Min Manzur Islami* (Beirut, 1979); M. Shams al-Din, *Bayna-l-Jahiliyya wa-l-Islam* (Beirut, 1975); M. Shams al-Din, *Al-Almaniyya* (Beirut, 1980), p. 8.
3. Maudoodi, *Al-Islam wa-l-Madaniyya al-Haditha* (Cairo, 1978); Khomeini, *Al-Hukuma al-Islamiyya* (Beirut ed., 1979).
4. A. Jarisha, *Shari'at Allah Hakima* (Cairo, 1977), chapter 2; *al-Da'wa*, February 1978; March, June 1979; *al-Nadhir*, August 31, 1980, p. 20; Y. al-'Azm, *Rihlat al-Daya' li-l-I'lam al-Arabi* (Jedda, 1980).

191

5. A. 'Abd al-Mu'ti, "Egyptian Broadcasting," *Dirasat 'Arabiyya*, October 1978, pp. 35–41.

6. *Al-Nadhir*, March 23, 1980, September 14, 1981; *al-Da'wa*, May 1977, p. 7; April 1977, p. 25; May 1978, p. 28; December 1978, p. 59; April 1979, p. 65; *al-I'tisam*, May 1977, pp. 7, 13; February 1978, p. 21; May 1978, p. 35; September 1978, pp. 31, 35.

7. *Al-Da'wa*, September 1976, p. 29; December 1976, pp. 28–29; January 1977, p. 11; March 1977, pp. 26–27; April 1977, pp. 26–27; *al-I'tisam*, April 1977, p. 27; March 1978, p. 20; May 1978, pp. 5, 20; February 1979, pp. 2, 31–32.

8. 'A. al-Mat'ani, *Azmat al-Tadayyun 'Inda-l-Shabab al-Mu'asir* (Cairo, 1978), pp. 108, 111, 117, 153.

9. *Al-Da'wa*, June 1979, pp. 26–27; *al-Nadhir*, October 22, 1979, p. 11.

10. *Al-Da'wa*, November 1976, pp. 12–13; March 1977, pp. 18–20; April 1977, pp. 16–17; July 1977, pp. 14–16; February 1979, pp. 28–29; *al-Nadhir*, September 28, 1980.

11. *Al-Da'wa*, March 1977, pp. 36–37; November 1978, pp. 41–43.

12. *Al-Irhab al-Nusayri*, pp. 51–55; *al-Nadhir*, September 14, 1981; M. Hilmi, *Al-Makhatir* (Cairo, 1977), pp. 28–29; 'A. Muhsin, *Al-Lugha al-'Arabiyya Bayna Shu'ubiyatayn* (Cairo, 1981).

13. *Al-Nadhir*, December 13, 1979, p. 10; *al-I'tisam*, June 1978, p. 31; June 1979, p. 21; *al-Da'wa*, August 1979, pp. 40–41.

14. *Al-Da'wa*, April 1977, pp. 4, 42.

15. *Al-Da'wa*, April 1978, pp. 44–45; June 1978, pp. 16–18, 42–43; July 1978, pp. 29, 30; December 1978, p. 23; February 1979, p. 33; *al-I'tisam*, April 1978, pp. 28–29.

16. *Al-I'tisam*, May 1978, p. 29; *al-Da'wa*, April 1977, pp. 36–38; June 1977, pp. 22–23; March 1978, pp. 42–43; June 1978, pp. 18–19; July 1978, pp. 10–11, 31; December 1978, p. 43; Jarisha, *Shari'at Allah Hakima*, chapter 6.

17. *Al-I'tisam*, September 1978, pp. 32–36; *al-Da'wa*, September 1979, pp. 28–29, 42–43.

18. I. 'Abduh, *Wad' al-Riba* (Cairo, 1977); J. J. Kishk, *Tariq al-Muslimin Ila-l-Thawra al-Sina'iyya* (Beirut, 1974).

19. *Al-Da'wa*, July 1978, pp. 30–31.

20. *Al-Nadhir*, May 2, 1981, p. 27; November 18, 1981, pp. 2–3; *al-Da'wa*, May 1978, p. 45; July 1978, p. 31.

21. M. A. Khamis, *Al-Harakat al-Nisa'iyya* (Cairo, 1978); Khamis, *Al-Mar'a bi-l-Tasawwur al-Islami* (Cairo, 1978); Y. al-Qardawi, *Al-Hulul*

al-Mustawrada (Beirut, 1977); al-Qardawi, Al-Hall al-Islami (Beirut, 1974); al-Nadhir, December 13, 1979; 'A. al-Jabari, Al-Muslima al-Misriyya (Cairo, 1979).

22. Al-Da'wa, July 1979, p. 18; May 1977, p. 30; August 1977, p. 10; January 1978, pp. 12–13; February 1978, pp. 44–45; May 1978, p. 28; February 1979, p. 57; al-I'tisam, May 1977, pp. 40–41.

23. Al-Da'wa, March 1977, p. 43; January 1978, pp. 22–24; May 1978, pp. 28, 46–47; al-I'tisam, June–July 1981, pp. 12–13.

24. Al-Nadhir, December 13, 1979, p. 9; al-I'tisam, May 1977, pp. 4–5; March 1978, p. 18; September 1978, pp. 5, 27; February 1979, p. 10; Khomeini, Al-Hukuma al-Islamiyya, pp. 72, 132, 141.

25. A. I. 'Ashur, Mutafarriqat fi-l-Din wa-l-Hayat (Cairo, 1978), pp. 67–68; Bahi, Mustaqbal al-Islam, p. 22; al-Nadhir, April 10, August 31, 1981.

26. Al-Da'wa, March 1977, pp. 13–15; June 1979, p. 20.

27. Al-Da'wa, January 1978, pp. 22–24; July 1978, pp. 6–7.

28. Al-Da'wa, December 1978, p. 8; December 1978, pp. 40–42.

29. Jarisha, Shari'at Allah, pp. 113, 120; al-I'tisam, April 1978, p. 20.

30. W. 'Uthman, Hizb Allah fi-Muwajahat Hizb al-Shaytan (Cairo, 1976).

31. Al-Nadhir, July 1982; al-Irhab al-Nusayri, pp. 40, 76; 'A. 'Uways, Al-Muslimun fi Ma'rakat al-Baqa' (Cairo, 1979), p. 133; al-I'tisam, November 1979, p. 10; February 1980, pp. 3–4; May–June 1980, pp. 16–17.

Chapter 2. Barbarity and Nationalism

1. S. al-Bahasnawi, "Behind Bars," al-'Arabi (Kuwait), June 1982, p. 45.

2. 'A. Jarisha, Fi-l-Zinzana (Cairo, 1979), p. 41; Jarisha, 'Indama Yahkumu al-Tughat (Cairo, 1975), pp. 48–49.

3. K. al-Faramawi, Yawmiyyat Sajin fi-l-Sijn al-Harbi (Cairo, 1976), pp. 170, 174; 'A. al-Sisi, Mina-l-Madhbaha Ila Sahat al-Da'wa (Cairo, 1978), p. 20; Jarisha, 'Indama, pp. 50–51.

4. Al-Ikhwan Amam al-Mashnaqa (Cairo, 1955).

5. J.Rizq, Madhabahat al-Ikhwan fi Liman Torra (Cairo, 1979), p. 47; Rizq, Madhabih al-Ikhwan fi Sujun Nasir (Cairo, 1977), p. 27. Both books are based on eyewitness reports. M. 'A. Fayid, Wa-bi-l-Haqq (Cairo,

1976), pp. 118–19; and on earlier dissensions see 'A. Khafaji, *'Indama Ghabat al-Shams* (Kuwait, 1979), pp. 276–78.

6. Trial proceedings quoted in H. Hassan, et al., *Muwajahat al-Fikr al-Mutatarrif* (Cairo, 1980), pp. 62–63.

7. Trial proceedings quoted in *al-Nadhir*, February 1, 1980.

8. *Al-Ahram*, July 12, 1974; *Akhbar al-Yawm*, May 31, 1975; Faraj's book as quoted by *al-Ahrar* (Cairo), December 14, 1981, and by M. 'Amara, *Al-Farida al-Gha'iba* (commentary) (Cairo, 1982), p. 23.

9. F. Yakan, *Mushkilat al-Da'wa wa-l-Da'iya* (Beirut, 1967), p. 250. See also 'A. Abu Khayr, *Dhikriyati Ma'a Jama'at al-Muslimin* (Kuwait, 1980), p. 112.

10. For example, T. Husayn, et al., *Ha'ula'i Humm al-Ikhwan* (Cairo, 1955); Higher Islamic Council, *Ra'y al-Din fi Ikhwan al-Shaytan* (Cairo, 1966); Faramawi, *Yawmiyyat*, pp. 161–63; 'A. Khafaji, *'Indama*, pp. 286–88; *al-Ahram*, November 12, December 24, 1982, January 21, 1983.

11. See Qutb's introduction to the second edition of Nadvi's *Madha Khasira*, and Nadvi's memoir *Mudhakkirat Sa'ih fi-l-Sharq al-Arabi* (Cairo, 1954), pp. 21–22, 26–27, 43–49, 166–67, 149, 150, 184–85.

12. *Fi Zilal al Qur'an*, commentary on sura V, 44–48. See M. 'A. Dannawi, *Kubra al-Harakat al-Islamiyya* (Cairo, 1978); M. M. Shams al-Din, *Bayma-l-Jahiliyya wa-l-Islam* (Beirut, 1975).

13. *Ma'alim fi-l-Tariq*, pp. 150–52, 30–33, 144–45, 165–66.

14. Rizq, *Madhabih*, pp. 139–41.

15. See below, chapter 4.

16. See Z. S. al-Bayyumi, *Al-Ikhwan al-Muslimun* (Cairo, 1975), pp. 157–58; I. Gershoni, "The Emergence of Pan-Nationalism in Egypt," *Asian and African Studies (AAS)* 16/1 (1982).

17. S. al-Husri, *Ara' wa-Ahadith fi-l-Wataniyya wa-l-Qawmiyya* (Beirut, 1944); Husri, *Al-'Uruba bayna Du'atiha wa-Mu'aridiha* (Beirut, 1952); Sh. Arslan, *Hadir al-'Alam al-Islami*, 3d ed. (Beirut, 1971), vol. 1, p. 342 (1st ed., 1925).

18. "The Principles of the Free World," *al-Risala*, January 5, 1953, p. 16.

19. *Ma'alim*, pp. 30–31, 194–95.

20. S. Jawhar, *Al-Mawta Yatakallamun* (Cairo, 1977), pp. 33–38, 86–87; *al-Ahram*, December 21, 1965, February 2 and April 11, 1966.

21. *Ma'alim*, pp. 196–97. The *Khayr umma* ("You are the best Nation") concept is criticized for other reasons by liberal and left-wing thinkers,

see "Arab Revisionist Historians," in my *Interpretations of Islam* (Princeton, N.J., 1984).

22. Jawhar, *Al-Mawta*, pp. 129, 135; see *al-Ahram*, February 5, 1966.

23. *Ma'a Allah* (Cairo, 1959), p. 254.

24. Ghazzali, *Haqiqat al-Qawmiyya al-'Arabiyya* (Cairo, 1961), pp. 9, 16; *Ma'a Allah*, p. 100.

25. See the 2d ed. of *Haqiqat* (1969), where the words *wa-Usturat al-Ba'th al-'Arabi* were added to the title. See the Syrian MB's publication, *al-Irhab al-Nusayri*, p. 52.

26. F. Yakan, *Risalat al-Qawmiyya al-'Arabiyya* (Beirut, 1959); M. M. al-Sawwaf, *Al-Mukhatatat al-Isti'mariyya li-Mukafahat al-Islam* (Cairo, 1979), pp. 48–50, 36.

27. 'A. Nasir al-Din, *Qadiyat al-'Arab* (Beirut, 1963) (introduction to 3d ed.), p. 19; *al-'Arabi* (January 1959), pp. 24–25; 'A. H. Kharbutli, *Muhammad wa-l-qawmiyya al-'Arabiyya* (Cairo, 1959); Kharbutli, *Al-Qawmiyya al-'Arabiyya mina-l-Fajr ila-l-Zuhr* (Cairo, 1961); Taymur quoted by Nadvi, *Al-'Arab wa-l-Islam* (Beirut, 1964), p. 11.

28. M. A. Bashmil, *Al-Qawmiyya fi Nazar al-Islam* (Beirut, 1960), pp. 40–42, 38; see 'A. Ibn al-Baz, *Naqd al-Qawmiyya al-'Arabiyya*, 2d ed. (Beirut, 1971).

29. Nadvi, *Al-'Arab wa-l-Islam*. The quotation is from p. 75, see also pp. 3, 85–86, 98–99. See his *Uridu 'an Atahaddath ila-l-Ikhwan* (Cairo, 1972); Nadvi, *Mudhakkirat*.

30. Nadvi, *Al-'Arab wa-l-Islam*, p. 15. See S. Hawwa, *Jund Allah: Thaqafa wa-Akhlaq* (Beirut, 1971), p. 205. On the impact upon youth, see the results of a 1968 survey carried out among Syrian students, which showed that most of them identified with Pan-Arabism and very few with Islam (R. H. Hinnebusch's article in Dessouki, ed., *Islamic Resurgence*, p. 155 (n); and H. Barakat, *Lebanon in Strife* [Austin, Texas, 1977]).

31. See M. al-Khatib, in *Majallat al-Azhar* 17 (1956), pp. 937–41; 18 (1957), pp. 337–44.

32. "The Umma of Monotheism Is Being Unified," *Majallat al-Azhar* 35/2 (1963), p. 4.

33. "Pan-Arab Nationalism," *al-'Arabi*, December 1958, pp. 22, 24.

34. Fayid, "Muhammad's Unity," *al-I'tisam*, August 1963.

35. *Bayna-l-Da'wa al-Qawmiyya wa-l-Rabita al-Islamiyya* (Beirut, 1967), p. 68. See Hawwa, *Jund Allah*, p. 204.

36. H. 'Ashmawi, *Al-Ikhwan wa-l-Thawra*, vol. 1 (Cairo, 1977), pp. 66–67.

37. H. 'Ashmawi, *Al-Ikhwan wa-l-Thawra*, p. 81; Jarisha, *Fi-l-Zinzana*, p. 15; Yakan, *Mushkilat*, p. 248.

38. *Bayan al-Thawra al-Islamiyya fi Suriya wa Minhajuha* (Damascus), November 9, 1980, p. 19.

39. *Bayan al-Thawra*, pp. 8–9; *al-Nadhir*, December 5, 1979.

40. Rizq, *Madhabih*, pp. 63–64, 136–37, 139; Rizq, *Madhbahat al-Ikhwan fi Liman Torra*.

41. Jarisha, *Fi-l-Zinzana*, pp. 22–23. See R. Ahmad, *Al-Bawwaba al-Sawda'* (Amman, 1974); Faramawi, *Yawmiyyat*; 'A. Sulayman, *Shuhada' wa-Qatla fi Zill al-Tughyan* (Cairo, 1979); 'U. al-Tilimsani, *Qala al-Nas . . . fi 'Abd al-Nasir* (Cairo, 1980), pp. 42–44, 103–14; Khafaji, *'Indama*, pp. 168–364.

42. Hawwa, *Jund Allah*, p. 17; Bitar as quoted below (chapter 5); Jundi quoted by E. Kedourie, *Arab Political Memoirs* (London, 1974), pp. 200–02; J. Rizq, *Al-Ikhwan al-Muslimun wa-l-Mu'amara 'Ala Suriya* (Cairo, 1980), pp. 129, 138.

43. *Al-Irhab al-Nusayri*, p. 92.

44. Yakan, *Mushkilat*, pp. 48–51, 229.

45. Hawwa, *Jund Allah*, p. 510. See al-Sisi, *Mina-l-Madhbaha*, p. 20.

46. Hawwa, *Jund Allah*, pp. 12, 59, 205. See M. 'A. Dannawi, *Al Tariq ila Hukm Islami* (Tripoli, Lebanon, 1970), pp. 163–71.

47. Hawwa, *Min Ajl Khutwa Ila-l-Amam* (Beirut, 1979), pp. 92–93.

48. *Mithaq al-Jabha al-Islamiyya fi Suriya*, January 17, 1981, pp. 4, 11; *Tishrin* (Damascus), March 31, 1982; *Bayan al-Thawra*, pp. 7, 51–53.

49. *Harakat wa-Madhahib fi Mizan al-Islam* (Beirut, 1970), pp. 104, 107. Among conservative authors writing in similar vein, see S. al-Munajjid, *A'midat al-Nakba* (Beirut, 1967).

50. Interview with *al-Shira'* (Beirut), November 21, 1983.

51. W. 'Uthman, *Asrar al-Haraka al-Tullabiyya* (Cairo, 1976), p. 21; S. Ibrahim, "The New Arab Order," *al-Siyasa al-Duwaliyya*, October 1980.

52. *Nazarat Mu'asira fi Turathina* (Muslim Students' Association, University of Cairo, 1975), p. 49; Fayid, *Wa-bi-l-Haqq*, pp. 12, 27.

53. Rizq, *Madhabih*, p. 120; Qutb's articles on Zionism and Judaism were collected in Jeddah in 1970 (*Sira'una ma'a-l-Yahud*).

54. Jarisha, *Fi-l-Zinzana*, p. 36.

55. *Al-Jihad fi Sabil Allah* (Minya University, Engineering School), pp. 9, 24–25, 40; *Nazarat*, p. 15; see W. 'Uthman, *Hizb Allah* (Cairo, 1975), p. 75.

56. 'A. 'Uways, *Al-Muslimun fi Ma'rakat al-Baqa* (Cairo, 1979), pp. 125–26. See A. al-Jindi, *Suqut al-'Almaniyya* (Beirut, 1973); M. Hilmi, *Al-Makhatir*, p. 44.

57. *Al-Irhab al-Nusayri*, p. 91; *al-Nadhir*, (clandestine organ of the Syrian MB), June 8, 1982, February 1, 1983.

Chapter 3. In Quest of Authenticity

1. Yakan, *Mushkilat*, p. 248. See MB memorandum to President Naguib (March 1953), in H. al-Hudaybi, *Al-Islam wa-l-Da'iya*, p. 180; Hawwa, *Jund Allah*, p. 74.

2. 'A. 'Awdah, *Al-Islam bayna Jahl Abna'ihi wa-Ajz Ulama'ihi* (Cairo, 1953); Z. S. al-Bayyumi, *Al-Ikhwan al-Muslimun* (Cairo, 1979), pp. 292–303; Shams al-Din, *Bayna-l-Jahiliyya*, pp. 175, 92–94; MB, *Nahwa Jil Muslim* (Cairo, 1954); Nadvi, *Mudhakkirat*, pp. 54–55.

3. *Al-Irhab al-Nusayri*, pp. 104–05, 24, 51–55; R. A. Hinnebusch, "The Islamic Movement in Syria," in Dessouki, ed., *Islamic Resurgence*; H. Batutu, "Syria's Muslim Brethren," *MERIP Reports*, November–December 1982.

4. Shams al-Din, *Bayna-l-Jahiliyya*, pp. 64, 66; Enayat, *Modern Islamic Political Thought*, pp. 118–19, 140–44; Bayyumi, *Al-Ikhwan al-Muslimun*, pp. 261–71.

5. M. A. A. Samman, introduction to Fayid, *Wa-bi-l-Haqq*, p. 19; M. A. 'Anbar, *Nahwa Thawra Islamiyya* (Cairo, 1979), p. 24; see *al-I'tisam*, November 1979, pp. 3–4; June–July 1980, pp. 12–13.

6. *Majallat al-Azhar* 23/9 (May 1952), p. 7; *Majallat al-Azhar* 32/2 (July 1960), pp. 128–32; *Al-Irhab al-Nusayri*, p. 30.

7. See *al-Nadhir*, November 5, 1981.

8. *Al-Nadhir*, December 5, 1979.

9. M. A. 'Ashur, introduction to Fayid, *Wa-bi-l-Haqq*, pp. 7–8; Fayid, *Wa-bi-l-Haqq*, pp. 193–94, 254–55; Jarisha, *Fi-l-Zinzana*, pp. 108–09. Jawhar, *Al-Mawta*, pp. 48–49; A. al-Naqqash, "Women's Liberation and the Call for Theocracy in Egypt," *Qadaya 'Arabiyya* (Beirut), July–August 1974.

10. Hawwa, *Jund Allah*, p. 68; Hawwa, *Min Ajl Khutwa*, p. 10.

11. Trial proceedings in *al-Siyasa* (Kuwait), October 27, 1979, and in Hassan, et al., *Muwajahat al-Fikr*, pp. 86–89. See *al-Liwa' al-Islami*, June 17, 1982 (debate between al-Azhar theologians and Takfir prisoners); see *Mayo* (Cairo), December 24, 1982.

12. Y. al-Qardawi, *Al-Sahwa al-Islamiyya bayna-l-Judud wa-l-Tatar-ruf* (Qatar, 1982), pp. 91–93.

13. *Minbar al-Islam*, January 1982, p. 87; *al-Ahram*, May 9, 1982. See Ibrahim's article in Dessouki, ed., *Islamic Resurgence*.

14. Information gleaned from *al-Nadhir*, 1979–83.

15. Jawhar, *Al-Mawta*, p. 137; see Rizq, *Madhbahat al-Ikhwan*, p. 17; Shams al-Din, *Bayna-l-Jahiliyya*, pp. 171–72; Abu Khayr, *Dhikri-yati*, pp. 48, 123; al-Bahi, *Mustaqbal al-Islam*; Hawwa, *Jund Allah*, p. 486; *Al-Rajul al-Sanam: Kemal Ataturk* (Beirut, 1977).

16. See his *Al-'Adala al-Ijtima'iyya fi-l-Islam* (Cairo, 1949).

17. 'A. Khafaji, *Hiwar ma'a-l-Shuyu'iyyin fi Aqbiyat al-Sujun* (Ku-wait, 1979).

18. See his *Ishtirakiyat al-Islam* (Damascus, 1958).

19. *Suriya mina-l-Dakhil* (MB, clandestine), February 1980; *al-Nad-hir*, February 23, April 7, October 22, 1980; September 14, November 18, 1981; February 4, June 8, 1982; *Bayan al-Thawra*, p. 7; *al-Da'wa* (Cairo), October 1980.

20. *Al-Nadhir*, March 23, August 3, 1980; August 1, 1981; *al-Fursan* (Damascus), February 12, 1980.

21. *Al-Nadhir*, March 3, 1980; Hawwa, *Min Ajl Khutwa*, pp. 12–13, 141, 211.

22. Yakan, *Mushkilat*, p. 228; *Al-Irhab al-Nusayri*, p. 72; Rizq, *Madhbahat al-Ikhwan*, p. 82; Jarisha, *'Indama*, p. 11; Jarisha, *Fi-l-Zin-zana*, pp. 84, 103; *al-Ahram*, August 30, 1965. On Iraq see al-Sawwaf, *Mukhatatat*, p. 20.

23. S. 'Ashmawi, in *al-Nadhir* (Cairo), July 20, 1946; H. Dawh, *Safahat Min Jihad al-Shabab* (Cairo, 1977), p. 25; W. 'Uthman, *Asrar*.

24. 'A. J. al-Sahhar, *Zikriyat Sinima'iyya* (Cairo, 1975); *Safir Amrika bi-l-Alwan al-Tabi'iyya* (Cairo, 1957); N. Hasan, *Al-Tilifizyun wa-Inhira-fat al-Shabab* (Cairo, 1975); A. Sa'd, *Al-Sinima wa-l-Shabab* (Cairo, 1971). See H. Enayat, *Modern Islamic Political Thought*, p. 91.

25. See Shams al-Din, *al-'Almaniyya*, p. 119; 'A. 'Ulwan, *Huum al-Islam fi-Wasa'il al-I'lam* (Hama, 1978), pp. 14–30; M. 'U. al-Dib, *Matariq al-Haqq* (Cairo, 1976), pp. 99–102. Qutb was preoccupied with the danger of the media already before 1954 (*Dirasat Islamiyya*, ed. Dar al-Shuruq, p. 141).

26. *Al-Ahram*, September 8, 1965; Jawhar, *Al-Mawta*, p. 76.

27. Fayid, *Wa-bi-l-Haqq*, p. 122; Jarisha, *Fi-l-Zinzana*, pp. 83–84.

28. Hawwa, *Jund Allah*, p. 47; see Abu Khayr, *Dhikriyati*, pp. 47, 50.

29. *Mithaq al-Jabha*, p. 10; *Bayan al-Thawra*, p. 45; *al-Nadhir*, August 11, 1980.

30. 'A. Faraj quoted in *al-Ahrar*, December 14, 1981.

31. For example, *Mayo*, February 7, 1983; *Sabah al-Khayr*, February 3, 1982; *al-Liwa' al-Islami*, June 10, 1982.

32. *Al-'Almaniyya*, pp. 119–20.

33. M. Qutb, *Hal Nahnu Muslimun*, 2d ed. (Beirut, 1968); Sh. Arslan, *Limadha Ta'khkhara al-Muslimun wa-Taqaddama Ghayruhum* (Cairo, 1939); see Nadvi, *Madha Khasira al-'Alam*.

34. M. al-Bahi, *Mustaqbal al-Islam*; A. 'Awdah, *Al-Islam wa-Awda'una al-Siyasiyya* (Cairo, 1951).

35. Hawwa, *Al-Islam*, vol. 2 (Beirut, 1970), p. 5.

36. Qutb, *Mustaqbal Hadha al-Din*; Hawwa, *Jund Allah*, p. 508; Yakan, *Mushkilat*, p. 51.

37. *Ma'alim* p. 58.

38. 'A. 'Uways, *Ma'rakat al-Baqa'*, p. 99; T. al-Tibb, *Al-Hall al-Islami* (Cairo, 1979), p. 33.

39. *Ma'alim*, pp. 214–15; see his *Ma'rakat al-Islam wa-l-Ra'smaliyya* (Cairo, 1951), pp. 25–26; *Fi-l-Ta'rikh* (Jeddah, 1967), p. 16. *Nahwa Mujtama' Islami* (Cairo), p. 9. See Qutb's "letters from America" in *al-Risala* (November, December 1951).

40. Shams al-Din, *Bayna-l-Jahiliyya*, pp. 301–05; Shams al-Din, *Al-'Almaniyya*, p. 49; Hawwa, *Jund Allah*, p. 68; H. M. al-Qa'ud, *Hurras al-Da'wa* (Cairo, 1979); Abu Khayr, *Dhikriyati*, p. 106.

41. *Al-Ahram*, December 21, 1965; April 10, 1966; S. Qutb, *Fiqh al-Da'wa* (Beirut, 1970); *Al-Siyasa* (Kuwait), October 22–25, 1979. See A. Jarisha, *Din wa-Dawla* (Cairo, 1979), p. 73; *al-Ahram*, December 12, 1982.

42. *Nazarat*, pp. 1–2, 7.

43. For example, Hawwa, *Jund Allah*. M. 'Ashur, *Abu Bakr* (Cairo, 1974); 'Ashur, *'Uthman* (Cairo, 1978).

44. *Nazarat*, p. 33; *Al-Jihad fi Sabil Allah*, p. 65.

45. *Al-Safahat al-Akhira min Ta'rikhina* (Cairo, 1978).

46. Bayyumi, *Al-Ikhwan al-Muslimun*, pp. 186–88, 214–18; Fayid, *Wa-bi-l-Haqq*, pp. 97–98; Maudoodi, *The Islamic Law and Constitution* (Lahore, 1977), pp. 211–12; F. 'Abd al-Sabbur, in *Al-Ikhwan al-Muslimun*, January 15, 1946.

47. *Tafsir Surat al-Shura* (Beirut, 1973), pp. 83–85; *Ma'alim*, p. 3. The latter is also reproduced verbatim in the Minya Muslim Students' *Al-*

Jihad fi Sabil Allah, p. 27. The letter to Naguib is in *al-Akhbar*, August 8, 1952.

48. Hawwa, *Jund Allah*, pp. 12–13.

49. Dannawi, *Al-Tariq ila Hukm Islami*, pp. 54–55; *al-Nadhir*, September 14, 1981.

50. 'Anbar, *Thawra Islamiyya*, p. 49; *al-I'tisam*, March–April 1980; *al-Nadhir*, March 3, 1981.

51. W. 'Uthman, *Hizb Allah fi-Muwajahat Hizb al-Shaytan*, p. 55; see Z. H. Faruki, *The Myth of Democracy* (Lahore, 1973).

52. *Mayo* (Cairo), June 7, 14, 21, 1982; see 'Anbar, *Thawra Islamiyya*, p. 48; *al-Nur* (Cairo), September 28, 1983.

53. Enayat, *Modern Islamic Political Thought*, pp. 151–53.

54. *Ma'alim*, pp. 32–33; see Dannawi, *Al-Tariq ila Hukm Islami*, pp. 176–77.

55. A. H. al-Zayyat's article in *al-Risala* (Cairo), March 4, 1965. See S. al-Munajjid, *Al-Tadlil al-Ishtiraqi* (Beirut, 1966), p. 46; Dannawi, *Al-Tariq ila Hukm Islami*.

56. Bashmil, *Ukdhubat al-Istishraqiyya al-'Arabiyya* (Beirut, 1962); S. al-Munajjid, *Balshafat al-Islam* (Beirut, 1966).

57. *Al-Nadhir*, April 7, 1980; *Mithaq al-Jabha*, p. 13; *Bayan al-Thawra*, pp. 22–23.

58. Hawwa, *Jund Allah*, p. 12; *Al-Irhab al-Nusayri*, pp. 52, 72; Jarisha, *'Indama*, pp. 11, 84, 103; see Sheikh Sha'rawi, *Fatawa*, vol. 1 (Cairo, 1981), p. 87.

59. Shabab Muhammad, "The Shari'a and the Non-Muslims," *Rasa'il al-Da'wa*, 1978; *al-Da'wa*, August 1981, pp. 28–29; Hawwa, *Jund Allah*, pp. 16, 430–31; *al-I'tisam*, May–June 1980, pp. 4–5, 8–9; see Y. al-Qardawi, *Ghayr al-Muslimun fi-l-Mujtama' al-Islami* (Cairo, 1977).

60. Yakan, *Harakat*, pp. 71–73; Nadvi, *Al-Arab wa-l-Islam*, pp. 14–18; Hawwa, *Jund Allah*, p. 205; Abu Khayr, *Dhikriyati*, p. 106; 'Anbar, *Thawra Islamiyya*, p. 20; 'Uways, *Ma'rakat al-Baqa'*, pp. 113–23; *al-I'tisam*, May–June 1980, p. 30.

61. Khalfallah's article in *al-Arabi*, December 1958; Bashmil, *Ukdhubat*, pp. 126–27; 'Anbar, *Thawra Islamiyya*; *al-Ahram*, September 8, 1981.

62. See, for example, M. 'I. I. al-Tahtawi, *Al-Nasraniyya wa-l-Islam* (Cairo, 1977).

63. *Mithaq al-Jabha*, p. 13; *Bayan al-Thawra*, pp. 18–19; *al-Nadhir*, August 11, 1980; Sa'd al-Din interview, *al-Nadhir*, September 14, 1981; Hawwa, *Min Ajl Khutwa*, pp. 6–7, 27–28.

64. Yakan, *Al-Masa'la al-Lubnaniyya min Manzur Islami* (Beirut,

1979); *al-Shira'*, November 21, 1983 (interview with Sha'ban); Mujahidun leaflet (March 1981), private collection. See H. M. al-Qa'ud, *Al-Harb al-Salibiyya al-'Ashira* (Cairo, 1981); Yakan *Abjadiyat al-'Amal al-Islami* (Beirut, 1981).

65. I have borrowed this term from J. Herf, "Reactionary Modernism," *Theory and Society* 10 (1981), pp. 805–43.

66. See, for instance, W. 'Uthman (an engineer), *Hizb Allah*, p. 76; *al-I'tisam*, December 1979, pp. 30–31. There are also conservatives who manipulate the media such as Sheikh Sha'rawi (television) and Sheikh Kishk (cassettes). See chapter 5.

67. *Al-'Almaniyya*, p. 49; *Al-Hall al-Islami*.

68. F. Zakariya, *'Ara' Naqdiyya fi-l-Fikr wa-l-Thaqafa* (Cairo, 1975); H. Hanafi, *Qadaya Mu'asira*, vol. 1 (Cairo, 1977); S. J. al-'Azm, *Al-Istishraq wa-l-Istishraq Ma'kusan* (Beirut, 1981).

69. See the account of 'A. Babti, political leader of the Jama'a in *al-Shira'*, December 5, 1983.

Chapter 4. The Sunni Revolution

1. In Iran only his earlier works were translated: *Al-'Adala* and *Mashahid al-Qiyama* as well as parts of his Koranic commentary.

2. Hawwa, *Jund Allah*, pp. 41–46; Yakan, *Mushkilat*, pp. 229, 251; Yakan, *Nahwa Haraka Islamiyya 'Alamiyya* (Beirut, 1971); Abu Khayr, *Dhikriyati*, p. 29; 'Amara, *Al-Farida al-Gha'iba* (Cairo, 1982), pp. 12–13.

3. Yakan, *Mushkilat*, pp. 251–53; 'Anbar, *Thawra Islamiyya*, pp. 21–22.

4. Abu Khayr, *Dhikriyati*, pp. 81, 91–94; S. Qutb, however, expressed deep respect for al-Banna (Jawhar, *Al-Mawta*, p. 138) and so do most other radicals, for instance, Yakan, *Mushkilat*, pp. 46–49; Dannawi, *Kubra Harakat*.

5. A. Kriegel, *The French Communists: Profile of a People* (Chicago, 1972), p. xxxi. See Dannawi, *Kubra Harakat*, pp. 266–67.

6. *Al-Ahram*, February 4, 5, 1966; Jawhar, *Al-Mawta*, p. 138; Abu Khayr, *Dhikriyati*, pp. 9–12.

7. Dannawi, *Al-Tariq ila Hukm Islami*, pp. 80–81 (following Qutb's *Ma'alim*, p. 20); *al-Nadhir*, April 7, 1980; *Mithaq al-Jabha*, p. 4.

8. Bahasnawi in *al-'Arabi*, January 1982, p. 46; H. Hasan, et al., *Muwajahat al-Fikr*, p. 58; *Akhbar al-Yawm*, May 31, 1975; 'Amara, *Al-Farida al-Gha'iba*, pp. 24–25.

9. For example, *Mayo*, September 7, November 16, 1981; *al-Gum-*

huriyya, November 20, 1981; *al-Ahram*, February 11, 1983; *al-Musawwar*, February 5, July 30, 1982; *Akhar Sa'a*, November 11, 18, 1981; Abu Khayr, *Dhikriyati*, p. 137.

10. Abu Khayr, *Dhikriyati*, p. 57.

11. Nadvi, *Mudhakkirat*, pp. 184–85. See Hawwa, *Min Ajl Khutwa*, p. 136.

12. Abu Khayr, *Dhikriyati*, pp. 29, 104, 123, 128–29; *Akhbar al-Yawm*, May 31, 1975; 'Amara, *Al-Farida al-Gha'iba*, p. 20; Hassan, et al., *Muwajahat al-Fikr*, pp. 41–88.

13. See his critique of the MB and of Qutb for precipitating into violent action in *Western Civilization and Islam* (Lucknow, 1969), pp. 110–13.

14. Events reconstructed by Jawhar, *Al-Mawta*, and Rizq, *Madhabih*. See *al-Ahram*, September 7, 1965 through April 11, 1966; A. Imam, *'Abd al-Nasir wa-l-Ikhwan* (Cairo, 1981).

15. Ibn 'Asakir, *Ta'rikh Madinat Dimashq* (Damascus, 1977), p. 182; Abu Yusuf, *Kitab al-Kharaj*, trans. Ben Shemesh (London, 1969), p. 43; Ibn Hanbal, *Kitab al-Sunna* (Cairo, n.d.), p. 35. See my "Ulama and Power," in *Interpretations of Islam*.

16. Jawhar, *Al-Mawta*, pp. 139–40.

17. *Al-Nadhir*, August 8, 1980.

18. Ibn Taymiyya, *Fatawa* (Cairo, 1909), vol. 4, pp. 198, 280–81. See Hassan, et al., *Muwajahat al-Fikr*, pp. 99–102.

19. *Al-Siyasa al-Shar'iyya*, English trans. (Beirut, 1966), p. 145.

20. 'A. al-Nafisi, *'Indama Yahkumu-l-Islam* (London, 1981), p. 144; see 'Amara, *Al-Farida al-Gha'iba*, p. 53.

21. S. Hawwa, *Jawla fi-l-Fiqhayn al-Kabir wa-l-Akbar* (Amman, 1980), p. 10.

22. *Ma'alim*, pp. 150–52, 30–33, 165–66.

23. For example, Shams al-Din, *Bayna-l-Jahiliyya wa-l-Islam*, p. 249; 'Uthman, *Hizb Allah*, p. 55.

24. *Mayo*, April 6, 1981.

25. *Al-Ahram*, April 11, 1966.

26. Excerpts of *The Absent Precept* (*al-Farida al-Gha'iba*) in *al-Ahrar* (Cairo), December 14, 1981; *al-Liwa' al-Islami* (Cairo), February 25, March 4, 11, 18, 1982; *al-Ahram*, March 25, 1982. Text with commentary in 'Amara, *Al-Farida al-Gha'iba*. On the assassins, see *Mayo*, November 2, 1981; *al-Ahram*, November 20, 1981; *al-Musawwar*, November 27, 1981.

27. *Al-Ahram*, September 8, 1981, February 4, 1983; *Mayo*, September 21, 1981; *Dirasat fi-l-Islam* 243 (September 1981), p. 74.

28. Hawwa, *Jund Allah*, p. 479; *al-Irhab al-Nusayri*, pp. 32, 37, 50.

29. *Al-Nadhir*, December 13, 1979, February 12, 1981; *Bayan al-Thawra al-Islamiyya fi Suriya wa-Minhajuha* (Damascus), November 9, 1980, pp. 1–2.

30. Hawwa, *Min Ajl Khutwa*, pp. 30, 34, 135, 170.

31. *Al-Nadhir*, February 1, 1980.

32. Rizq, *Al-Ikhwan al-Muslimun wa-l-Mu'amara 'Ala Suriya*, pp. 25–28, 87–97; 'A. al-Sayyid, *Al-Nusayriyya aw al-'Alawiyyun* (Cairo, 1980); 'A. al-Husayni, *Al-Judhur al-Ta'rikhiyya li-l-Nusayriyya* (Cairo, 1980).

33. *Al-Ahram*, April 11, 1966; Supreme Council for Islamic Affairs, *Ra'y al-Din fi Ikhwan al-Shaytan* (Cairo, 1966); Abu Khayr, *Dhikriyati*, p. 66; M. H. al-Dhahabi, *Al-Ittijahat al-Munharifa fi Tafsir al-Qur'an* (Cairo, 1976), p. 63 (written in 1966); Egyptian Ministry of Waqfs, *Dirasat Fi-l-Islam* 243 (September 1981), pp. 82–83; 'A. Imam, *Al-Ikhwan wa-'Abd al-Nasir* (Cairo, 1981), p. 118.

34. *Akhar Sa'a*, September 23, 1981; *al-Ahram*, February 18, June 25, 1983; 'Amara, *Al-Farida al-Gha'iba*, p. 50; *al-Musawwar*, June 4, 1982; *Mushkilat al-Da'wa wa-l-Du'at* (Cairo, 1977); *al-Liwa' al-Islami*, April 22, June 10, July 29, 1982; see M. H. al-Dhahabi, *Al-Ittijahat*; *Mayo*, February 7, 1983. On the leftist interpretation of the Kharijites see my "Arab Revisionist Historians," in *Interpretations of Islam*.

35. Bayyumi, *Al-Ikhwan al-Muslimun*, pp. 127, 156; Hudaybi, *Al-Islam wa-l-Da'iya*, pp. 197–99; Hudaybi, *Dusturuna* (Cairo, 1978); see *al-Ahram*, September 7, 1965.

36. "Seven questions inside the Torra Prison," in his *Al-Islam wa-l-Da'iya*, pp. 183–87; see his *Du'at La Qudat* (Cairo, 1969).

37. *Al-Islam Da'wa wa-Laysa Thawra* (Cairo, 1979); *Al-Qur'an fi Muwajahat al-Madiyya* (Cairo, 1978). See 'U. Tilimsani, in *al-Hilal*, April 1982; *al-Siyasa* (Kuwait), March 16, 1982; *al-Musawwar*, February 9, 1982; M. A. Ahmad, *Hayat al-'Aqida wa-Rijaliha* (Cairo, 1980).

38. See Qardawi's article in *al-Muslim al-Mu'asir* (Beirut), April 1977; Sisi, *Mina-l-Madhbaha*; Y. 'Azm, *Al-Shahid Sayyid Qutb* (Beirut, 1980); A. A. 'Abd al-Ghaffar, *Al-Jahiliyya Qadiman wa-Hadithan* (Kuwait, 1980).

39. M. Qutb's letters to *al-Shihab* (Beirut), September 1, 1975, and *al-Mujtama'* (Kuwait), October 21, 1975.

40. *Al-Ahram*, November 12, 1982; *al-Liwa' al-Islami*, March 25, 1982.

41. M. Hilmi, *Al-Usul al-Ta'rikhiyya li-Mas'alat Takfir al-Muslim*.

42. Sisi, *Mina-l-Madhbaha*, pp. 53, 57; see Nadvi, *Western Civilization and Islam*, p. 110.

43. H. al-Banna, *Risalat al-Mu'tamar al-Khamis* (Cairo, 1938); Bayyumi, *Al-Ikhwan al-Muslimun*, p. 127.

44. Yakan, *Mushkilat*, pp. 236–37; see interview of Tahrir party leader with *al-Shira'*, December 22, 1983.

45. Yakan, *Mushkilat*, p. 234; Dannawi, *Al-Tariq ila Hukm Islami*, pp. 234–35.

46. Hawwa, *Min Ajl Khutwa*.

47. Hawwa, *Jund Allah*, pp. 446–47, 478, 484; Yakan, *Mushkilat*, p. 232.

48. Yakan *Abjadiyat* (Beirut, 1981), pp. 48, 97.

49. *Al-Nur* (Cairo), June 1, 8, 15, 1983. Abu Isma'il was reelected to parliament, on the Wafd slate, in May 1984.

50. *Al-Ra'id*, June 28, August 3, November 17, 1979.

51. *Nazarat*, pp. 54, 58; *Al-Jihad fi Sabil Allah*, p. 32. See Sheikh Tantawi in *Al-Irhab al-Nusayri*, p. 106; A. Jarisha, *Shari'at Allah* (Cairo, 1977), pp. 113, 120; Hawwa, *Jund Allah*, pp. 451–53; Ibrahim in Dessouki, ed., *Islamic Resurgence*, p. 127.

52. K. Mannheim, *Essays on the Sociology of Knowledge*, ed. P. Kecskemeti (London, 1952), pp. 304–12; N. Ryder, "The Cohort as a Concept of Social Change," *American Sociological Review* 30 (1965), pp. 843–61.

·53. *Al-Ahram*, February 4, 1966. In a sample of MB prisoners in 1957 one finds only 40 percent students and professionals (Rizq, *Madhbahat*, p. 168).

54. *Al-Ahram*, May 9, 1982; S. Ibrahim's article in Dessouki, ed., *Islamic Resurgence*, pp. 117–27.

55. *Al-Nadhir*, 1979–83, passim.

56. Hassan, *Muwajahat al-Fikr*, p. 51.

57. Khafaji, *'Indama Ghabat al-Shams*, p. 278.

58. Jarisha, *'Indama*, pp. 81, 62.

59. Sisi, *Mina-l-Madhbaha*, p. 20.

60. *Al-Irhab al-Nusayri*, pp. 92–93, 75, 51–55; *al-Nadhir*, July 1982, December 1982, January 1983; *Fi Sujun al-Ba'th al-Nusayri* (n.p., 1980).

61. M. al-Dib, *Matariq al-Haqq* (Cairo, 1976), pp. 99–101; see Abu Khayr, *Dhikriyati*, pp. 47, 50.

62. *Akhbar al-Yawm*, May 31, 1975; *al-Musawwar*, September 21, 1981; Shabab Muhammad, *Jund al-Da'wa* (Cairo, 1979), chapter 7.

63. Students' petitions to Sadat to apply the Shari'a in Jarisha, *Din wa-Dawla*, pp. 88–92; on the neo-Pharaonism see 'Uways, *Ma'rakat al-Baqa'*, p. 117; Qardawi in *al-Da'wa*, October 1979.

64. *Al-Nadhir*, January 8, February 27, May 8, 1982.

65. "Takfir without Proof," *Dirasat fi-l-Islam* 243 (September 1981), pp. 77, 85; Hawwa, *Jund Allah*, p. 76.

66. Abu Khayr, *Dhikriyati*, pp. 38–39.

67. *Al-Siyasa* (Kuwait), October 26, 1979; *Mayo*, November 18, 1981; *Akhar Sa'a*, November 11, 1981; Dannawi, *Kubra al-Harakat al-Isla-miyya*, ed. Muslim Students' Association (Cairo, 1978); M. 'A. al-Sam-man, *Al-Islam wa-Makanat al-Shari'a*, ed. Muslim Students' Association (Cairo, 1977).

68. *Al-Gumhuriyya*, July 2, 1975; *Akhar Sa'a*, September 23, 1981; *al-Musawwar*, October 30, 1981.

69. B. Yasin, "Marriage Crisis in Syria," *Dirasat Arabiyya* (Beirut), August 1978; *Mithaq al-Jabha*, p. 10; *Bayan al-Thawra*, p. 47; *al-Nadhir*, March 3, 1980. See *al-Ahali* (in Egypt), August 11, 1982.

70. *Al-Ahrar* (Cairo), December 14, 1981; 'Amara, *Al-Farida al-Gha'iba*, pp. 15–18.

Chapter 5. The Conservative Periphery

1. Ratio of religious books computed on the basis of the annual reports of *Nashrat al-Ida' li-l-Matbu'at* (Cairo: Dar al-Kutub). See H. Hamon and P. Rothman, *Les Intellocrates* (Paris, 1981), p. 76. On *al-Liwa'* circulation: *al-Gumhuriyya*, June 3, 1982.

2. S. Ibrahim, "The New Arab Social Order," *al-Siyasa al-Duwa-liyya*, October 1980.

3. *Al-Ahram*, May 5, 1968.

4. *Al-Ahram*, November 28, 1973.

5. *Al-Liwa'*, March 7, April 6, August 5, 1982, November 17, 1983; Sha'rawi, *Fatawa* (Cairo, 1981), vol. 1, p. 97; vol. 2, p. 12; vol. 3, p. 47; vol. 4, pp. 40, 84; vol. 6, pp. 16–17; A. Zayn, *Hiwar ma'a-l-Sheikh al-Sha'rawi* (Cairo, 1977), pp. 58–71; *al-Nur*, September 21, 1983.

6. *Al-Liwa'*, January 29, June 3, July 22, August 26, 1982, Decem-ber 12, 1983; Sha'rawi, *Fatawa*, vol. 1, pp. 54, 59; vol. 6, pp. 10–11. See S. 'Uways, *Al-Khulud fi-l-Turath al-Sha'bi al-Misri* (Cairo, 1966).

7. *Al-Liwa'*, April 15, 1982, February 2, 1983; see *al-Liwa'*, No-

vember 11, 1982; Sha'rawi, *Fatawa*, vol. 4, p. 55; *Ruz al-Yusuf*, April 26, 1982; *al-Nur*, August 3, 1983; see Sheikh Kishk, *Tariq al-Najat* (Cairo, 1979), pp. 66–75 (sermons, also available on tape cassettes).

8. *Al-Liwa'*, August 12, 1982; Sha'rawi, *Fatawa*, vol. 1, p. 91; vol. 2, p. 72; vol. 3, p. 66. See M. Hilmi, *Al-Makhatir*, pp. 108–10.

9. *Al-Nur*, December 1, 1982, October 12, 1983; *al-Liwa'*, July 13, 1981, March 4, April 15, May 6, 1982; Sha'rawi, *Fatawa*, vol. 6, p. 31.

10. *Al-Liwa'*, February 4, March 11, 25, April 1, July 8, 1982; *al-Nur*, June 1, August 10, 1983.

11. *Al-Nur*, October 19, 1983; *al-Gumhuriyya*, September 10, 1983; see H. Khalafallah, "Unofficial Tape Cassette Culture in the Middle East," *Index* 2/5 (1982), pp. 10–12.

12. Sha'rawi, *Fatawa*, vol. 1, p. 65; on the polls see the one published by *Al-Idha'a wa-l-Tilifizyun*, May 15, 1982 (showing a majority of respondents demanding more religious programs).

13. *Al-Liwa'*, February 25, 1982. For the more optimistic view see the June 3, August 23, 1982 issues.

14. Sha'rawi, *Fatawa*, vol. 3, p. 38; vol. 4, pp. 33, 36; *al-Liwa'*, February 18, April 1, 1982; February 24, May 19, 1983.

15. *Al-Liwa'*, March 18, April 8, May 6, June 17, 1982; see *al-Siyasa* (Kuwait), October 26, 1979.

16. *Al-Liwa'*, March 25, June 24, 1982. Sha'rawi, who is a former minister of waqfs, is, however, highly critical of the ulama; see his *Qadaya al-Islam* (Cairo, 1980). For similar views on the Left see H. Hanafi, "What Is the Islamic Left?" *Al-Yasar al-Islami*, January 1981, pp. 30–32.

17. *Al-Liwa'*, March 18, April 29, May 20, September 2, October 28, 1982. See the special issue of *Majallat al-Azhar*, July 1982; Sha'rawi, *Fatawa*, vol. 1, pp. 94, 104.

18. *Al-Liwa'*, August 17, 1981, July 29, 1982; Sha'rawi, *Fatawa*, vol. 1, pp. 125–26; *Mayo*, June 28, 1982.

19. *Al-Liwa'*, February 25, March 4, July 8, August 26, October 7, 1982; *al-Nur*, June 6, October 5, 1983.

20. *Al-I'tisam*, November 1979, p. 5; *al-Liwa'*, September 21, 1981; April 8, May 27, August 26, 1982; June 23, 1983; *al-Nur*, July 20, September 28, October 19, 1983; *al-Siyasi*, May 11, 1983; *Aktubar*, July 17, 1983.

21. Sha'rawi, *Fatawa*, vol. 2, p. 45; *al-Liwa'*, May 6, July 15, November 18, 1982; *al-Nur*, December 7, 1983; *Sabah al-Khayr*, February 3, 1983.

22. *Al-Liwa'*, March 4, 11, April 1, 29, July 8, 22, 1982; Sha'rawi,

Fatawa, vol. 1, pp. 21, 35–36; vol. 3, pp. 32, 38; *al-Nur*, November 17, 1983.

23. *Al-Nur*, August 3, December 1, 1983.

24. *Al-Liwa'*, January 29, February 18, 25, June 7, August 18; *al-Nur*, December 8, 1982; August 3, 1983; Sha'rawi, *Fatawa*, vol. 1, pp. 18–20; vol. 2, pp. 17, 21; vol. 3, pp. 26–30. See Sheikh Saqr, *Al-Hijab wa-'Amal al-Mar'a* (Cairo: Ministry of Religions, 1982); *Al-I'tisam*, November 1979, p. 5.

25. *Al-Nur*, May 4, 1983.

26. *Mayo*, July 27, 1982; *al-Liwa'*, February 18, April 22, June 3, August 5, 1982; Sha'rawi, *Fatawa*, vol. 2, p. 34; Sha'rawi, *Al-Islam wa-Harakat al-Hayat* (Cairo, 1980), pp. 55–57, 81–84 (which also comprises a nonapologetic view of jihad). See N. 'Abd al-Fattah, "Islam and the Religious Minority in Egypt," *al-Mustaqbal al-'Arabi*, August 1981.

27. *Al-Gumhuriyya*, March 7, 1982; *al-Liwa'*, September 14, November 9, 1981; March 25, April 22, July 11, November 11, 1982; *al-Nur*, June 1, 1983; October 12, 1983 (editorial). The conservatives are joined on this point by the Muslim Left; see M. 'Amara, "Islam and the Sword," *al-'Arabi* (Kuwait), June 1982.

28. *Mayo*, June 7, 1982 and his *Fatawa*, vol. 1, pp. 125–26.

29. *Al-Ahram*, October 18, November 18, 1981. But see his reservations on the Takfir (*Fatawa*, vol. 2, pp. 27–28).

Chapter 6. Assessment by the Left

1. See "Arab Revisionist Historians," in my *Interpretations of Islam*.

2. See S. J. al-'Azm, *Al-Naqd al-Dhati Ba'da-l-Hazima* (Beirut, 1968); S. J. al-'Azm, *Naqd al-Fikr al-Dini* (Beirut, 1969).

3. M. Masmuli, "Sowing to the Wind," *al-Fikr* (Tunis), December 1978, pp. 88–89; A. Iskandar, *Sira' al-Yamin wa-l-Yasar* (Beirut, 1977), pp. 5–6, 89–90.

4. *Tahawwulat*, no. 1 (summer 1982), pp. 3–4; see *al-Adab*, special issue, January–March 1983.

5. Adonis, *Al-Nahar al-'Arabi wa-l-Duwali* (hereafter NAD), June 16, 1980; on Gh. Shukri compare his articles in *Dirasat 'Arabiyya* (hereafter DA), September 1979 and *al-Tadamun*, December 1979.

6. *Al-Ahali*, September 3, 1983.

7. M. 'Abd-al-Fadil, "The Arab World in the Seventies," *al-Mus-taqbal al-'Arabi* (hereafter MA), May 1979, p. 165; see interview with M. Wahbah, *Qadaya 'Arabiyya* (hereafter QA), June–September 1978;

S. Yasin, "The Arab Intellectual," *QA*, February 1980. See B. al-Bakr's inquiry in *al-Hayat al-Jadida* (Beirut), no. 3 (1981), p. 152.

8. F. Zakariya, "The Cultural Crisis," *al-'Arabi*, February 1980; F. A. Hadi, "The False Paradise," *Mawaqif* (winter 1980); H. Barakat, *Lebanon in Strife*, p. 199. See *MA* symposium, May 1983.

9. Adonis, "From Military Intellectual to Military Faqih," *NAD*, July 7, 1980; S. al-Bitar, symposium of *al-Ihya al-'Arabi*, November 17, 1979; H. Hanafi, "Arab National Thought in the Balance," *QA*, April 1978; Hanafi, *Dirasat Islamiyya* (Beirut, 1982), esp. pp. 299–346.

10. Zurayq in *MA* symposium, March 1980, p. 154; Mahmud quoted in *al-Yasar al-'Arabi* (hereafter *YA*), July 1977, p. 30.

11. A. al-Shaykh, "The Rationality Campaign," *DA*, October 1980; S. 'Isa, "Taha Husayn and the Ordeal of Reason in Egypt," *al-Katib*, January 1974; *YA*, April 1977, p. 27; interview with Zakariya, *YA*, June 1980; Kh. Mansur, "Apologetic Thought and Cultural Decline," *YA*, September 1977; R. al-Sa'id, "The Tragedy of Arab Thought," *DA*, January 1981.

12. Interview in *QA*, July–September 1978.

13. S. J. al-'Azm, *Al-Naqd al-Dhati*; S. J. al-'Azm, *Naqd al-Fikr al-Dini*; M. Harbi, *Le FLN: Mirage et realité* (Paris, 1980).

14. G. Corm, *Contribution à l'étude des sociétés multi-confessionnelles* (Paris, 1971), pp. 287, 285, 249 (defended as Ph.D. thesis, 1969; published in Arabic, Beirut, 1979); G. Corm, "Myth and Reality," *Mawaqif*, September–October 1970; G. Corm, "The Lebanese Civil War in Perspective," *al-Bahith*, April–June 1978; B. Ghaylun, *Al-Mas'ala al-Ta'ifiyya* (Beirut, 1979).

15. W. Khalidi, *Conflict and Violence in Lebanon* (Cambridge, Mass., 1979); S. Nasr, "Rapports entre confessions et societé Libanaise," in J. Beauberot, *Palestine et Liban* (Paris, 1977); J. Toubi, "Social Dynamics in War-Torn Lebanon," *The Jerusalem Quarterly* 17 (1980); G. Corm, "Lebanon: Dilemma and Solution," *QA*, October–December 1978.

16. H. Barakat, *Lebanon in Strife*; H. Barakat, "Lebanese Society: Mosaic or Pluralism?" *Mawaqif*, January–April 1968; H. Barakat, "The Future of Social and Political Integration in the Arab World," *MA*, June 1980.

17. "Reflections on Co-existence in Lebanon," *NAD*, July 30, 1979.

18. Survey by A. Farraj, *NAD*, November 17, 1980, p. 40.

19. "The West, Islam and Secularization," *QA*, October–November 1977.

20. Interview in *NAD*, January 15, 1979; see his "Specificity and Authenticity," *al-Adab*, May 1974.

21. H. Saghiya, *Sira' al-Islam wa-l-Batrul* (Beirut, 1978); H. Fahs in *al-Safir*, February 12, 1979; M. al-Sulh, "Islam of the Ruler and Islam of the Masses," *NAD*, January 29, 1979. See A. S. al-Dajani, "The Future of the Relationship Between Arabism and Islam," *MA*, February 1981.

22. Compare his articles in *Mawaqif*, summer 1974, winter 1979.

23. Review of Saghiya's book in *al-Katib al-Filastini*, February 1979; A. al-Shaykh, "The Political and Cultural Exploitation of the Iranian Revolution," *YA*, April 1979; Adonis, "Reflections on the Islamic Revolution in Iran," *Mawaqif*, winter 1979; 'A. M. Ahmad, "Contemporary Islamic Currents," *QA*, March 1980; see Abdelmalek's contradictory statement in *MA* symposium, December 1980.

24. B. Ghalyun, "Social Struggle and Islam," *NAD*, April 22, 1979; see A. Dimitri, "The Present Crisis," *YA*, January 1980, and his recent, *YA*, February 1981.

25. For example, *YA*, February 1979, pp. 22–24; *al-Tadamun*, August 1979, pp. 41–43.

26. For example, H. Kurum, "Jama'at at-Takfir wa-l-Hijra," *DA*, March 1978; A. Yusuf, "Jama'at at-Takfir wa-l-Hijra," *YA*, September 1977; I. Sarkis, "Religious Ideology and Leftist Thought," *DA*, June 1980; Gh. Shukri, "At the Crossroads," *DA*, December 1980; R. al-Sa'id, *Hasan al-Banna* (Cairo, 1977); S. Ibrahim, "The New Arab Social Order," *al-Siyasa al-Duwaliya*, October 1980; N. 'Abd al-Fattah, "The Fundamentalist Resurgence," *QA*, February–April 1982; J. Amin, *Mihnat al-Iqtisad wa-l-Thaqafa fi Misr* (Cairo, 1982), pp. 185–89.

27. Interview with Zakariya, *YA*, June 1980.

28. Corm interview with *DA*, January 1980; *DA* editorial, June 1979; Sharara, *Al-Dawla fi-l-Thaqafa al-'Arabiyya* (Beirut, 1980), p. 155.

29. "The Comrades," *DA*, July 1980, pp. 6–7.

30. T. Farah, "Politics and Religion in Kuwait," in Dessouki, ed., *Islamic Resurgence*, p. 173; W. A. al-Tamimi, "The Attitude of Arab Public Opinion Towards the Resolution of the Arab-Israeli Conflict," *MA*, November 1980; S. Ibrahim, *Ittijahat al-Ra'y al-'Amm al-'Arabi wa-Qadiyat al-Wahda* (Beirut, 1980), pp. 140–44; K. al-Manufi, *Al-Thaqafa al-Siyasiyya li-l-Fallahin al-Misriyyin* (Beirut, 1980); B. Sarhan, *Al-'A'ila wa-l-Qaraba 'inda-l-Filastiniyyin fi Kuwait* (Kuwait, 1977). See 'A. al-Mashat's article in *The Middle East Journal* 37/3 (1983), table 9.

31. A. Maroun, "Un Islam crispé," *Esprit*, January 1980; A. Iskandar, *Sira' al-Yamin wa-l-Yasar*.

32. S. 'Isa, "Taha Husayn"; S. 'Isa, "The Question of Theocracy," *MA*, May 1978; interview with J. al-Shaykh, *al-Ihya' al-'Arabi*, March 28,

1980; H. Hanafi, "Historical Origins of our Crisis of Freedom and Democracy," *MA*, January 1979.

33. N. al-Qazzi, "The Genesis of Secularism," *al-Ihya' al-'Arabi*, September 30, 1979.

34. S. Yasin, *Tahlil Madmun al-Fikr al-Qawmi al-'Arabi* (Beirut, 1980); S. Ibrahim, "Sociology of Minorities in the Arab World," *QA*, April–September 1976. See Adonis's article in *Mawaqif* (spring 1983), pp. 147–48.

35. For example, Kh. Muhi al-Din, et al., *Al-Mas'ala al-Ta'ifiyya fi Misr* (Beirut, 1980); special section in *YA*, July–August 1980; I. Khuri, ed., *al-Masihiyyun al-'Arab* (Beirut, 1981).

36. 'A. al-Rabi'u, "Islam and Secularism," *QA*, July 1980; Paris: M. Arkoun (see n. 40); Gh. Shukri (see n. 3); A. Iskander (see n. 3); J. al-Shaykh (see n. 32); M. A. 'Alim (see n. 44); T. Ben Djelloun (*Le Monde*, July 30, 1980); Lyon: A. Merad (*Le Monde*, June 1, 1980); Göttingen: B. al-Tibi (*QA*, March 1980); London: N. al-Khallaj (see n. 39); Washington: Barakat (see n. 8).

37. *Ta'rikh al-'Arab wa-l-'Alam*, symposium, March 1980; *MA*, symposium, March 1980; R. al-Sa'id, "Arab Nationalism: Three Questions in Search of an Answer," *MA*, September 1979.

38. Rabi'u, "Islam and Secularism," *QA*, July 1980; see S. Yasin, "The Arab Intellectual," *QA*, February 1980.

39. Kh. al-Nu'aymi, "Arab Political Thought and Islam," *YA*, August 1979; N. al-Khallaj, "Contemporary Islamic Currents," *al-Ghad*, April–June 1980.

40. "L'Islam et la laicité," *Bulletin du Centre Thomas More* 24 (1978); "The Relationship between Islam and Politics," *al-Bahith*, July–August 1980.

41. Interview with *QA*, March–May 1978.

42. M. Sulh in *NAD*, November 3, 1980; 'Abbas in *MA* symposium, December 1980, p. 141; S. Karam, *MA*, November 1980; Gh. Shukri in *al-Tadamun*, December 1979, p. 38. Empirical findings on the qutriyya in S. Ibrahim, *Ittijahat*, pp. 271–75. See *MA* symposium, March 1981.

43. J. Mughayzil, *Al-'Uruba wa-l-'Almana* (Beirut, 1980); K. Pakraduni in *NAD*, November 3, 1980.

44. M. A. 'Alim, "Islam and Revolution," *YA*, March 1979 and his earlier critique on the same writer, *al-Adab*, May 1974; Corm, interview with *DA*, January 1980.

45. Introduction to his edition of *Al-Hukuma al-Islamiyya* (Cairo,

1979), p. 29; see his "Right and Left in Religious Thought," *al-Tali'a*, October 1976; G. Zaynati, "Western Methodology and Arab Realities," *al-Fikr al-'Arabi al-Mu'asir*, December 1980–January 1981.
46. Adonis, in *NAD*, July 7, 1980; S. Ibrahim, *Ittijahat*, p. 76.

Conclusion

1. J. Pitt-Rivers, *The Fate of Shechem* (Cambridge, England, 1977), pp. vii–viii.
2. S. 'Uways, *Hutaf al-Samitin* (Cairo, 1971); S. 'Uways, *Al-Khulud fi Hayat al-Misriyyin al-Mua'sirin* (Cairo, 1972); N. Sa'adawi, *Al-Mar'a al-Arabiyya wa-l-Jins* (Beirut, 1973); N. Sa'adawi, *The Hidden Face of Eve* (London, 1980); A. al-Naqqash, "Women's Liberation and the Call for Theocracy in Egypt," *QA*, July–August 1974.
3. H. Sharabi, "Family and Cultural Development in Arab Society," *al-Ma'rifa* (Damascus), June 1974; B. Yasin, *Al-Thaluth al-Muharram* (Beirut, 1973).
4. Sultan's report in *al-Majalla al-Ijtima'iyya al-Misriyya*, January 1972; Hantura's article in *al-Majalla al-Ijtima'iyya al-Misriyya*, 1968 (fasc. 1); Suwayf, *Al-Tatarruf ka-Uslub li-l-Ijaba* (Cairo, 1968).
5. S. J. al-Azm, *Al-Naqd al-Dhati*; S. J. al-Azm, *Naqd al-Fikr al-Dini*; the quotations are from H. Barakat, "Alienation and Revolution in Arab Life," *al-Mawaqif* (Beirut), 1969, pp. 18–44.
6. "Major Causes of Arab Political Physiognomy," *QA*, May 1979.
7. C. Geertz, *Islam Observed* (New Haven, 1968), chapter 3.
8. Qa'ud, *Hurras*; Rizq, *Madhabih*, pp. 150–58; *al-Ahram*, September 9, 1965; Bayyumi, *Al-Ikhwan al-Muslimun*, pp. 271–75. See Abu Khayr, *Dhikriyati*; and Hassan, et al., *Muwajahat al-Fikr*, pp. 73–75 on "Maraboutist" qualities attributed to Shukri Mustafa by his votaries (and see *al-Ahram*, July 9, 1979). Qutb's letters to his sister (*al-Fikr*, Tunis, 1959) breathe the same martyrological notions as does 'Isam al-'Attar, *Azma Ruhiyya* (Cairo, 1979), pp. 25–29.
9. For example, *al-I'tisam*. January 1980, pp. 28–29; March–April 1980, p. 5; *Al-Irhab al-Nusayri*, pp. 20–21; M. 'Anbar, *Nahwa Thawra Islamiyya* (Cairo, 1979), pp. 86–90.
10. *Al-Nadhir*, August 11, 1980.
11. Proceedings quoted in *al-Safir*, May 28, 1982.
12. Interview of 'A. Babti in *al-Shira'*, December 5, 1983.

13. Interview in *al-Watan al-Arabi*, April 16, 1982; see *al-Nadhir*, May 2, 1981; March 27, May 8, 1982; see *al-I'tisam*, February 1980, pp. 6–7.

14. Interview in *al-Shira'*, November 21, 1983. For further elaboration on the issue discussed in the last three pages see my "Radicals: Shiite and Sunni," AAS, forthcoming.

Index

The Arabic definite article al- has been omitted in surnames.

214